The Minority Body

Studies in Feminist Philosophy is designed to showcase cutting-edge monographs and collections that display the full range of feminist approaches to philosophy, that push feminist thought in important new directions, and that display the outstanding quality of feminist philosophical thought.

STUDIES IN FEMINIST PHILOSOPHY
Cheshire Calhoun, *Series Editor*

Advisory Board

Recently Published in the Series:

Visible Identities: Race, Gender and the Self
Linda Martín Alcoff

Women and Citizenship
Edited by Marilyn Friedman

*Women's Liberation and the Sublime:
Feminism, Postmodernism, Environment*
Bonnie Mann

Analyzing Oppression
Ann E. Cudd

*Ecological Thinking: The Politics of Epistemic
Location*
Lorraine Code

*Self Transformations: Foucault, Ethics, and
Normalized Bodies*
Cressida J. Heyes

Family Bonds: Genealogies of Race and Gender
Ellen K. Feder

*Moral Understandings: A Feminist Study in
Ethics, Second Edition*
Margaret Urban Walker

The Moral Skeptic
Anita M. Superson

*"You've Changed": Sex Reassignment and
Personal Identity*
Edited by Laurie J. Shrage

*Dancing with Iris: The Philosophy of Iris
Marion Young*
Edited by Ann Ferguson and Mechthild Nagel

Philosophy of Science after Feminism
Janet A. Kourany

*Shifting Ground: Knowledge and Reality,
Transgression and Trustworthiness*
Naomi Scheman

The Metaphysics of Gender
Charlotte Witt

Unpopular Privacy: What Must We Hide?
Anita L. Allen

*Adaptive Preferences and Women's
Empowerment*
Serene Khader

*Minimizing Marriage: Marriage, Morality,
and the Law*
Elizabeth Brake

*Out from the Shadows: Analytic Feminist
Contributions to Traditional Philosophy*
Edited by Sharon L. Crasnow and Anita
M. Superson

*The Epistemology of Resistance: Gender and
Racial Oppression, Epistemic Injustice, and
Resistant Imaginations*
José Medina

*Simone de Beauvoir and the Politics of
Ambiguity*
Sonia Kruks

*Identities and Freedom: Feminist Theory
Between Power and Connection*
Allison Weir

*Vulnerability: New Essays in Ethics and
Feminist Philosophy*
Edited by Catriona Mackenzie, Wendy
Rogers, and Susan Dodds

*Sovereign Masculinity: Gender Lessons from
the War on Terror*
Bonnie Mann

Autonomy, Oppression, and Gender
Edited by Andrea Veltman and Mark Piper

*Our Faithfulness to the Past: The Ethics and
Politics of Memory*
Sue Campbell
Edited by Christine M. Koggel and Rockney
Jacobsen

The Physiology of Sexist and Racist Oppression
Shannon Sullivan

The Minority Body

A Theory of Disability

Elizabeth Barnes

OXFORD
UNIVERSITY PRESS

Great Clarendon Street, Oxford, OX2 6DP,
United Kingdom

Oxford University Press is a department of the University of Oxford.
It furthers the University's objective of excellence in research, scholarship,
and education by publishing worldwide. Oxford is a registered trade mark of
Oxford University Press in the UK and in certain other countries

First Edition published in 2016

Impression: 1

Published in the United States of America by Oxford University Press
198 Madison Avenue, New York, NY 10016, United States of America

British Library Cataloguing in Publication Data
Data available

Library of Congress Control Number: 2015953286

ISBN 978-0-19-873258-7

Printed in Great Britain by
Clays Ltd, St Ives plc

*To Clay Barnes—Thanks for these wacky genes,
and for teaching me how to live with them*

Table of Contents

Preface

This book is personal. Maybe it's strange to admit that about a philosophy book, when we so easily buy into the myth that philosophy is supposed to be a purely rational endeavor unclouded by messy things like emotions. But there's no point in hiding it. I'm disabled, and this is a book about disability. Of course it's personal.

I used to think I couldn't philosophize about disability precisely because the topic is so personal. But on reflection, that's absurd. Disability is a topic that's personal for everyone. The last time I checked, most non-disabled people are pretty personally invested in being non-disabled. The fact that this sort of personal investment is so easy to ignore is one of the more pernicious aspects of philosophy's obsession with objective neutrality. It's easy to confuse the view from normal with the view from nowhere. And then it's uniquely the minority voices which we single out as biased or lacking objectivity. When it comes to disability, I'm not objective. And neither are you. And that's true whether you're disabled or (temporarily) non-disabled.

My introduction to disability as an area of academic study was as an undergraduate, through the English department. It was there that I encountered the cross-disciplinary conversation in the humanities and parts of the social sciences that gets labeled disability studies. The ideas I discovered there were, with no exaggeration, life-changing. My disability (which is called Ehlers-Danlos syndrome, if you're curious) is complicated, and requires ongoing complex medical care. I see a lot of doctors, I've had a lot of surgeries, I take a lot of medicine. And like many people with complicated and rare conditions, I spent a lot of time bouncing around from misdiagnosis to misdiagnosis. In short, my experience of disability was extremely medicalized.

The ideas I encountered in disability studies were—or at least felt—radical. It had never occurred to me that there might be a social dimension to the difficulties I was experiencing. That my disability might be something more than my own sad, little tragedy was a revelation. It wasn't exactly that I became convinced by the books I read arguing for disability pride and inclusion. It was more that reading these things made clear, for the first time, something I had always felt, but had never been able to express—even to myself. That experience was transformative.

But as much as the work I found through the English department moved me, I was already in love with analytic philosophy. So I enrolled in an applied ethics class, eager to discover what insight philosophy would offer into disability. I encountered two philosophical arguments, as an undergraduate, that dealt specifically with disability—Peter Singer's argument for the permissibility of infanticide and Derek Parfit's 'handicapped child' case. To say that I was disappointed would be a massive understatement. 'Heartbroken' might be closer to the truth.

My disappointment with much of the philosophical engagement with disability I encountered only strengthened in grad school. Of course there were amazing exceptions—Eva Kittay, Anita Silvers—but most of the philosophical work on disability that I managed to find seemed to focus primarily on who can do what to which kinds of fetuses in which very abstract circumstances. So I kept my head down, kept reading non-philosophy disability studies on the side, and mostly focused on metaphysics.

I decided that I could actually do philosophy about disability when I read Sally Haslanger's work on adoption. She openly acknowledges that the topic is personal for her—that the moral significance of her own family is at stake in the debate. And then she proceeds to give completely clear and compelling arguments. Reading Sally's work taught me several crucial things. The first is that it's possible to do excellent philosophy on topics in which you're personally invested. The second, and perhaps more important, is that philosophy needs the voices of those who are personally invested. The literature on adoption wouldn't be complete without the perspective of adoptive mothers. Likewise, there's a reason why much of the philosophical engagement with disability didn't resonate with me. It's dominated by non-disabled people. And philosophical discussion of disability is always going to be incomplete if disabled people are largely on the sidelines. A key slogan of the disability rights movement is 'Nothing about us without us.' That includes philosophy. If I didn't like what I was reading—and I didn't—I needed to get involved. So here we are.

Portions of chapters 2 and 5 were previously published in Elizabeth Barnes, 'Valuing disability, causing disability', *Ethics* 125 (1) (2014), pp. 88–113; sections of chapter 4 were previously published in Elizabeth Barnes, 'Disability and adaptive preference', *Philosophical Perspectives* 23 (1) (2009), pp. 1–22.

I have benefited, over the course of writing this book, from the help and insight of more people than I am going to remember to acknowledge. Thanks for helpful comments and feedback to Kate Abramson, Joel Anderson, Teresa Blankmeyer-Burke, Tim Button, Steve Campbell, Ben Caplan, Ruth Chang, Shannon Dea, Tom Dougherty, Janice Dowell, Daniel Elstein, Delia Graff Fara, Miranda Fricker, Brie Gertler, Elizabeth Harman, Sally Haslanger, Jonathan Jacobs, Katharine Jenkins, Jeff King, Eva Kittay, Meena Krishnamurthy, Gerald Lang, Rae Langton, Heather Logue, Ofra Magidor, Kris McDaniel, Jeff McMahan, Trenton Merricks, Sarah Moss, Daniel Nolan, Laurie Paul, John Protevi, Mike Rea, Jonathan Schaffer, Miriam Schoenfield, Alex Skiles, Paulina Sliwa, David Sobel, Joe Stramondo, Eric Swanson, Amie Thomasson, Kevin Timpe, Christina Van Dyke, Pekka Vayrynen, David Wasserman, and audiences at Cambridge University, Durham University, Leeds University, MIT, Ohio State University, Oxford University, Rutgers University, Syracuse University, the University of Virginia, and the Arizona Ontology Conference. I'm also very grateful to the amazing students I had the opportunity to interact with at Leeds University and the University of Virginia, most especially Dani Adams, Sarah Adams, Richard Caves, Jim Darcy, Matt Duncan, Fran Fairbarn, Jade Fletcher, Derek Lam, Robb Muckle, Nick Rimmel, Alex Roberts, Adam Tiller, and Carl Warom. I'm sure I learned more from getting to teach each of them than they could possibly have learned from getting taught by me. Thanks also to the Mind Association for funding a semester of research leave in order for me to work on this book.

I'm especially grateful to Jenny Saul. I would have been completely at sea, in writing this book, without the help and insight of feminist philosophy. And it was Jenny who (gently, patiently) encouraged me to give feminist philosophy more than a passing glance. She also challenged me, pushed me, and helped me—in the best ways—on so many sections of this book. I can't even begin to thank her for everything she's done, both for this book and for me as a person.

And then there are my dear friends, my best allies, my partners in crime—Jason Turner and Robbie Williams. The best philosophers are the ones who can have amazing, insightful things to say about pretty much anything, whether it's their area or not. The best friends are the ones who always make you feel accepted, encouraged, and valued. Jason and Robbie are the best philosophers and the best friends. There's no way in hell I'd have had the guts to write this book without them.

And finally, thanks to my other half, my love, and my favorite thing in the world—Ross Cameron. Ross has read and commented on multiple drafts of everything in this book, and there isn't an idea in here that hasn't benefited from discussion with him. He has been unfailingly supportive, unfailingly generous, unfailingly obnoxiously smart. And he has always loved me just the way I am.

Introduction

There is a massive disconnect between the way disability is understood in the disability rights and disability pride movements and the way disability is understood within analytic philosophy. The former see being disabled as primarily a social phenomenon—a way of being a minority, a way of facing social oppression, but not a way of being inherently or intrinsically worse off. But while this view of disability has been widely incorporated into academic disability studies, it remains at the margins of analytic philosophy. The idea that disability is not inherently bad or suboptimal is one that many philosophers treat with open skepticism, and sometimes even with scorn.

The goal of this book is to articulate and defend a version of the view of disability that is common in the disability rights movement. I will argue that to be physically disabled is not to have a defective body, but simply to have a minority body.

0.1 The Relationship Between Disability and Bioethics

Philosophical work on disability is often assumed to be 'applied ethics' or 'bioethics'. And this is unsurprising, given that many philosophers adopt a medicalized view of disability, according to which disability is nothing more than a kind of biological disorder. (I'll discuss the inadequacy of this conception of disability in chapter 1.) I don't deny that there are many interesting disability-centric issues which can usefully be described as bioethics. But this book isn't (or isn't primarily) about them. The issues I'm going to focus on are to my mind more foundational. They are the kinds of things that need to be addressed before we can grapple with the complicated questions of, for example, healthcare resource allocation or who can select what type of fetus under what circumstance.

What is disability? What is its connection to well-being? What would it mean—and what would it entail—to say that disability isn't something that's inherently bad or suboptimal? These issues are, in my opinion, crucial topics for any philosophical analysis of disability, and they aren't—again, in my opinion—topics that are well described as bioethics. Or at least I don't think they deserve the label 'bioethics' if we don't also describe Sally Haslanger's work on gender, for example, as bioethics.

For lack of a better term, I think of these as issues in social philosophy, and so I think of this book as a work of social philosophy. My own discussion of these issues is heavily influenced by feminist philosophy. Whether this book also therefore deserves to be called feminist philosophy is a taxonomical question that probably isn't very interesting.

0.2 Varieties of Disability, and Why I'm Not Talking About Some of Them

This book is about physical disability. There are, of course, other forms of disability—including psychological and cognitive disability. But unfortunately I'm not going to talk about them.

The primary reason for this is simplicity. The task of saying what (if anything) disability is, or what its connection to well-being is, gets complicated enough given the heterogeneity of things we classify as physical disability. Including cognitive and psychological disability in the mix increases that complexity (and heterogeneity) exponentially. So my tentative suggestion is that the way to approach theories of disability is 'ground-up' rather than 'top-down'. We first need to see whether workable accounts can be had of physical disability, psychological disability, and cognitive disability, respectively—or whether, indeed, this tripartite grouping is just mistaken. And then we need to ask whether and to what extent these categories might be usefully unified. Perhaps, for example, some things we think of as psychological disabilities have more in common with physical disabilities than they do with other psychological disabilities. Or perhaps the tripartite distinction is right and we need separate, unrelated theories of physical, psychological, and cognitive disability, respectively. Or perhaps there's a single notion of disability that covers physical, psychological, and cognitive forms of disability. Or perhaps instead these categories are unified by analogy.

(To borrow an example from Kris McDaniel, exercise, broccoli, Stephen Curry, and my marriage are all healthy—but arguably there's no single property that they all share in virtue of which they are healthy.[1] 'Healthy' is a concept that's unified by analogy. 'Disability' might be as well.) I don't have a settled view on any of these incredibly complex questions. But I do think it's worth talking about physical disabilities as a group, while remaining agnostic about whether and to what extent what I want to say about physical disability should be extended. I'm thus going to proceed by focusing exclusively on physical disability and seeing what progress I can make.

The other main reason for focusing on physical disability has to do with the epistemology of testimony. Throughout the book, I'll be appealing to—and relying on—the first-person testimony of disabled people, and I'll specifically argue (in chapter 4) that this testimony is reliable (or, more carefully, that we don't have special reason to think it's unreliable). But psychological and cognitive disabilities raise complicated issues for the reliability of testimony that simply aren't present in the case of physical disability. So—again, mostly for simplicity—I'm going to restrict my attention to physical disability as the easiest and most straightforward test case. That's not to say that the testimony-based arguments I give here don't work for other forms of disability. It's just to say that more work would need to be done to show whether they do, and the book is already long enough as it is.

So in what follows, I focus on physical disability without taking a view on what the connection is between physical disability and other forms of disability. I think simplifying in this way is warranted, regardless of the fact that we have a single word—'disability'—that can refer to all the different varieties of disability. That is, I don't think we should infer that there is a unified category—or a unified connection to well-being— covering psychological, physical, and cognitive forms of disability simply because our word 'disability' can refer to physical, cognitive, or psychological disability. Modifiers like 'physically', 'mentally', 'psychologically', etc. can do a lot of work. Suppose we say of Anna that she is mentally restrained, and of Ben that he is physically restrained. We are saying that Anna is calm, collected, and focused, whereas we are saying that Ben is

---

[1] McDaniel (2010).

tied up. These cases might be unified by analogy, but it doesn't seem like there's obviously any particular feature or property that they have in common. Nevertheless, we can say of each of Anna and Ben simply that they are restrained, without explicitly specifying whether they are physically or mentally restrained. Context does a lot of work.

That's not to deny that there is such a unified category. It's just to say that our use of the word 'disability' doesn't by itself show or suggest that there is. Again, I think the best way to approach the question of whether and to what extent different types of disability form a common kind or have a common connection to well-being is by first engaging in detailed analysis of the different varieties of disability and then exploring the potential commonalities (and differences). We should also be open to the possibility that such commonalities might cut across the way we standardly divide disabilities. That is, we shouldn't assume that either all psychological or cognitive disabilities share a common feature with physical disability or none of them do. Nor should we assume that a particular psychological or cognitive disability will have more in common with other such disabilities than it will with physical disabilities. Certainly the neurodiversity and autism acceptance movements (as well as similar campaigns for Down syndrome) seem to have a lot in common with the disability pride campaigns that have more traditionally been associated with physical disability. It might be that autism simply has a lot more in common—at least with respect to well-being—with physical disability than it does with, say, schizophrenia.

Again, I don't want to take a stand on these issues, nor do I want to take a stand on whether the physical/cognitive/psychological classification of disabilities is a helpful one. I'm going to argue that we should re-evaluate much of the way we think about the connection between disability and well-being *at least* for what we think of as physical disability. I'm neutral on whether these arguments extend to other cases (that is, whether or not they apply at most to physical disability). My sincere hope, in exploring these issues for physical disability, is that similar projects for other forms of disability arise in tandem. That— rather than an attempt at a global theory of anything and everything that gets labeled 'disability'—is, I think, the best way forward for philosophical analysis of disability.

As Eva Kittay often says, disability needs to be a 'big tent', including a lot of diverse perspectives and experiences. In focusing on physical disability, it's not my intention to exclude or marginalize other forms of disability. I simply want to start small (or small*er*), with the hope that others can engage in similar projects in other areas, and then connections can be explored.

In what follows I will, for the sake of simplicity, use the term 'disability' to refer to physical disability.

0.3 Terminology

Like many cases in which we're discussing social kinds and marginalized groups, word choice when it comes to talking about disability is a vexed issue. I know of no terminology in the area that isn't offensive or upsetting to someone. So rather than trying to find terminology that is universally acceptable, I've simply tried to settle on terminology that is principled.

I use the term 'ableism' to mean social prejudice and stigma directed against the disabled in virtue of the fact that they are disabled, just as people use the term 'racism' to mean social prejudice and stigma directed against those of a particular race in virtue of the fact that they are members of that race. But this prejudice encompasses more than just personal attitudes—it can include the way our society is structured and organized. So, for example, a world free of ableism is not simply a world where no individuals harbor prejudiced thoughts about the disabled, it's also a world that doesn't contain massive accessibility barriers for the disabled. (I'm sometimes tempted by the view that ableism—like racism—is best understood as entirely structural, rather than a matter of individual belief and attitude, but I won't take a stand on that here.)

I use the word 'disability' to refer to particular bodily features or conditions. I give an account of what I take these bodily features to be in chapter 1. Because I think that 'disability' refers to the physical states of bodies—to particular bodily features—my usage of 'disability' is closer to what is often meant by 'impairment' in the literature on disability. I explain in chapter 1 why I think a distinction between disability and impairment isn't necessary, and since 'disability' is the more familiar term, that's the one I'm using.

I use 'disabled people' to refer to people who have the sorts of bodily features or conditions picked out by the term 'disability'. I use 'disabled people' rather than 'people with disabilities' because 'disabled people' mirrors our usage of other terms which pick out minority social groups—for example, we say 'gay people' not 'people with gayness'. It's sometimes suggested that we should say 'people with disabilities' because 'disabled people' suggests that disability somehow defines the person. But I simply don't think that's true. Saying that someone is a disabled person doesn't mean that disability defines who they are any more than saying that someone is a gay person means that sexuality defines who they are.

I am using 'disabled' rather than a replacement term like 'differently-abled'. Words are hard to replace. I think it's easier to shift meanings. It's probably a presupposition of the common usage of 'disabled' and 'disability' that being disabled is bad, and that disabilities are bad. But—as 'reclaiming' projects have taught us—presuppositions can be objected to, and they can be changed.

It used to be a presupposition of the common usage of 'queer' that it was bad to be queer. It isn't any more. Likewise, the origin of its use as a term for describing sexuality is bound up in a lot of anti-gay prejudice. But its contemporary usage isn't. I think we can do the same thing for 'disabled' (and, similarly, for terms like 'crip'). Changing the received presuppositions and implicatures—and getting away from the unfortunate roots of these words—is, I think, an easier task than getting people to stop using words like 'disabled' and 'disability'. So I'll proceed with the common-usage terms.

0.4 The Plan

I'm going to defend the idea that being disabled is not something that by itself or intrinsically makes you worse off. Being disabled is, I'll argue, a way of being a minority with respect to one's body, just as being gay is a way of being a minority with respect to sexuality. It is something that makes you different from the majority, but that difference isn't by itself a bad thing. To be disabled is to have a minority body, but not to have a broken or defective body.

So that's the destination. Here's the roadmap.

Chapter 1: Constructing Disability—The things we group as 'disabilities' are strikingly heterogeneous. The first task of any philosophical theory of disability is thus to argue that there is something unifying these disparate cases to which philosophical analysis can be usefully applied.

Many accounts of disability attempt to explain what unifies individual disabilities via reference to specific features of disabled bodies, but I argue that such accounts fail. There is no objective feature(s) of disabled bodies such that all and only bodies with that feature(s) count as disabled. Instead, I argue that disability is socially constructed. On my view, we should care about disability—and care about philosophical analysis of disability—primarily because disability is a way that people have grouped themselves when organizing a civil rights struggle. This basic idea yields a social constructionist account that is importantly different from the more familiar social model of disability, as well as from other familiar social constructionist projects in philosophy, such as Sally Haslanger's account of race and gender.

Chapter 2: Bad-Difference and Mere-Difference—In this chapter, I elaborate on the distinction between what I call the 'mere-difference' conceptions of disability and the more familiar 'bad-difference' conceptions of disability (which maintain that disability is something inherently bad for you). The distinction is a complex one, because the key issue is the relationship between disability and well-being. There are various theories of well-being, and no single way of characterizing the bad-difference/mere-difference distinction cuts across them all. Instead of offering a single distinction, I offer multiple ways of characterizing bad-difference and mere-difference views of disability. These characterizations are independent of one another—they each offer sufficient but non-necessary conditions for maintaining bad- and mere-difference views. I argue that these various characterizations combine to form a composite picture of the family of views I am labeling 'mere-difference' and 'bad-difference'. I then further argue that no version of the 'bad-difference' view should be considered obvious or common sense.

Chapter 3: The Value-Neutral Model—Here I articulate and defend a particular way of holding a mere-difference view of disability, which I call the 'Value-Neutral Model' of disability. The goal of this account is to give a model of disability according to which disability is mere-difference, and yet may still be viewed as (in a restricted sense) a harm. Based on this model, I argue that one needn't say that all the harms associated with being disabled are socially mediated or caused by social injustice (that is, one needn't deny that disability might involve harms even in an ideal, ableism-free society) in order to maintain a mere-difference view of disability. Likewise, I argue that it's consistent to think both that disability is not in general something bad and that disability is bad *for some people* or *in some circumstances*.

Chapter 4: Taking Their Word for It—The arguments in chapters 2 and 3 rely heavily on the first-person testimony of disabled people who claim to value being disabled. This chapter focuses on the epistemological issues surrounding such testimony. It's sometimes suggested that this sort of testimony is unreliable because it is based on adaptive preference. Drawing on the influential work of Miranda Fricker, I argue that this dismissal of disabled people's testimony is unwarranted, and that discounting the testimony of disabled people in this way is a type of testimonial injustice.

Chapter 5: Causing Disability—This chapter examines two major, interrelated objections to any mere-difference view: that it makes it permissible to cause disability, and that it makes it impermissible to remove disability. I attempt to unpack both these objections. I argue that in neither case does the mere-difference view generate a universal response. That is, it doesn't tell you whether, regardless of the circumstances, it is always permissible to cause disability or impermissible to remove it. I further argue that neither the case of causing nor the case of removing provide effective objections to the mere-difference view.

Chapter 6: Disability Pride—In conclusion, I defend the epistemological importance of disability pride. Disabled people—in addition to being subject to testimonial injustice—are subject to the other form of epistemic injustice Miranda Fricker identifies: hermeneutical injustice. Parts of their own experience are obscured or made difficult to articulate because of dominant stereotypes and assumptions about disability. Disability pride is, I argue, essential to combating this.

1

Constructing Disability

> Sometimes we who are activists and thinkers forget about our bodies, ignore our bodies, or reframe our bodies to fit our theories and political strategies. For several decades now, activists in a variety of social change movements, ranging from black civil rights to women's liberation, from disability rights to queer liberation, have said repeatedly that the problems faced by any marginalized group of people lie, not in their bodies, but in the oppression they face. But in defining the external, collective, material nature of social injustice as separate from the body, we have sometimes ended up sidelining the profound relationships that connect our bodies with who we are and how we experience oppression.
>
> Eli Clare (2001)

1.1 The Problem

The things we group together under the label 'disability' are strikingly heterogeneous. Spinal chord injuries are very different from deafness. Deafness is very different from MS. MS is very different from achondroplasia. And so on. The goal of this book is to explore the connection between disability and well-being. I'm going to pursue the idea that disability, like other minority features, is (by itself) *neutral* with respect to well-being. But the first hurdle that greets any such project is simply this: Does it make any sense to ask philosophical questions about *disability* per se, rather than about individual disabilities? Is there anything unifying the disparate cases of individual disabilities, such that it's worth talking about disability as a kind?

Certainly, philosophers often do talk about disability as a kind. We ask under what conditions, if any, it's permissible to knowingly bring a disabled child into existence. We ask what duties societies have toward disabled people. We ask whether disabled people pose a problem for certain theories of justice. And so on. But the question is whether this practice is in good standing. To say that it is, we need to be able to say that there's something unifying the heterogeneous group of things we label 'disabilities', such that it makes sense to engage in philosophical questions about disability in general, rather than about individual disabilities.

In what follows, I focus specifically on the question of what—if anything—unifies particular instances of *physical* disability (see the discussion in section 2 of the introduction). I take no stand on whether what I say here will generalize to other forms of disability, such as cognitive disability or psychological disability.

1.2 Criteria for Success

I want to figure out what disability is. This is a project in social metaphysics—I'm not investigating what our word 'disability' means, nor trying to give a theory of our folk concept of disability. I'm asking *what it is* for something to be a disability. But I first need to briefly set out what I take to be the major criteria of success for any such account of disability. None of these criteria are uncontroversial. But (as I'll explain) I take them to be desiderata of an account of disability that does the work I want an account of disability to do.

(i) Delivers correct verdicts for paradigm cases

A successful account of disability needs to say that paradigm cases of disability are in fact disabilities (and that paradigm cases of non-disability are not). I would hazard a guess that most of us didn't begin an interest in disability by interest in the abstract concept. We begin with an interest by ostension. We want to know what *these kinds of things—* deafness, blindness, paralysis, achondroplasia, MS, etc.—are, such that they have something in common with each other.

Consider someone who wants to give an account of what it is to be a mammal. Such an account needn't respect *all* paradigm or intuitive judgements. There can be some surprises (dolphins and whales, perhaps) that make sense on reflection and there can be some hard cases (such as the noble platypus). But any successful account is constrained to not stray *too far* from the class of animals we began being interested in. An account of mammals that delivers the result that snakes, lizards, frogs, and earthworms are mammals is not a successful account of mammals. Likewise, an account that says that bears, horses, dogs, and chipmunks are not mammals is similarly unsuccessful.[1]

Similar points apply for the case of disability. A successful account of disability needn't match up exactly with pre-theoretic judgements. The class of invisible disabilities might be on similar footing, for example, to the class of aquatic mammals. There will, furthermore, be hard cases which an account of disability might usefully help us adjudicate. Is epilepsy completely controlled by medication a disability? Is in-remission MS a disability? And so on.

But an account that says of many paradigm cases of disability that they are not in fact disabilities is a non-starter, as is an account which says of many paradigm cases of non-disability that they are in fact disabilities.

(ii) Doesn't prejudge normative issues

A successful account of disability should also not make stipulations about normative issues. It should not be built into the very definition of disability that disability is something that's bad or suboptimal. The reason for this is simply that any such account of disability risks being unable to maintain condition (i). I'm assuming here that the disability rights movement has taught us, at the very least, that it is not analytic or a priori that physical conditions such as deafness, achondroplasia, etc. are bad. It should be an open question—at least as we begin inquiry—that some of these conditions are *not* bad. Any account that builds in normativity—that defines disability as a kind of negative or bad state— thus risks the consequence that many paradigm cases of disability are in fact not disabilities after all. And that's something a successful account of disability shouldn't leave open.

---

[1] I can imagine someone protesting at this point that the cases of mammals and disabilities are strongly disanalogous, because mammals constitute a natural kind, whereas disabilities do not. But similar points apply to cases that are clearly not natural kinds. Suppose I wanted to give an account of what it is to be an artwork. Again, in such a case I am constrained at least to some extent by paradigm cases. There will be puzzling cases— such as 'found art'—and questions of whether every minor doodle in a sketchbook counts as an artwork, but my account is unsuccessful if I say that chickens are works of art, or if I say that the ceiling of the Sistine Chapel is not a work of art.

Some accounts of disability are happy to reject (ii), even with the consequence that it will mean rejecting (i). Perhaps the most prominent of these is Guy Kahane and Julian Savulescu's (2009) 'welfarist account' of disability, according to which disability is understood as anything that makes your life go worse for you. Kahane and Savulescu acknowledge that this account leaves open that what we think of as paradigm cases of disability might, in some circumstances, not count as disabilities. And that's because there might be circumstances in which these features don't make people worse off (though they assert that *most* paradigm disabilities will be disabilities in their sense *most* of the time).[2] But lots of things that we don't think of as disabilities have a negative impact on welfare. And any such feature, according to the welfarist account, should in fact count as a disability. Kahane and Savulescu are happy to accept the radically revisionary nature of their account. But for the purposes here, I am going to simply assume that a successful account of disability should not—absent further compelling argument—be revisionary in this way, not the least because I think that a philosophical theory of disability shouldn't be in the business of claiming that much of what is said about disability within the disability rights movement is analytically false.

(iii) Is unifying or explanatory

The search for a philosophical account of disability is not merely the search for an account of disability that is extensionally adequate. We're not simply asking which things count as disabilities. We're asking what disability *is*. Individual disabilities do not, prima facie, have that much in common with each other. A successful account of disability needs to tell us what unifies these disparate cases—it needs to explain what (if anything) it is that individual disabilities have in common with each other.

This is one point at which different goals may yield different success conditions. Many legal definitions of disability seem primarily concerned with extensional adequacy, rather than with overarching explanation. And rightly so—the task of a legal definition of disability is to tell us who should count as disabled in the eyes of the law. A legal definition is not trying to tell us what disability *is*, it is trying to tell us whom the state should classify as disabled. The latter doesn't obviously give us insight into the former.

---

[2] Kahane and Savulescu (2009), (2011).

(iv) Is not circular

This one may be obvious, but it's worth stating explicitly. A successful account of disability cannot appeal—tacitly or otherwise—to the things it wants to explain in order to do its explanatory work. A successful account of disability cannot say that what unifies individual disabilities is that they are all disabilities.

It's sometimes been suggested, for example, that what unifies disabilities is that they are the sorts of things subject to ableism.[3] But such an account—at least if it is intended as explanatory, rather than simply extensionally adequate—is circular. Ableism *just is* prejudice and discrimination against disability and disabled people. So we don't get any further grip on what disability is by saying that disability is all and only the things subject to ableism, since we define ableism as the types of prejudice directed specifically at disability.

1.3 Naturalistic Accounts of Disability

In light of these stated criteria, we can now proceed to evaluate candidate accounts of disability. Obviously, I won't be able to canvass every account of disability, but I'll discuss some of the most significant ones. Hopefully, what I have to say about these cases will be illustrative of the sorts of problems that can arise for accounts of disability. To begin with, let's consider accounts of disability that attempt to explain what disability is in terms of natural or objective features of disabled bodies.

1.3.1 Disability is a departure from normal functioning or species norm

Perhaps the single most dominant idea within naturalistic accounts of disability is *normal functioning*.[4] The basic idea here is that there is a standard of normal functioning for humans, and that deviations from that norm are disabilities (or diseases). The normally functioning human can see, the blind person cannot—so the blind person is disabled. The

---

[3] This is more or less the account of disability given in Wendell (1997).

[4] This conception of disability has roots that trace back to Aristotle, but it owes its modern popularity within philosophy most notably to Norman Daniels. See especially Daniels (1985). Daniels takes his concept of normal functioning from the work of Christopher Boorse. See, for example, Boorse (1976).

normally functioning human can hear, the Deaf person cannot—so the Deaf person is disabled. And so on.[5]

There are reasons to be skeptical about the very idea of 'normal functioning' for a species.[6] But I'm going to set this sort of skepticism aside, and grant for the sake of argument that normal functioning is a concept in good standing. Even granting this much, normal functioning can't provide the basis for a successful account of disability. And that's simply because it overgeneralizes—there are many departures from normal functioning that are not disabilities.

Consider Michael Phelps. Michael Phelps has hypermobile joints, an arm span three inches longer than his height, unusually large feet, and muscles that produce a surprisingly small amount of lactic acid compared to normal ranges.[7] Michael Phelps is quite clearly a departure from normal species functioning, but he is also quite clearly not disabled.

But as Norman Daniels remarks, the concept of normal functioning needed here is 'not merely a statistical notion . . . Rather, it draws on a theoretical account of the design of the organism.'[8] Disabilities are *negative* departures from statistically typical functioning, where 'negative' means deviation from the organism's design, rather than something normative or value-laden.[9] It's often suggested that those functionings that might benefit the survival of the species should count as 'normal', whether or not they are (currently) had by the majority of species members.[10] Likewise, functioning is non-normal insofar as it impairs or hinders survival and reproduction.

But this doesn't address the case of Michael Phelps. It's very far from obvious that Phelps's abnormal functioning promotes long-term

---

[5] It's important to distinguish the sense of 'departure from normal function' intended here from the idea—common within critical disability studies—that disability is deviation from normalcy. Within critical disability studies, normalcy is understood as a socially constructed concept—whether something is 'normal' is a matter of how we think about it. So, e.g., Rosemarie Thomson (2012) says that 'the human variations we think of as disability are interruptions or departures from a standard script of human form, function, behavior, or perception that in contemporary thought we call normal.' I'll discuss social constructionist accounts in more detail later, though I won't be engaging directly with much of the critical disability studies literature.

[6] See, for example, Kingma (2010), Krag (2013), and Amundson (2000).

[7] Siebert (2014).   [8] Daniels (1985), p. 28.

[9] Though it's unclear whether there is any such value-free sense of 'negative'. See Ananth (2008).

[10] For discussion and an overview, see Satz (2006).

survival. In fact, some of the features that make him such an unusually good swimmer—particularly his lanky physique, known as 'marfanoid habitus'—also put him at higher risk for various cardiac problems.[11] Unsurprisingly, what helps humans survive longest may well come apart from what helps them swim very, very fast. And yet, risk of heart problems notwithstanding, Michael Phelps is not disabled.[12] More generally, marfanoid habitus is not (by itself) a disability, even though it's a departure from normal functioning that doesn't promote survival; one can have marfanoid habitus and its only effects be an unusually lanky physique.

But the overgeneralization problems get worse. On this account, a function is *normal* if it makes 'a statistically typical contribution . . . to individual survival and reproduction'.[13] Functions are *abnormal* when these goals of reproduction and survival are impaired in some way. If sexual orientation is at least in part biologically influenced (that is, if there are at least biological factors that predispose you to certain sexual orientations) then it looks like the normal function account might classify being gay as a disability, since being gay is statistically atypical and does not contribute to reproduction.[14] I'm happy to assume that it's a requirement of any successful theory of disability that it can distinguish between being disabled and being gay.

Although its proponents claim otherwise, it seems that often the normal functioning account is implicitly normative. Disabilities are *negative* departures from normal functioning—where 'negative' cannot

---

[11] Phelps discusses the fact that he goes for yearly cardiac exams in his autobiography. See Phelps and Cazeneuve (2008), p. 66. Individuals like Phelps, with some of the clinical features of Marfan syndrome, are often carefully monitored, as there is indication that they are at greater risk of some Marfan-like cardiac problems, regardless of whether they in fact have Marfan syndrome. See Pyeritz (2012).

[12] Phelps also presents a good counterexample to other attempts at amending the normal functioning account. We might say that to be disabled is to depart from normal functioning in a way that substantially affects your daily life—but certainly Phelps's departures from normal functioning have substantially affected his daily life. Or we might say that to be disabled is to depart from normal functioning in a way that inhibits what your body can do—but Phelps's muscles cannot make lactic acid at the same rate that most people's muscles can make lactic acid. And so on.

[13] Ananth (2008), p. 130.

[14] Boorse, in later work (e.g. (1997), (2014)), develops a much more substantial theory of 'normal function' than the one incorporated by Daniels—and this more substantial theory of normal functions can address problems like this one. The more Boorse develops his account of functions, however, the more they look implicitly normative.

simply be interpreted by biological criteria such as propensity to benefit survival and reproduction. It's worth noting, though, that even if we were to ignore (ii) and allow an account of disability to be explicitly normative, the normal functioning account would *still* overgeneralize. For example, recent scientific research has identified a variety of genes—or gene combinations—that cause an unusual predisposition to cancer.[15] The presence of these genes represents a *negative*—in whatever sense of 'negative' you want—departure from normal species functioning. And yet merely having a predisposition to cancer does not make you disabled.

There are other constraints that might be placed on the normal functioning account—we might say, for example, that disability is departure from normal functioning that substantially restricts daily activities. But such restrictions face the same sorts of problems that the next account we'll look at—the *lack of ability* account—faces, so I won't address them twice over.

1.3.2 Disability is the lack of a physical ability that most people have

Another familiar way of characterizing disability is via lack of ability. A basic version of such an account would be simply: To be disabled is to lack a physical ability which most people have. But that's a non-starter. Most people can 'roll' their tongues. To not be able to roll your tongue is to lack an ability which most people have. And yet those of us who can't roll our tongues are not disabled in virtue of that lack of ability.

So the lack-of-ability approach needs to be qualified. Perhaps the claim should be that disability is the lack of a *significant* ability that most people have.[16] Or we might say that disability is the lack of an ability that most people have, *the lack of which has a substantial impact on daily life*. The main problem with these accounts, though, is that there are many disabilities that aren't correlated with a specific lack of ability. Some conditions we class as disabilities have fluctuating physical

---

[15] Turnbull and Hodgson (2005).

[16] Not all such accounts are naturalistic, however. For example, Ron Amundson (1992) characterizes disability in terms of lack of significant 'personal abilities', but on his account these lacks are often socially mediated.

manifestations—you may be unable to do something one day, perfectly able to do it the next. And conditions that affect energy levels or cause chronic pain often don't cause the lack of any one particular ability, though they may affect how quickly you can perform a task, whether you can perform the task pain-free, or how much you can do in a given time period before needing to rest. There isn't always a neat correlation between disability and de re lack of ability. So, for example, someone with rheumatoid arthritis may be able to carry out the same types of everyday tasks that most other people can—she may just do them more slowly and with more pain, and not be able to do as many of them at any given time. Likewise, there's not a particular ability lacked by someone with achondroplasia. Someone with achondroplasia navigates the world very differently than someone who is six feet tall, but it's hard to quantify that difference via the lack of some ability. Conversely, there seem to be some disabilities that arise due to *enhanced* ability, rather than lack of ability. For example, in some forms of peripheral neuropathy, nerves become hyper-sensitized, to the point where even mild touch is painful.[17]

Perhaps the solution is to make abilities very fine-grained. Being able to reach a standard-height kitchen counter without a step is an ability. Being able to put your suitcase in the luggage compartment on an airplane without assistance, and without stepping up on anything (like the seats) is an ability. And so we can point to lots of abilities that someone with achondroplasia lacks. Lacking any of these very fine-grained abilities doesn't make a substantial impact on daily life, though. So we need to say something like this: Disability is the lack of some abilities, the cumulative effect of which makes a substantial impact on daily life. But if we're understanding abilities in this very fine-grained way, we're once again left with an account that overgeneralizes. Being a petite woman can involve the lack of many such fine-grained abilities— you can't reach things most people can reach, you can't lift things most people can lift, you can't see from theater seats most people can see from, etc. And the cumulative effect of this lack of ability has a substantial effect on your daily life—being a petite woman substantially affects the way you navigate daily tasks. And yet being a petite woman is not a disability.

---

[17] Decosterd, Allchorne, and Woolf (2002).

And so lack of ability accounts get increasingly complicated. Here, for example, is the World Health Organization's definition of disability from their 1980 International Classification of Impairments, Disabilities, and Handicaps.[18] Disability is 'restriction or lack (resulting from an impairment) of ability to perform an activity in the manner or within the range considered normal for a human being'. Such an account needs to make reference to impairments in order to have any hope of distinguishing disabilities from other social categories. If not for the impairment clause, being Black in 1950s America would count as a disability. But there's a serious worry here that accounts that need to make appeals to impairments will not be appropriately explanatory (thus violating (iii)), because they simply shift the burden of explanation from 'what is disability?' to 'what is impairment?' (see 1.4.1). The WHO 1980 account defines impairments as 'any loss or abnormality of...structure or function', which simply brings us back to the problems of the normal functioning account.

Worries about 'impairment' aside, though, the account still doesn't work. Imagine someone who has absolutely no desire to have children and then finds out via happenstance that they are infertile. It would be strange to say that this person has just discovered that they are disabled (and, unbeknownst to them, have been disabled for however long they've been infertile, though they will cease to be disabled once they pass normal childbearing years). More generally, it's strange to say that someone could have a disability they aren't aware of and which has no effect on their life. We do sometimes say of infertility that it can be disabling for people who very much want to have their biological children (although it isn't clear whether this usage is meant to describe physical or psychological disability). But someone who doesn't want children isn't disabled simply because they lack the ability to reproduce.[19]

---

[18] The WHO has since replaced this account of disability with one more influenced by the social model of disability. The UN, however, apparently still employs the 1980 definition. See http://www.un.org/esa/socdev/enable/dis50y10.htm.

[19] The 1980 definition makes a further distinction between disability and handicap—so its defender might contest that the infertile person who doesn't want children is disabled but not handicapped by that disability. I maintain, however, that any account of disability that classes this person as disabled is overgeneralizing.

Another—even more complicated—attempt at suitably qualifying the lack of ability account comes from Buchanan, Brock, Daniels, and Winkler (2000):

> To have a disability is to be unable to perform some significant range of tasks or functions that individuals in someone's reference group (e.g., adults)[20] are ordinarily able to do, at least under favorable conditions, where the inability is not due to simple and easily corrigible ignorance or to lack of the tools or means ordinarily available for performing such tasks or functions. (p. 286)

The proviso 'under favorable conditions' is in place to differentiate disability from limitations due to social prejudice. It would be true of a Black person in 1950s America that they were 'unable to perform some significant range of tasks or functions that individuals . . . are ordinarily able to do'. (That is doubtless still true for Black Americans today—but the Jim Crow laws made the limitations particularly explicit.) But we shouldn't thereby conflate race and disability.[21] Being Black limited what public transportation you could utilize, what public spaces you could inhabit, whether you could register to vote, etc.—but all in conditions that were highly unfavorable (i.e., highly racist). I take it that the idea is something like this—it's extrinsic features (such as racism) that placed functional limitations on Black Americans, whereas it's intrinsic features (such as lack of physical ability) that place limitations on disabled people. Someone who is blind simply cannot see—and cannot accomplish all the functions associated with seeing—no matter what her external surroundings are like.

This is, it's fair to say, an extremely controversial way of understanding disability. As proponents of the social model of disability (which we'll

---

[20] The clause about 'reference groups' is ostensibly in place to prevent it coming out that, e.g., toddlers are disabled because there are a lot of things they can't do that most people can do. But there are clearly going to be problems specifying what is meant by 'reference group' precisely. There is not much difference, physiologically, between seventeen year olds and eighteen year olds—but there's a tremendous difference, in our society at least, between them socially. Eighteen year olds can do many things that seventeen year olds can't, and it isn't clear that we can attribute this difference to 'unfavorable conditions' (at least, we'd need to learn more about what counts as favorable and unfavorable conditions). It seems that reference groups would need to be very fine-grained to get the right results for children and adolescents (as growth and development are rapid at this stage). But reference groups can't be too fine-grained if the account is going to work. Most people in their eighties are disabled in some way or other. But if we're comparing them to other people in their eighties, this account won't deliver the result that they are disabled.

[21] As we sometimes have—see especially Baynton (2013).

discuss in 1.4.1) have gone to great lengths to emphasize, many disabled people's limitations are due in large part to the way that our society is organized, rather than to anything intrinsic to the persons themselves. So if we understand 'favorable conditions' broadly enough to include conditions favorable to disabled people, there are many who will argue that this account rules out as disabilities lots of the things we would think of as paradigm cases of disability.[22]

But let's leave this issue to the side for now. Whether the functional limitation involved in disability is socially mediated notwithstanding, this account still fails condition (i). Once again, there are many disabilities for which there are no specific functions or tasks that a person with that disability cannot perform—though the tasks may be painful, or they may be able to do fewer of them in a given time period, or they may require assistive devices to accomplish them. In the other direction, there are conditions that meet the criteria given by Brock et al. that are not disabilities. Consider again the case of a petite woman. Depending on how we construe 'significant range',[23] there may well be a significant range of everyday tasks or functions that most people are able to do, but which she cannot do. She may not be able to open jars by herself, or reach the top shelf at the supermarket, or buy standardly sized clothing, and so on. That's certainly not to say that *all* petite women can't do these things—but there are definitely some petite women who can't, although most people in their reference group can. And yet such a woman is not disabled.

1.3.3 Disability is the interaction between impairment and social environment

Before shifting my focus to social constructionist accounts of disability (section 1.4), it's important to note that there is a family of accounts of disability—most notably the capabilities account, the revised WHO

[22] Similar points apply to the restriction to the 'tools or means *ordinarily available*' (my emphasis). Proper assistive devices and technology for disabled people are often not ordinarily available. But the disability rights movement stresses that this is a matter of social injustice.

[23] Perhaps the following activities don't count as a 'significant range' of tasks and functions. But the more stringently we understand 'significant range', the less chance the account has of adequately characterizing disability—there are many disabilities that don't preclude a 'significant range' of tasks or functions, in this stronger sense.

account, and the account offered by sociologist Tom Shakespeare—that seek to offer a middle ground between social constructionist and naturalistic approaches.[24] On all these views, disability is a multifaceted phenomenon in which disabled people face limitations partly due to intrinsic features of their bodies and partly due to barriers in their environment. On Shakespeare's model, for example, disability is limitation due to impairment, where 'impairment' is understood as departure from normal functioning (in the Boorse–Daniels sense). But this could be due to intrinsic features of the impairment, the interaction between impairment and social environment, or both.

I bring up these views simply to set them aside, since what I have to say about them overlaps with what I say about the normal functioning account (section 1.3.1) and the social model (section 1.4.1). My central concern with all these views is their reliance on a distinction between disability and impairment.[25] As I'll argue in section 1.4.1, there are major worries for views that rely on a disability/impairment distinction, particularly when (as is often the case) impairment is defined as departure from normal functioning. Such accounts inherit the problems of the normal functioning account. Moreover, as I'll argue in section 1.5, I think invoking a disability/impairment distinction makes views of disability more complicated than they need to be.

1.4 Social Constructions

So far, we've examined accounts of disability that attempt to answer the question 'what is disability' by focusing—at least primarily—on disabled bodies. What unifies individual disabilities, on these accounts, is something about what disabled bodies are like. Disabled bodies are bodies that function abnormally, or disabled bodies are bodies that lack some ability that normal bodies have, and so on. And I have argued that these accounts fail. I'm now going to make a further conjecture. Any such account of disability—that is, any account that says that what disabilities have in common is some specific feature of disabled bodies—will fail.

---

[24] See especially Mitra (2006) and Shakespeare (2006).
[25] E.g., Do we end up classifying limitation due to social prejudice against trans people or gay people as disability? If not, why not?

Obviously, I have not given arguments sufficient to support this conjecture (which is why I'm labeling it a conjecture). But the arguments I've given do make this conjecture seem, at least to me, quite plausible. Attempts to explain disability in terms of some feature that disabled bodies share are plagued by problems of over- and under-generalization. We specify some feature we think is distinctive of disabled bodies. But on closer examination, we see that non-disabled bodies can also have that feature, or that disabled bodies can lack that feature. I am skeptical that there is any feature of human bodies we can point to that is had by all and only disabled bodies, such that we can explain disability in terms of that feature. And if that's right, then there's nothing about disabled bodies that by itself explains what disability is.

It might be protested that disability is a disjunctively unified category—like jade. There isn't any single mineral composition that all and only instances of jade have in common, and that's because something can be jade by being either jadeite or nephrite.[26] Perhaps, similarly, there's no feature that *all* disabled bodies have in common. But certainly there are bodily features that some disabilities have in common—some disabilities involve loss of a sensory modality, other disabilities involve the inability to use some portion of the body, yet others involve chronic pain, and so on. Perhaps we might give a disjunctive account of disability based on these individual similarities, just as we give a disjunctive account of jade.

But the trouble with this approach is that I cannot see how it can meet criterion (iii). Some disabilities have physical or bodily features in common with each other. But suppose we then tried to give a disjunctive account of disability by listing those individual commonalities (in the precarious hope that the resulting disjunction would give us an extensionally adequate account of disability that wouldn't overgeneralize). We would say that disability is the loss of a sensory modality or the inability to use a part of the body or the absence of a limb or a physical condition that causes substantial chronic pain or a physical condition that causes

---

[26] See Kim (1992). Even in this case, though, it's plausible that the category is socially unified, rather than (disjunctively) naturally unified. Jadeite and nephrite have different mineral compositions, different physical characteristics (jadeite is harder than nephrite), and come in a different range of colors. What seems to unify them is not something natural, but rather that we have attached particular cultural meaning and significance to them.

reduced mobility or . . . and so on. But it then looks as though we simply encounter our original question—what, if anything, do the individual things we call 'disabilities' have in common with each other?—at this next level of abstraction. The question now simply becomes: What do the loss of a sensory modality, the inability to use a part of the body . . . etc. have in common with each other? What makes us think this heterogeneous group of features form a philosophically interesting kind?

So once again, my conjecture is this: There is no good answer to that question that explains the commonality solely in terms of what disabled bodies are like. There is nothing about what disabled bodies are like that *by itself* unifies or explains the category of disability. Disability is not a natural kind, and it cannot be explained via objective features of disabled bodies.

The claim that there is no physical or objective feature(s) had by all and only disabled bodies isn't particularly radical. Our own (contemporary, Western, industrialized) concept of disability is both relatively new and still in flux. For example, our contemporary understanding of disability groups together congenital and acquired disability, but throughout much of European history these wouldn't have gone together so clearly. Congenital disability was often considered deeply morally laden, much more so than acquired disability (which might be merely an unhappy accident).[27] And although the understanding of disability adopted by the disability rights movement, as well as contemporary medical and legal understandings of disability, explicitly allow for invisible disabilities, it's not clear that our folk conception of disability does. People with invisible disabilities often report that they feel stigmatized or marginalized when they identify as disabled, because people assume that if you are disabled this will be readily apparent.[28]

And just as there is historical variation in our understanding of disability, there is cross-cultural variation as well. For example, in the Democratic Republic of the Congo the Songye people distinguish between, roughly translated, 'bad' and 'faulty' people.[29] To be 'faulty' is to have some sort of physical defect or deformity which can be congenital or acquired, but which is not particularly marginalized in society. The group 'faulty' includes many of the things we classify as disability, but also seems to include some

---

[27] See especially Metzler (2005) and Holmes (2004).
[28] See especially Stone (2005).   [29] Devlieger (1995).

things we would think of as aesthetic features. Traits that are 'bad' likewise include many things we would classify as disabilities, but are only congenital (one cannot acquire a 'bad' trait), and are the subject of severe social marginalization. The Songye would recognize no category that lumps together the 'faulty' and the 'bad'. Likewise, some cultures see certain conditions we typically classify as disabilities as markers of special, privileged status. In Hmong culture, for example, most conditions we think of as disabilities are considered unfortunate accidents, or perhaps results of malevolent influence. But some conditions—in particular seizure disorders such as epilepsy—are seen as signs of divine favor and special wisdom.[30]

None of this, of course, shows that disability is not a natural kind. I'm happy to grant that we can make epistemic progress about natural kinds—we can *discover* natural kinds previously unknown to us. Disability could be one such kind. The point is simply that in denying that disability is a natural kind, and in denying that there is some feature(s) of disabled bodies that explains what disability is, I'm not thereby going against thousands of years of 'common sense' tradition. Whatever other objections there might be to such a view, it can't be objected to on the basis that societies everywhere throughout history have divided people into the disabled and the non-disabled.

With all this in mind, I'm now going to shift consideration to characterizations of disability according to which what individual disabilities have in common is not a feature of disabled bodies, but rather a feature of social interaction or social structures. That is, I'm going to focus on views that say disability is *socially constructed*.

1.4.1 The social model

A social constructionist approach to categories like race, gender, and disability seeks to explain such categories via appeal to social facts rather than natural facts. Social constructionism maintains that 'although it is typically thought that what unifies the instances of such categories is some set of *natural* or *physical* properties, instead their unity rests on *social* features.'[31]

---

[30] See especially Fadiman (1997).   [31] Haslanger (2014), p. 381.

The most familiar social constructionist approach to disability is doubtless the social model of disability. It's probably more accurate to say that the term 'the social model' picks out a family of views, as proponents of the model adopt a variety of (sometimes opposing) stances on points of detail. But I'm here understanding the social model as any of a range of views which maintain two hallmark tenets: a distinction between disability and impairment, and a further claim that disability is entirely constituted by social prejudice against persons with impairments.[32]

According to the social model, disability is the disadvantage produced by social prejudice against certain types of persons (persons with impairments). Were society not organized in a way that penalizes people with impairments, there would be no disabled people. Disability *just is* the negative net effects of having an impairment in a society that discriminates against those with impairments.

The social model has been tremendously influential, but I find it unsatisfactory for straightforward reasons.[33] Firstly, it's not clear that the account can meet criterion (iii)—that is, it's not clear that the social model is properly explanatory. We're told that disability arises due to social discrimination against those with impairments, but we are told relatively little about the impairments themselves.[34]

The worry here is that attempts to give a satisfactory account of impairment are likely to encounter all the problems discussed above for accounts of disability. It is no easier to say what physical feature(s) bodies with impairments have in common than it is to say what physical feature(s) bodies with disabilities have in common. Indeed, it's common to characterize impairments via exactly the sort of accounts—lack of

---

[32] Oliver (1996); Oliver and Barnes (2012).

[33] Amusingly, though, I am sometimes taken to be a major defender of it. Julian Savulescu (2015) cites me as one of the 'disability activists...who advance a social constructivist model of disability. Their central claim is that there is nothing inherently bad about disability, and people with disability are *only* disadvantaged either because of social prejudice/injustice or transition costs.' I have, to be clear, never defended any such view about disadvantage, and as chapter 3 makes clear this is not my view at all. Moreover, as the subsequent discussion emphasizes, social construction and the social model are not equivalent.

[34] Indeed, the lack of discussion of impairment within the social model is a recurring complaint—with some critics worrying that the resulting picture of disability is overly disembodied. See, for example, Hughes and Patterson (1997).

ability and departure from normal function—that we've already seen overgeneralize for disability.

It's sometimes suggested instead that impairment, like disability, is also socially constructed—'impairments' are those physical features that we stigmatize as being bodily defects or lacks, for example.[35] I won't discuss such views in much detail, but I think they face several serious problems. The most significant, to my mind, is that it isn't clear how such accounts can non-circularly distinguish impairments from other physical traits that give rise to prejudice and stigma—female sex organs, dark skin, etc. Such views will also face the kind of 'passing' worries discussed for Haslangerian and identity-based accounts in sections 1.4.2 and 1.4.3.

Is being gay an impairment, since it's a departure from 'normal function' that provokes discrimination? Is being petite an impairment, since it is a way one's body can be that restricts daily activities given the way society is structured? Is having female sex organs an impairment since it's a way your body can be which makes you subject to stigma and discrimination? It's not clear to me that either naturalistic or social constructionist accounts of impairments offer non-circular answers to such questions. And if we can't give a satisfactory account of what impairments are, then an account of disability that appeals to the impairment/disability distinction isn't adequately explanatory.

But the problems for the social model extend beyond the characterization (or lack thereof) of impairments. There's also the very straightforward worry that the characterization of disability offered by the social model is unsatisfactory and implausible. The social model says that disability *just is* the effect of discrimination. An ableism-free society is a society without disability. It's not, of course, a society without impairments. But impairments would, in such a society, not be disabling, and they would not constitute disabilities.

There are two ways of reading this claim. On the first, the social model says all the bad effects of *disability* are socially mediated (because disability is nothing more than the net effect of prejudice), but says nothing at all about whether impairments can or would have bad effects in the absence of such prejudice. On this reading, the only commitment the social model makes about impairments in an ableism-free world is

---

[35] For a defense of social constructionist accounts of impairment, see Tremain (2002); Vehmas and Mäkelä (2009).

that we shouldn't describe them as 'disability'. But on this reading, it seems that many of the philosophical questions we're interested in then become questions about impairment, not about disability. Is impairment something that's (by itself or intrinsically) bad for you? Should we try to eliminate impairments? Is it ever permissible to knowingly cause impairments? Would an ideal future society be one that's free, not just of social discrimination (and thus of disability, according to the social model), but also one that's free of impairments? The upshot of this reading of the social model is that we've moved the goalposts of inquiry (or perhaps simply renamed them). What we then need is a robust theory of impairments, and coming up with that will land us back with the same problems we started with.

But there's a stronger reading of the social model's claim, which often seems to be the reading intended by many of its proponents. According to this stronger reading, disability is the result of social prejudice against people with impairments, and furthermore all—or at least all the *substantial*—bad effects of impairments are due to this sort of prejudice. Impairments, in the absence of such prejudice, would be insignificant.

But this stronger reading is deeply implausible when we consider the full spectrum of disabilities. Perhaps it could be motivated for some paradigm cases of disability—some mobility or sensory impairments, for example. Although even for cases like these, it's hard to see why we should deny that, say, being unable to visually experience the faces of your loved ones or auditorily experience birdsong are bad effects of blindness and deafness, respectively—bad effects that would persist in the absence of ableism. Or consider cases of disability that involve chronic pain, or require continued medical monitoring, or are progressive. Society could be perfectly accepting of such conditions and they would still have a dramatic effect on the lives of those that have them.[36] The social model often seems committed, fallaciously, to the idea that if we want to say that disability is not bad, we have to say that disabilities would, in the absence of ableism, not have any bad effects (that is, would not be disabilities, but merely impairments). Chapter 3 argues in detail that these claims come apart.

---

[36] Based on these sorts of worries, it's sometimes been objected that the social model creates a 'disability hierarchy' between different forms of impairment. See Shakespeare (2013).

Proponents of the social model often set up a dichotomy—a choice between social and so-called 'medical' models of disability. The proposed dichotomy suggests that either we attribute all the bad effects of disability to social prejudice, or we accept an account of disability according to which disability is an individual matter (a 'personal tragedy').[37] But this dichotomy is a false one. There is wide variation—and divergence—in the characterization of disability that deserves the appellation 'social constructionist'. We can accept that what unifies disability is not objective similarity between disabled bodies without thereby committing to the social model.

1.4.2 A Haslangerian model

Perhaps the best-known proponent—and most careful expositor—of social constructionism in analytic philosophy is Sally Haslanger. Haslanger (2000) offers a version of social constructionism based on social hierarchies within social structures. When applied to disability, it gives a usefully different picture than that offered by the social model.

According to Haslanger (2000), a person, S, is a woman iff:

(i) S is regularly and for the most part observed or imagined to have certain bodily features presumed to be evidence of a female's biological role in reproduction;

(ii) that S has these features marks S within the dominant ideology of S's society as someone who ought to occupy certain kinds of social position that are in fact subordinate (and so motivates and justifies S's occupying such a position); and

(iii) the fact that S satisfies (i) and (ii) plays a role in S's systematic subordination, i.e., along some dimension, S's social position is oppressive, and S's satisfying (i) and (ii) plays a role in that dimension of subordination (p. 42).

And conversely, S is a man iff:

(i) S is regularly and for the most part observed or imagined to have certain bodily features presumed to be evidence of a male's biological role in reproduction;

---

[37] Oliver and Barnes (2012).

(ii) that S has these features marks S within the dominant ideology of S's society as someone who ought to occupy certain kinds of social position that are in fact privileged (and so motivates and justifies S's occupying such a position); and

(iii) the fact that S satisfies (i) and (ii) plays a role in S's systematic privilege, i.e., along some dimension, S's social position is privileged, and S's satisfying (i) and (ii) plays a role in that dimension of privilege (p. 42).

Similarly, a group G is *racialized* relative to a context C iff: members of G are (all and only) those:

(i) who are observed or imagined to have certain bodily features presumed in C to be evidence of ancestral links to a certain geographical region (or regions);

(ii) whose having (or being imagined to have) these features marks them within the context of the background ideology in C as appropriately occupying certain kinds of social position that are in fact either subordinate or privileged (and so motivates and justifies G's occupying such a position); and

(iii) whose satisfying (i) and (ii) plays (or would play) a role in their systematic subordination or privilege in C, i.e., who are *along some dimension* systematically subordinated or privileged when in C, and satisfying (i) and (ii) plays (or would play) a role in that dimension of privilege (p. 44).

Haslanger's approach to social construction is thus explicitly concerned with social position and social hierarchies. Our racial and gender categories are socially constructed insofar as *what those categories are* are dimensions of privilege or subjugation.

Let's examine these definitions in stages—looking at the definition of *woman* in particular—to get a clearer picture of what's going on. Condition (i) is meant to fix the class of people we're interested in—we're considering the group of people assumed to have bodily features we associate with a female's role in reproduction. The wording here is important; the people in this class are presumed to have such features, but they may not in fact have them. For Haslanger, to be a woman is to be treated as a woman (and this can and does come apart from being a clear case of female sex). A trans woman or an intersex woman can be *presumed* to have features such as a uterus and ovaries, though she might not in fact have them.[38] Likewise, the features can be real *or imagined*. Medieval anatomists thought that women's reproductive organs were basically inverted penises where babies could grow (women, being inferior creatures, had less 'internal fire' and so the penis was never pushed to the outside of the body, and remained internal).[39] No one has ever in fact had such a reproductive organ. What matters, for Haslanger's purposes, is that women were assumed to have such (imagined) bodily features and that these features were assumed to be part of a female's biological role in reproduction.

Condition (ii) picks out situations in which members of the class of people picked out by (i) are socially disadvantaged *because they are members of that class*. This is not to say that members of class (i) are always and in every way socially disadvantaged compared to non-members. It is simply to say that the fact that someone is a member of class (i) marks them out for certain specific kinds of social subordination. Which kinds of social subordination the members of (i) are marked out for might vary.

Finally, condition (iii) says that the fact that someone satisfies conditions (i) and (ii) will play a role in that person's being systematically socially oppressed along some dimension. There will be some aspect(s) of her social life in which she is continually disadvantaged and disempowered because she satisfies (i) and (ii). And this combination of (i)–(iii) is *what it is* to be a member of the social class woman. To be a woman is to occupy a subordinate social position—to be disadvantaged, along some dimension, with respect to men.

Haslanger is not saying that any and all women are socially disadvantaged compared to any and all men. Intersectionality matters—wealthy white women occupy a more privileged social position than poor Black men. Nor is she saying that there is a single dimension of disadvantage,

---

[38] This is where the 'regularly and for the most part' clause comes into play. A transvestite man might occasionally be taken to have such features when dressed as a woman, and a butch woman might similarly be on occasion taken to not have such features. But it doesn't follow that they are, in that context or for that period, the gender they are perceived to be. Haslanger is thus best understood as giving a theory of gender role—there might be other important aspects of gender, such as gender identity, which her view doesn't encompass. See especially Jenkins (forthcoming).

[39] See especially Miller (2010). The medieval view of female anatomy was apparently heavily influenced by Aristotle's view of women as 'deformed men'.

or a single subordinate social role, that is distinctive of being a woman. What she is saying is that to be a woman is to be marked for disadvantage *along some dimension*—what that dimension is can vary, and there might be other dimensions along which a woman is privileged.

Jane Austen's Emma Woodhouse and Greek tragedy's Iphigenia have very different social roles, and very different experiences of oppression. And different still are the role and oppression of Alice Walker's Celie. But all three are disadvantaged, and occupy subordinate social roles *along some dimensions*. Emma Woodhouse is rich and privileged, and people defer to her. But her options are severely constrained by gender roles. Iphigenia is likewise extremely privileged, more so even than Emma—she is the daughter of a king—but she is also more constrained than Emma; her gendered social role mandates meek obedience, even to the death. Unlike Emma and Iphigenia, Celie is oppressed racially and economically. But she's also oppressed in virtue of her gender. The Black men in *The Color Purple* are likewise disadvantaged racially and economically, but Celie's subordination has an added, gendered dimension (she is oppressed by and relative to the Black men in the story).

For Haslanger, to be a woman is to be socially subordinated—to occupy a place in a social structure such that you are disadvantaged (along some dimension) in comparison to men. Our gender categories—men and women—are hierarchical categories. They are ways we divide people based on perceived bodily characteristics that privilege some and disenfranchise others. And so the goal of feminism is to get rid of these entrenched hierarchies. This means, perhaps somewhat surprisingly, that the goal of feminism is to get rid of women (and men). To be clear, the goal is not, of course, to get rid of the people who are in fact categorized as women and men, but rather to get rid of the categorizations (that is, to eliminate the social hierarchy that constitutes the gender divide). The goal of feminism on the Haslangerian model is to make it such that, in the future, there aren't any women or men, and the categories 'man' and 'woman' are of purely historical use.

Might a Haslangerian approach to social constructionism work for disability?[40] Here's how this might go. A person, S, is disabled iff:

---

[40] A version of this view of disability seems, for example, to be what Anita Silvers (1998), p. 81 might have in mind when she says that 'disablement is not produced by the [physical] condition, but rather by the character of the conduct to which [people are] subjected.'

(i) S is regularly and for the most part observed or imagined to have certain bodily features presumed to be evidence of defective bodily functioning;

(ii) that S has these features marks S within the dominant ideology of S's society as someone who ought to occupy certain kinds of social position that are in fact subordinate (and so motivates and justifies S's occupying such a position); and

(iii) the fact that S satisfies (i) and (ii) plays a role in S's systematic subordination, i.e., along some dimension, S's social position is oppressive, and S's satisfying (i) and (ii) plays a role in that dimension of subordination.

But this straightforward translation of the Haslangerian model doesn't work, because (i) doesn't successfully pick out the right group of people. And that's primarily because whether someone is disabled and whether they are regularly and for the most part *observed* to have the bodily features we associate with disability are two different things. Being observed to have such bodily features is neither necessary nor sufficient for being disabled. Some disabilities—particularly those that usually involve the use of mobility aids like wheelchairs—are easily observable. Others are less so—you can't tell that someone is Deaf from a distance, for example, though deafness can often become apparent once, for example, someone begins a conversation. Yet others are variably observable—someone with MS might use a mobility aid on some occasions but not on others, walk with an unsteady gait on some days but not others, etc. Yet others are usually unobservable, but sometimes dramatically observable—epilepsy, to give a prime example. And others still—invisible disabilities—are almost always unobservable.

Conversely, one can regularly and for the most part be observed to have features associated with defective bodily functioning and yet not be (physically) disabled. Factitious disorder is a psychological condition in which a person goes to great lengths to fake the appearance of an illness or disability. In cases where the person fakes a disability, they can regularly be observed to have bodily features presumed to be evidence of defective bodily functioning.[41] They may even suffer social discrimination or

---

[41] There have been documented cases in which, for example, people convinced legal and medical professionals, as well as family and friends, that they were deaf-blind for several years. See Milner and Feldman (1998).

disadvantage because they are observed to have such features. And yet it's an odd result—to say the least—that a person with factitious disorder is physically disabled just because she pretends to be. (She may well be psychologically disabled—I leave that question to the side.) Indeed, in saying that a person with factitious disorder is disabled you would lose the very element of pretense that's constitutive of factitious disorder. By the very act of (successfully) *pretending* to be disabled, the person with factitious disorder would thereby *be* disabled.

1.4.3 Identity-based social construction

Perhaps, instead of focusing on social interaction and social roles, the salient thing to capture in a theory of disability is *group identity*.[42] Disability, on this view, would be important precisely insofar as people self-identify as disabled. It's an important category because it's a category that people have found useful and meaningful to self-identify as members of.

An analogous view of gender is sometimes advocated, particularly by those who want a theory of gender that accommodates the first-person testimony of some trans people.[43] Though it's certainly not the case that all trans people accept a binary gender identification, many do. And for at least some of these people—though again certainly not all—their binary gender identification is something they've felt strongly from a young age. A Haslangerian model of gender allows that, for example, someone who is sex male can be a woman. If such a person presents as female and is treated (regularly and for the most part) as female, then according to Haslanger they are a woman. But some people want to be able to say something stronger—they want to be able to say not only that such a person is a woman, but also that she has been a woman for as long as she has self-identified as one, even if there was a period of time at which she was treated like a man. It's this motivation that then leads to the adoption of an identity-based theory of gender.[44] Facts about gender,

---

[42] I'm going to specifically discuss views of gender that equate gender with gender identity. But other identity-centric versions of social constructionism—more familiar from philosophy of race (see especially Jeffers (2013))—aren't quite so strong. Their focus is on shared cultural identity, but self-identifying as a particular race can be a sufficient condition for being a member of that race. Similar points would apply, however, even to these views.

[43] See, for example, Bettcher (2009).

[44] Though, again, some argue that a theory of gender needs to accommodate *both* gender role *and* gender identity—that these are simply two different aspects of gendered experience; Jenkins (forthcoming).

on this view, are nothing more than facts about personal self-conception or self-identity. If you self-identify as a woman, you are a woman; if you self-identify as a man, you are a man; if you self-identify as non-binary or genderqueer, you're non-binary or genderqueer; etc. So the question is whether an analogous view might work as a theory of disability. I take no stand on whether such a view is adequate for gender, but I think that it is *in*adequate for disability. We can't explain what disability is simply by appeal to self-conception or self-identity.

The trouble with an identity-based theory of disability is that there are cases where people with conditions that are paradigm cases of disability do not self-identify as disabled, and there likewise seem to be cases where people who are paradigm cases of non-disability self-identify as disabled. *Self-identifying* as disabled is neither necessary nor sufficient for *being* disabled.

People involved in the Deaf pride movement want better understanding and respect for Deaf people. But in order to accomplish this, they have sometimes attempted to distance deafness from other disabilities. They take on board the common assumption that disability is bad, but want to argue that deafness is not bad. And this sometimes results in claims like 'Deafness is not a disability.' But it's not at all clear that we should take these claims as veridical and conclude that (some) Deaf people are not disabled. Claims such as these are often made out of ignorance of—and perhaps prejudice against—disabilities other than deafness.[45] Other disabilities are bad, sad, and tragic, deafness is not, so deafness must not be a disability. But other disabled people reject this characterization of their disabilities—indeed, the entire disability pride movement is centered around celebrating disability in general, just as the Deaf pride movement is centered around celebrating deafness. It seems like the most straightforward thing to say in this case is simply that some people in the Deaf community are wrong about what disability is like, rather than that Deaf people are not disabled if they don't self-identify as disabled.

Similarly, as we'll discuss in detail in chapter 6, many high-achieving people with paradigm instances of disability—paralysis, limb loss, etc.—will sometimes make claims like 'I've never thought of myself as

---

[45] See Atkinson (2008).

disabled.'[46] Again, such claims are often rooted in a stigmatized conception of disability. Disability is limitation or lack—it is being *less than* the non-disabled in some relevant sense—and so the high achiever who doesn't see themselves as limited or lacking feels pressure to say that they don't think of themselves as disabled. But again, the better response in this case seems to be rejecting the characterization of disability as nothing more than loss or lack, rather than granting that such people are not in fact disabled simply because their positive self-conception doesn't match their negative conception of disability.

On the flip side, there seem to be people who—at least plausibly— ought not to be classified as (physically) disabled, but who self-identify as (physically) disabled. To begin with, the case of factitious disorder is once again relevant. A curious feature of a small percentage of people with factitious disorder is that they will refuse to admit deception—to admit that they do not have the physical condition that they have been presenting themselves as having—even when confronted with compelling evidence of that deception.[47] It's not clear, in such cases, whether the person is simply refusing to admit that they are faking, or instead genuinely believes that they are not faking. So it's at least consistent with the evidence that some people with factitious disorder self-identify as disabled, and see themselves as making efforts, not to deceive, but rather to have their disability recognized. Suppose that this is true of some people with factitious disorder. It shouldn't follow that they are (physically) disabled, even if they believe themselves to be.

A more complex case is what often gets called body integrity identity disorder (BIID)—though activists prefer the term 'transabled'.[48] People who are transabled believe very strongly that in some sense their body *ought* to be disabled. The most familiar presentation is when a person believes that one of their limbs is not a part of their body, but BIID/ transability can also manifest as a persistent desire for paraplegia or other

---

[46] This claim is common among Paralympians, for example. See especially Glasgow Media Unit's report 'Bad News for Disabled People: How the Newspapers Are Reporting Disability' (http://www.gla.ac.uk/media/media_214917_en.pdf). For further discussion, see Howe (2011).

[47] Krahn et al. (2003).

[48] For an excellent overview see Blorn et al. (2012). See also Bosveld (2015).

specific disabilities.[49] Transabled people are generally in other respects completely psychologically typical, but they will go to great lengths—often endangering their lives—to make their body match their self-conception of the way their body ought to be.

In the case of transability, a person self-identifies (very strongly) as disabled, and typically has done so since childhood or early adolescence. But that self-conception doesn't match up to what their body is like, and so they will make great efforts to get their body to conform to their self-conception. Perhaps controversially,[50] I want to say that people who are transabled want to *become* disabled, and often successfully do so, but that before they undergo a body-altering procedure, they are not disabled. That is, I don't think that their self-identification as a disabled person is sufficient to make them disabled.

To press this point, it's worth noting that people who are transabled don't identify as disabled in the abstract. They identify as people with a *particular* disability—as amputees, as paraplegics, etc. And in general, we don't think people can be disabled in the abstract. You're disabled in virtue of having some disability or other. But it would require a fairly extreme amount of conceptual revision to say that, pre-transition, transabled people really are amputees, really are paraplegics, etc. And so I'm inclined to say that, pre-transition, they aren't disabled.

1.4.4 Social construction and the disappearing body

We can see, at this point, a recurring problem for traditional social constructionist models when applied to disability. The push toward social constructionism comes from thinking that there is no objective feature(s) of bodies that unifies individual disabilities. But though disability doesn't seem to be entirely explained by what disabled bodies are like, it's also not entirely separate from what disabled bodies are like. And that makes many standard social constructionist models inadequate as accounts of disability.

For example, the main component of the Haslangerian model is interpersonal social interaction. What gender you are is not a question

---

[49] Or, in some cases, that their body has/ought to have a specific disability, such as paraplegia. See First and Fisher (2012).

[50] It may be controversial because there are incredibly striking parallels between transability and the experience of some transgender people. See Lawrence (2006).

of what your body is like—what sexual organs or chromosomes you have—but is rather a question of what social position you occupy. It seems, though, that whether or not this holds for gender and race, it cannot be true of disability. There is more to being disabled than being treated in a specific way. Some people are treated as disabled who are not disabled (e.g., people with factitious disorder, as well as the occasional benefit fraudster). And some people are disabled who are not—or not usually—treated as disabled.[51]

Crucially, the disadvantages faced by disabled people are not simply a function of how people treat each other. Our society as a whole places normative expectations on bodies—what they can do, how they can do it, and in what amounts. Having a disability is—at least in part—having a body that fails to meet these norms. You can be socially disadvantaged because of what your body is like even if no one knows that's what your body is like, and even if no one treats you, interpersonally, as though your body is 'abnormal'. Moreover, some bodies come with unique challenges and difficulties, regardless of what the social norms are.

I've argued that there's no objective feature(s) that all and only disabled bodies share. But the worry is that standard models of social construction, when applied to disability, go too far in the other direction—the body drops out from them entirely. We may not be able to give an account of disability based on objective similarities shared by disabled bodies. And yet what your body is like *matters* to whether you are disabled. It might not matter for gender or race—I take no stand on that here—but it does matter for disability.

According to Rosemarie Garland Thomson (1997a), to say that disability is socially constructed is to say that 'disability is the attribution of corporeal deviance—not . . . a property of bodies [but] a product of cultural rules about what bodies should be or do.'[52] But this needn't be how we understand social construction. Being disabled is not *merely* a matter of what your body is like, but we can still allow that it is *partly* a matter of what your body is like. Disability could be a socially constructed property of bodies.

In *Blackness Visible*, Charles Mills argues that the social reality of race makes it possible to ask, of a person's race, 'what are they *really*?' There

---

[51] See especially Samuels (2013).   [52] Thomson (1997a), p. 7.

are questions of how the person is treated, how they are racialized, how they self-identify, etc.—but for Mills none of these questions exhaust the social reality of race. There remains a further question—do they *really have* the objective features we consider necessary or sufficient for being a member of a particular race? Mills makes it very clear that in saying this he doesn't thereby endorse a naturalistic or biological account of race. He thinks the reason that particular objective features are necessary and sufficient for racial classification is that society has placed cultural importance on these features. That is, social norms and attitudes determine which—of a diverse, arbitrary collection of objective properties, which by themselves have nothing to do with each other and have no socially independent significance as a group—matter for racial classification. Nevertheless, given the cultural importance society in fact places on these features, we can then ask the 'what are they *really?*' question. That is, we can ask whether an individual really does have the particular features that society has given social importance to as the hallmarks of racial classification.

In a similar vein, I suggest that the question of whether someone is disabled ought to be a question of what their body is (really) like. That is, whether someone is disabled is not merely a matter of how they are treated or how they self-identify. It's a matter of whether they in fact have particular objective bodily features. But the fact that these bodily features are important to us—the fact that they matter, and are considered relevant to the classification of someone as disabled—is due to the way we think about bodies, rather than some objective similarity between such bodies. And that's what it is, on my view, for disability to be socially constructed.

1.5 A Moderate Social Constructionism

Thus, following Mills, I propose that what we need is a moderate social constructionism—a view that says that disability is socially constructed, but which places greater importance on objective features of bodies (rather than how bodies are perceived or treated). That is, I propose that we need a social constructionism that still allows us to say that whether you are disabled is in part determined by what your body is (objectively) like.

1.5.1 The ameliorative project

In her discussion of social construction, Sally Haslanger introduces what she calls *the ameliorative project*. The basic idea behind the ameliorative project is this: When we are asking what social kinds like race and gender are, we should (at least in part) be asking what we *want them to be*. Why and how are these categories useful? Why should we care about them? How can they help us to accomplish our legitimate political and social goals? According to Haslanger, the ameliorative project for social categories 'seeks to identify what legitimate purposes we might have (if any) in categorizing people on the basis of [such categories], and to develop concepts that would help us achieve these ends'.[53]

There's a reading of the ameliorative project that takes it as a *truth-making* claim. Consider the true theory, T, of gender. Part of what makes T true is that T will help us achieve our political and social goals. If our (legitimate) goals with respect to gender involve gender justice and the end of patriarchy, then part of what makes T true is that T helps us to undermine the patriarchy (and no rival theory would help us more).

On this (very strong) reading of the ameliorative project, I don't find it plausible. It seems like the correct theory of a social kind and the most pragmatically useful theory of a social kind could, at least in principle, come apart. Suppose Haslanger is right about gender. What it is to have a gender is to occupy a space in a hierarchical social structure—to be privileged or subordinated along some dimension because of observed or imagined bodily characteristics associated with reproductive role. Gender justice, on this view of gender, mandates getting rid of these essentially hierarchical categories. The way to achieve gender justice is to no longer divide people in this way. But it seems like an open possibility that, for example, error theory might be a more useful theory in working toward this goal than is Haslanger's own theory. I don't want to argue that error theory is in fact more effective. My claim is this: If it turned out that error theory was actually a more effective tool for eliminating gender categories, it doesn't seem like that should automatically falsify Haslanger's account (or, for similar reasons, make it the case that error theory is true). A theory might be pragmatically effective for lots of reasons— because it is easy to understand, because it is compelling, etc. And it isn't

---

[53] Haslanger (2014), p. 386.

clear to me why any of these factors should bear on whether a theory is *true*, even when we are dealing with theories of social kinds.

So insofar as the ameliorative project should be understood in this truthmaking way, I'm unsympathetic to it. But there's a nearby idea to which I'm very sympathetic, and which I think is a plausible interpretation of Haslanger's ameliorative project.[54] Let's take as a starting point that—for whatever reason—a particular social category (gender, race, disability, etc.) doesn't correspond to anything natural or objective. At this point, error theory becomes a looming option for the category. In many such cases, we started out assuming the category was a natural category. But that assumption turned out to be untenable. So it's then tempting to move from 'category x doesn't correspond to anything natural or objective' to 'category x doesn't correspond to *anything at all.*' That is, once the assumption that a category like race, gender, or disability is a natural category is shown to be mistaken, there's a temptation to say that the category itself isn't in good standing.[55]

This is, famously, the approach to race taken by, inter alia, Anthony Appiah (1996) and Naomi Zack (1997). Appiah argues that because our folk concept of race is mistaken, we should say that there is no such thing as race, and that all attributions of race are false.[56] Haslanger finds this eliminativist approach to such social categories unsatisfying. And it's in arguing against eliminativism about categories like race and gender—and in favor of social constructionism—that she develops the idea of the ameliorative project.

Given this context, one way of interpreting the ameliorative project—the idea that we should ask what we want such categories to be, what the point of having such categories is, etc.—is as emphasizing the need to explain what we would be missing (if anything) if we adopted an error theory. On this reading, the ameliorative project looks like a species of a very familiar model of theory choice. When deciding between theories,

---

[54] See Barnes (forthcoming).

[55] 'Deconstructionist' projects—which attempt to show that disability, as a category, isn't in good standing—are increasingly common within critical disability studies. I'm not sure whether these projects deserve the label 'error theories,' but they do often make claims such as 'there's no such thing as disability.' For a brief overview see Shakespeare (2014), pp. 56–68.

[56] Appiah doesn't think we should forgo racial talk entirely, but argues that we should replace talk of races with talk of 'racial identities.'

we need to decide which theory gives us the best overall explanatory picture. We want our theories to be parsimonious, but not so parsimonious as to be expressively inadequate. We want our theories to be simple, but not overly simplified. And so on. A constraint on any successful theory is explanatory adequacy. So when we're considering theories that say that there is no such thing as gender or there is no such thing as race, we need to be able to say what, if anything, the (simpler, more parsimonious) error theories are missing out. *What would be lost* if we adopted an error theory of such categories?

What's distinctive about the ameliorative project, on this reading, is that it adds a new dimension to what we're paying attention to when we ask whether a theory is explanatorily adequate. Typically, the factors we consider when evaluating explanatory adequacy are things like: whether the theory makes sense of our communication practices, whether it can ascribe a reasonably high degree of rationality to agents, whether it explains the truth of the natural language sentences we assume are true, and so on. The ameliorative project asks us to look at more than these familiar considerations when evaluating explanatory adequacy. When evaluating theories of social categories, the ameliorative project asks us to consider what role these categories have to play in social progress—with the background assumption that understanding and explaining social injustice is part of what will help us to address it. Everyone agrees that we evaluate a theory partly by judging how well that theory does the work we need a theory of its kind to do. The ameliorative project tells us to expand our traditional concept of the work a theory needs to do. When we're dealing with theories of social kinds and social categories, part of the work such a theory needs to do is distinctively *social* work.

It's through this lens that I think we should view the question 'what is disability?' Why is it important to have a theory of disability? Why is disability per se something we should be interested in as philosophers, rather than simply focusing on individual disabilities? What would be lost if we were to simply adopt an error theory, and say that there is no such thing as disability?

What is interesting, worthwhile, useful, etc. about disability as a category is, I contend, that it's a social category people have found useful when organizing themselves in a civil rights struggle. It's a social category that people have used to explain what their experiences of social oppression have in common, and it's a social category people have used to group themselves together to work for progress and change. The social category of disability is philosophically interesting, that is, because of the disability rights movement. And so what *we want*—to use the terms of the ameliorative project—from a philosophical theory of disability is something that captures this aspect of disability.

But if that's why we're interested in disability, then another problem emerges for standard social constructionist pictures. A striking feature of the disability rights movement over the last twenty years has been an evolution from simply demanding equality to actively *celebrating* disability. The movement now includes not just protests and demands for legislation, but disability pride parades, disability-centric art and theater, and an emphasis on shared community.[57] *Disability culture* is an increasingly vivid part of the disability rights movement.[58]

But this leaves the emerging conception of disability within the disability rights movement—sometimes called an *affirmational* conception of disability[59]—at odds with many of the most popular versions of social constructionism. According to accounts like the social model (as well as 'mixed' accounts like those mentioned in section 1.3.3), disability is something entirely negative—it is an improper imposition of social norms upon bodies or a mismatch between expectations about what bodies should be like and what some bodies are like. Similarly, a Haslangerian model says that disability is the social subordination of bodies marked as deviant in some way.[60] For all these views, disability is something we should want to go away (even if we don't want 'impairments' to go away).

---

[57] Brown (2002); Sandhal and Auslander (2005).

[58] Analogies are often drawn here to the role that *gay culture* has played in the gay rights movement. Corbett (1994); McRuer and Wilkerson (2003).

[59] Swain and French (2000).

[60] The upshot of Haslanger's view of gender is that genders as we know them—the categories man and woman—should be eliminated. And Haslanger uses the ameliorative project to motivate this view of gender. (Re)conceptualizing gender as inherently hierarchical—and thus inherently problematic—helps us, she argues, to work toward equality, in part by transforming the way we think about what gender *is*. But regardless of whether this is correct in the case of gender, it's worth noting that the issue might play out very differently for disability. Most people *already* think disability should be eliminated. So the claim that the category should be eliminated—while it might be transformational and radical in the case of gender—is utterly mundane in the case of disability. A Haslangerian model of disability would, of course, contend that disability should be eliminated *for reasons other than what most people assume*. But that's not re-conceptualization to nearly the same extent.

It's difficult to maintain, simultaneously, that disability is something to be celebrated and that disability is something we ultimately want to get rid of. And so familiar social constructionist accounts have a hard time accommodating the affirmational conception of disability characteristic of disability pride. In this sense, standard social constructionist views of disability prejudge the normative issues just as much as the normative reading of Daniels's normal functioning account or Kahane and Savulescu's 'welfarist' account.

I'll argue in chapter 6 that a concept of disability pride is essential to combating a specific type of *epistemic injustice* that disabled people are subject to. But my claim here is simply that a successful answer to the question 'what is disability?' shouldn't stipulate that disability is bad, harmful, etc. We first need to say what—if anything—unifies individual disabilities. Then we can begin to investigate the question of what the relationship is between disability and various normative issues. It might be protested that what unifies individual disabilities is, in fact, something normative. But, viewing the question 'what is disability?' through the lens of the ameliorative project, I'm skeptical about this. I've claimed that what's interesting about disability—why we want and need an account of disability—is that it's a category that people have found useful when organizing themselves in a civil rights movement. And so I think that an account of disability needs to at least *leave open* that the affirmational characterization of disability increasingly common within that civil rights movement is correct. That is, it should be left open that disability pride makes sense and that people might have reason to self-identify as disabled even in a world free of prejudice against the disabled.

1.5.2 Disability as solidarity

I've proposed that what matters about disability as a category—why it's interesting, and why we should care about it—is that it's a category people have found useful when organizing themselves in a civil rights struggle. Now I want to take that idea and run with it. I'm going to present an account of disability on which disability *just is* whatever the disability rights movement is promoting justice for.[61]

---

[61] This phrasing is a bit strained—the disability rights movement doesn't promote justice for disabilities, it promotes justice for disabled people. But I'll explain later why I want to focus specifically on disabilities, rather than on the people that have disabilities.

Our modern conception of disability is relatively new. And there's a substantial amount of evidence that the development of this way of thinking about disability has been heavily influenced by the emergence of the disability rights movement—and further codified through the laws that the disability rights movement lobbied for.[62] So it's not terribly radical to go a step further: The disability rights movement didn't just influence the category disability, they *created* it.

I want to say that disability is socially constructed from group solidarity.[63] A group of people with a variety of physical conditions got together and observed that their experiences of their bodies had something in common. They used that commonality to organize themselves in a civil rights struggle aimed at promoting justice for people with bodies they judged to be importantly similar (and to give rise to importantly similar experiences) to their own. Disability, as a category, is constructed from that solidarity among people with physically non-standard bodies.

Here's a first pass. A person, S, is physically disabled iff:

(i) S has physical condition x
(ii) Members of the disability rights movement judge that x is among the physical conditions that they are seeking to promote justice for.

This gets at the basic idea: You're disabled just in case you have the sort of body that the disability rights movement is promoting equality for. But it's too simple to work. To begin with, no social movement is monolithic in its judgements (or in its constituents—see section 1.5.3). There is disagreement within the disability rights movement about which conditions should count as disabilities, just as there is

---

[62] For discussion see especially Linton (1998). See also Scotch (1988).

[63] I don't here have the space to delve into a discussion of what group solidarity consists in. For a philosophical theory of solidarity I particularly recommend Tommie Shelby's *We Who Are Dark*. Shelby identifies (2005, pp. 69–70) five central features of group solidarity: (i) identification with the group ('[the] tendency of members of the group to identify . . . with each other and with the group as a whole'); (ii) special concern ('a disposition to assist and comfort those with whom one identifies'); (iii) shared values and goals ('more or less vague ideals, specific policies, practical principles, broad social programs, political ideologies, or utopian social visions'); (iv) loyalty ('faithfulness to the group's values . . . and a willingness to exert extra effort . . . to advance the group's interests'); (v) mutual trust ('reason to believe that the others will not let him down, betray his trust, or free ride').

disagreement within feminism about which persons should count as women. We can't simply say that you're disabled iff: the disability rights movement says you are, any more than we can say you're a woman iff: feminism says you are.

Moreover, it seems strange to postulate members of the disability rights movement as inviolable disability detectors. (Or better: inviolable disability *determiners*.) They should be able to sometimes be wrong about whether something is a disability. There are many conditions that are poorly understood or carry associated stigma—obesity, chronic fatigue syndrome, sexually transmitted diseases, etc. It seems like members of the disability rights movement might judge that such conditions aren't disabilities for all sorts of reasons (prejudice, stigma, misinformation) that ought to be orthogonal to whether such conditions are in fact disabilities. But the simple model above can't allow for that.

So here's what I suggest. The disability rights movement doesn't make judgements about what is and what isn't a disability at random. Their judgements are rule-based[64] (even if the rules are not explicit or transparent, and even if the rules are sometimes incomplete). It doesn't matter, for my purposes, what those rules in fact are. But I suspect that they are something like cluster-concept reasoning. The disability rights movement tends to count a physical condition as a disability (and therefore as something they're working to promote justice for) if it has some sufficient number of features such as: being subject to social stigma and prejudice; being viewed as unusual or atypical; making ordinary daily tasks difficult or complicated; causing chronic pain; causing barriers to access of public spaces; causing barriers to employment; causing shame; requiring use of mobility aids or assistive technology; requiring medical care; and so on. As with most cluster concepts, there will no doubt be vagueness and borderline cases. But the idea is that it's this sort of (familiar) cluster-concept reasoning that's employed.

---

[64] In roughly the sense of 'constitutive rules' developed by Searle (1969) and Rawls (1955). For Searle, the paradigm locution of a constitutive rule is 'x counts as Φ in context C.' Rules of this kind are rules determined by social practice—things like the rules of chess, or the offside rule in soccer.

With that in mind, we can say the following. A person, S, is physically disabled in a context, C, iff:

(i) S is in some bodily state x[65]

(ii) The rules for making judgements about solidarity employed by the disability rights movement classify x in context C as among the physical conditions that they are seeking to promote justice for.

Here's the idea, in a nutshell. A collection of people got together and identified a form of group solidarity. Although they had a strikingly heterogeneous range of physical conditions, they perceived a commonality in how those physical conditions were stigmatized, how people treated them because of those physical conditions, how those physical conditions made it difficult to access public spaces, to complete everyday tasks, to get adequate healthcare, get full-time employment and benefits, etc. And so despite having very different bodies, it made sense to think of their experience of their bodies as having something in common, and it made sense to think of themselves as working toward a common goal. This all involved judgements of solidarity (shared experience, shared struggle, shared goals). Those judgements of commonality are (implicitly) rule-based. The application of those rules determines what counts as a disability. Disability is all and only the things that the disability rights movement ought[66] to consider as things they are promoting justice for—it is rule-based solidarity among people with certain kinds of bodies.[67]

But this allows that the disability rights movement can be mistaken—even systematically mistaken—about whether a given physical condition is a disability. And that's because they can deploy their own rules

[65] I intended clause (i) to range over particular bodily states or features, rather than family groupings of physical traits, illnesses, etc. So the kind of physical conditions I have in mind would be, e.g., the particular bodily state of someone with MS—the particular condition of their nerves and muscles—rather than MS as a kind.

[66] 'Ought' in the sense of applying their own rules for judgements about commonality and solidarity correctly and rationally.

[67] Crucially, the suggestion here is not—as social constructionism is sometimes accused of doing—to ignore intersectionality and suggest that there is some experience of disability that all disabled people have or could have in common. Rather, it is to suggest that there are some physical conditions that a particular social movement can make (rule-based) judgements about as being the kind of physical conditions they are trying to make it easier to live with. See especially Devlieger and Albrecht (2000).

incorrectly. Likewise, the disability rights movement can be ignorant about whether something is a disability. A given condition can in fact be something that the movement is promoting equality for without the movement realizing this.

On this account, whether you have a disability is partly determined by what your body is like (and not merely by how your body is perceived or treated by others). Like Mills's view on race, on this view of disability it makes sense to ask whether someone is *really* disabled. The person with factitious disorder doesn't count as disabled, because they don't in fact have a physical condition that the disability rights movement is promoting justice for (even if they are often perceived to have such a condition). But it's still the case that disability is socially constructed. A group of people make solidarity judgements based on things their bodies, and their experience of those bodies, have in common. Those judgements are rule-based, and it's the application of those rules that determines what counts as a disability. So it's the application of social features (judgements about solidarity) to objective features of bodies that creates disability.

It's also important to note that these solidarity judgements needn't neatly classify *types* of physical conditions as disabilities. We're often tempted—perhaps as a legacy of naturalistic accounts of disability—to ask questions like 'is asthma a disability?' or 'is psoriasis a disability?' But there needn't be any general answer to such questions. Perhaps severe asthma definitely is a disability, while mild asthma is not. There's no need to deliver a yes/no verdict to the question of whether asthma is *in general* a disability. (Nor is there a need to invoke a disability/impairment distinction in order to allow for this.) Someone with severe asthma will be in a different bodily state than someone with mild asthma. The kinds of efforts made by the disability rights movement for accessibility, accommodation, acceptance, etc. may be relevant to someone whose body is severely affected by asthma in a way they simply aren't for someone whose body is only mildly affected by asthma.

Context also matters. A condition that is barely noticeable to someone working a relaxed desk job might present extreme barriers for and have profound impact on the daily life of someone whose livelihood depends on manual labor. Likewise, a condition that is nothing more than an annoyance in one community might be the kind of thing that affects nearly every aspect of daily life in a community in which it is deeply stigmatized. Again, we can allow for this kind of flexibility without needing a distinction between disability and impairment, or between disability and handicap. Whether the way your body is will give rise to experiences that have important commonalities with the experiences of other people we think of as disabled will depend, at least in part, on your circumstances.

I've suggested that disability-related judgements of solidarity are based around a cluster of central concepts. Why not instead simply say that disability is the cluster concept that the judgements of solidarity are based on? Because although such an account would have the same extension, I don't think it's as explanatory. We need an account of what unifies individual instances of disability—we need to explain what such individual conditions have in common. But the cluster concept itself might not explain this. For all I know, it's a gerrymandered, unnatural cluster. So what unifies disability as a category isn't obviously the cluster concept itself. Rather, what unifies the category (and what makes the cluster concept interesting, whether or not it's gerrymandered) is the underlying social solidarity—these individual conditions are *the kind of thing* that the disability rights movement is trying to make the world a better place to live with.

1.5.3 On circularity and vagueness

I've tried to give an account of disability by appealing to the practices of the disability rights movement. But doesn't that make my account circular, thereby violating condition (iv)? I don't think that use of the term 'disability' is enough to render the account circular. Civil rights movements are individuated by what they do, not by their names. So, for example, there is a civil rights movement that focuses on mass incarceration, police violence, unequal sentencing, 'stop and frisk' rules, and impediments to voter registration, among many other things. There is another that focuses on marriage equality, sexuality-related hate crimes, equal access to partner benefits, and HIV awareness, among many other things. And then there is yet another that focuses on access to public spaces, opposition to eugenics, accommodations in the workplace and in education, availability of assistive technology, affordable access to care (both healthcare and personal assistance), and whose slogan is 'Nothing about us without us.' One doesn't need to appeal to a prior understanding of disability to tell the difference between the disability rights movement and other social movements, or to single out the disability rights movement.

That being said, my account appeals to *the* disability rights movement as though it was a single thing. That's a convenient simplification—but it is also an *over*simplification. I don't have an underlying theory of civil rights movements to offer, but it's plausible that there might be lots of distinct (or partially distinct) social groups that fall under the broad heading of disability rights movements. I'm happy with the idea that there might be lots of different disability rights movements, or that— more parsimoniously—it's simply vague or indeterminate which social group is referred to by 'the disability rights movement'.

Suppose we took the first alternative—allowing that there are many different (perhaps overlapping) social groups and that 'the disability rights movement' picks out different ones in different contexts. On this way of thinking about things, there would then be many different (similar, over-lapping) social categories created by these different (similar, overlapping) social groups. We could then adopt David Lewis's famous solution to the problem of the many—there are many social categories here, but there is *almost* one. Which of the various social categories in the vicinity deserve the name 'disability',[68] on this view, is underdetermined—but it also doesn't matter very much. To rephrase Lewis, 'which one deserves the name ["disability"] is up to us. If we decline to settle the question, nothing else will settle it for us. We cannot deny the arbitrariness. What we can deny, though, is that it is trouble.'[69] We can still continue to do interesting philosophy about disability in general (rather than individual disabilities), because on the Lewis-style view, although there's no one thing that uniquely counts as disability, the differences between the candidates are philosophically insignificant.

Alternatively—and my own preferred option—we could instead say that this entire domain (like most any aspect of social ontology) is riddled with indeterminacy. It's indeterminate which social group should count as the disability rights movement (it's indeterminate what the group's members are, what its membership conditions are, what its temporal and cross-cultural extension is, etc.). Similarly, it's plausibly

---

[68] Where 'disability' is being used as a technical term—again, I'm not here trying to give a theory of our ordinary language usage of 'disability'.

[69] Lewis (1999), p. 172.

indeterminate which rules for solidarity-based judgement are *the* rules employed by whatever social group counts as the disability rights movement. That will mean that it's indeterminate which physical conditions count as disabilities. (That is, it's indeterminate what the extent of the relevant social category is.)

But rather than being a problem, I think that's exactly what we should expect for a category as messy as disability. I don't want to take a view here on what the best thing to say about such indeterminacy is. I just want to register that I don't see it as a drawback of the view. Indeed, it would strike me as deeply implausible that any aspect of our complex, multifaceted social reality had fully determinate boundaries.[70]

1.5.4 Other worlds and other times

Richard III was disabled. But Richard III lived long before the emergence of the disability rights movement. Does this model allow us to say that Richard III was disabled? Yes. Richard III had a physical condition such that the (actual, present) rules for making judgements about solidarity employed by the disability rights movement classify *that condition* as something the disability rights movement is promoting justice for. And so Richard III counts as disabled, even though the disability rights movement never promoted justice *for him*.

That is, my view allows me to say that disability *travels*. It's often assumed that social kinds shouldn't travel,[71] but I think that at least in the case of disability the anti-travel motivations are mistaken. It's true that historically we wouldn't have thought in terms of disability or divided people up along disabled/non-disabled lines the way we do now. And Richard III wouldn't have self-identified as disabled. But there's a difference between saying 'historically we didn't have the concept of disability' or 'historically, we wouldn't have divided people up in this way' and saying 'historically, no one was disabled.' Richard III had a physical condition that marked him out for stigma and social

---

[70] There's sometimes a suggestion that areas where there is a lot of vagueness or indeterminacy are areas we should treat with less metaphysical seriousness—the important questions, for example, are just a matter of how we use our words. But I don't think the inference from 'is vague' to 'isn't metaphysically robust or interesting' is a good one, and I think it's especially one that should be rejected by those interested in social ontology. See Barnes (2014).

[71] See especially Mallon (2004).

prejudice and which affected his daily life. That's the kind of physical condition the disability rights movement is promoting justice for (even though they weren't doing so during his lifetime). And so Richard III was disabled.[72]

What about non-actual (rather than non-present) scenarios? Blindness is a paradigm case of disability. But consider the case of Geordi La Forge—the blind character from *Star Trek: The Next Generation*. In the technologically advanced future, Geordi has access to a device that allows him to process visual information. Is Geordi disabled? There's often an assumption in discussions of disability that to be disabled is to be substantially disadvantaged or stigmatized in some way. And if that's right, then Geordi isn't disabled.

But on my view, there's no essential link between disability and disadvantage or stigma. Although Geordi is in a context that's very different than the actual, present contexts in which people experience blindness, his experience of blindness still has a profound impact on his life. It makes him reliant on assistive technology, it makes his daily experience of processing visual information strikingly different than that of most people, it makes him go about many daily tasks in unusual ways, and it makes him feel like he sticks out. The disability rights movement seeks to promote awareness of—and celebration of—bodily difference. Those kinds of efforts are relevant to Geordi's experience of blindness, even though Geordi isn't substantially disadvantaged by his blindness. So Geordi's blindness can still be considered a disability, even in such a futuristic context. It's not analytic or necessary of disabilities that they be disadvantageous.

Theories of disability have standardly maintained much more contextual flexibility than this. On the social model of disability, for example, you stop being disabled if you stop being socially marginalized because of an impairment. The thought has traditionally been that conditions are disabilities only insofar as they are disadvantageous or harmful in some way. To account for this, layers of complexity are often introduced—we distinguish between disability and handicap, handicap and impairment, and so on.

---

[72] Saying this allows us to make important claims like 'Richard III faced prejudice because of his disability' and 'Shakespeare's play *Richard III* is an important historical example of literary stigma about the disabled.'

The view I'm defending here presents a simpler picture. I favor this approach in part because it's more parsimonious—we don't need to distinguish between separate categories of disability, impairment, handicap, etc. But a further advantage is that this approach leaves room for an affirmational model of disability. It's an open question, on this account, whether in a society free of prejudice against the disabled people there might still be disabled people. The *essential* link between disability and disadvantage is broken. Yes, most disabilities are in fact (actually, presently) disadvantageous. But maybe they don't have to be. And maybe they wouldn't cease to be disabilities simply by ceasing to be disadvantageous.

I'm identifying the social category disability by rigidifying on the actual, present rules for making solidarity judgements. But, crucially, whether this category is of interest to us can vary—both across times and across worlds. Perhaps the world in which, for example, mobility differences are not in any way stigmatized is a world in which a different social category matters to us, and a different social category deserves the name 'disability'. Likewise, perhaps one hundred years from now—if we have progressed in our treatment of disabled people—a different category might be of interest to us (or our current category will be primarily of historical interest). Or maybe we'll be interested in exactly the same category. This account makes no predictions at all about that. What this picture entails is that if you've got a substantial mobility difference one hundred years from now, you'll be a member of the social category we currently call 'disability'. But whether we will still call that category 'disability', or whether that category will be of interest to us at all, is left open.

Standard accounts of disability also include large amounts of contingency. It's common to say that if circumstances had been different—if there had been ramps everywhere, or we all spoke a signed language instead of a spoken language, or we made different daily demands on our bodies—then a different group of people would have been disabled. Disability, on my view, is still a deeply contingent matter, but the contingency is located elsewhere. There could have been no disability rights movement (either because there could have been no social movement for disabled people, or because a social movement for disabled people could have been combined with another social movement, such that there was no distinctively disability-focused movement). Likewise, the disability rights movement might easily have employed different rules for judgements about solidarity. And so that there is a category of disability and that it includes the physical conditions it does are both, on this account, deeply contingent. But again, I allow for this without introducing complex distinctions between disability, impairment, and handicap. Such distinctions aren't necessary for the contingency and contextual variation we want from a theory of disability.

1.6 Stacking the Deck?

The rest of the book is about the connection between disability and well-being. But you might worry that, at this point, I've stacked the deck. If disability is socially constructed in the way I argue, doesn't that help the case of those who say disability isn't something bad? I don't think that the kind of social constructionism I defend here stacks the deck in favor a disability-positive view, so much as it levels the playing field. Many naturalistic accounts of disability make disability-negative views seem plausible, maybe even obvious. If disability *just is* the lack of a substantial ability or a negative departure from normal functioning, it makes perfect sense to think that disability is bad. But disability isn't anything so simple, and the fact that we've tended to view it as such is perhaps part of the reason why we tend to think it's obvious that disability is bad.

Plenty of social kinds which we think are bad and ultimately want to get rid of are (plausibly) socially constructed. Being a victim of domestic violence, being a refugee, being an addict—these are all kinds that are amenable to a social constructionist analysis, but they are also the kinds of thing that we think are clearly harmful. So saying that a kind is socially constructed doesn't, by itself, in any way suggest that there's no connection between being a member of that kind and net reduction in well-being. Nor does a solidarity-based version of social constructionism suggest this. Various victims rights groups, for example, seem to be formed from a kind of solidarity-based social constructionism, and yet we definitely wouldn't infer from that that being a member of such a group isn't thereby something harmful. So the question of whether and to what extent there is a connection between disability and well-being isn't settled by saying that disability is socially constructed (or even socially constructed based on group solidarity).

2

Bad-Difference and Mere-Difference

Are we 'worse off'? I don't think so. Not in any meaningful sense. There are too many variables. For those of us with congenital conditions, disability shapes all we are. Those disabled later in life adapt. We take constraints that no one would choose and build rich and satisfying lives within them. We enjoy pleasures other people enjoy, and pleasures peculiarly our own. We have something the world needs.

Harriet McBryde Johnson (2005)

Let's assume that I have convinced you, in the previous chapter, that it makes sense to give a philosophical account of *disability* in general, rather than of individual disabilities—or at least that you are happy to keep reading, even if I haven't convinced you. The core question of this book involves the connection between disability and well-being. Is disability simply another way of being a minority—something that makes you *different* but not something that makes you worse off? Or is disability something that's bad for you—not merely something that makes you different, but something that makes you worse off because of that difference? I'm going to defend the view—common within the disability rights movement, but often dismissed as incredible by philosophers—that disability is *neutral* with respect to well-being.

The goal of this chapter, though, is not to address the question of whether disability is bad or neutral. The goal is, rather, to characterize this distinction. (Readers should note that some of the discussion in sections 2.1–2.3 is intricate, and perhaps a little dry. Those not fond of the minutiae of philosophical distinctions should feel free to assume the basic moral 'it's complicated' and proceed directly to section 2.4.)

Let's call views that maintain that disability is by itself something that makes you worse off 'bad-difference' views of disability. According to bad-difference views of disability, not only is having a disability a bad thing, having a disability would still be a bad thing even if society was fully accommodating of disabled people. In contrast, let's call views that deny this 'mere-difference' views of disability. According to mere-difference views of disability, having a disability makes you physically non-standard, but it doesn't (by itself or automatically) make you worse off. This rough-and-ready distinction highlights the basic ideas, but it needs to be explained in much more detail if it's going to be put to work.

In what follows, I'll refer to *the* mere-difference view and *the* bad-difference view, mostly for simplicity's sake. I'm using these descriptions to pick out two exclusive—though not exhaustive—options for how disability interacts with well-being: either disability (by itself or intrinsically) makes you worse off, or it simply makes you different. The former is what I call the bad-difference view, the latter is what I call the mere-difference view. But I'm not thereby suggesting that these terms pick out unique theories of disability. There are lots of distinct views of disability that count as mere-difference views—the social model of disability, as well as the view I'll be defending in chapter 3 are two such views. And there are likewise lots of distinct views of disability that count as bad-difference views—a utilitarian like Peter Singer will have a very different view of disability than a neo-Aristotelian like Philippa Foot, but they both defend bad-difference views.

2.1 What the Mere-Difference View is Not

First, let me explain why the bad-difference/mere-difference distinction is complicated. There are a lot of claims easily confused with the basic statement of the mere-difference view, but which are not commitments of the mere-difference view. Working out what the commitments of the mere-difference view really are, as we shall see, is a tricky matter.

2.1.1 Average well-being

The mere-difference view isn't simply the view that, on average, disabled people aren't any worse off than non-disabled people. It's perfectly consistent with the mere-difference view that the actual well-being of disabled people is, on average, lower than that of non-disabled people, simply because of how society treats disabled people. Indeed, given that our culture assumes that disability is a bad thing, and does not do a particularly good job of accommodating or accepting people with disabilities, it might be reasonable to expect on those grounds alone that disabled people would have, on average, lower levels of well-being than non-disabled people.[1] Whether they do seems to tell us nothing about whether disability *itself* negatively affects personal well-being. And that's because the negative effects on well-being could be largely or entirely determined by ableism, rather than by disability itself.

Most people hold a mere-difference view of gayness. And yet gay people tend to be at higher risk of depression, anxiety, self-harm, and suicide.[2] It could well be the case that gay people have, *on average*, lower levels of well-being than straight people. But such discrepancy would not be remotely mysterious, nor would it in any way threaten a mere-difference view of gayness. It's not easy to be gay in contemporary society. Straightness is the perceived norm, and gayness is discriminated against. Most of us, I'd wager, would attribute any discrepancy in well-being between gay people and straight people to the way society treats gay people, not to gayness itself. That is, we don't think such a discrepancy (if there is one) tells us anything about the effect gayness itself has on well-being.

For similar reasons, a discrepancy in well-being between disabled and non-disabled people can't by itself support a bad-difference view of disability. Nor is the mere-difference view of disability committed to the claim that disabled people are no worse off, in the actual world, than non-disabled people.

2.1.2 Intrinsic goods

The mere-difference view also needn't deny that disability involves the loss of intrinsic goods or capabilities. Many people are attracted to the idea that things like hearing, seeing, walking, etc. are intrinsic goods—or at least facilitate intrinsic goods (such as, perhaps, auditory

---

[1] Though it should be mentioned that at least the *perceived* well-being of disabled people often doesn't match up to what non-disabled people expect it to be—there's a substantial body of research that suggests that disabled people's perception of their own happiness and contentment is relatively similar to that of non-disabled people, whereas non-disabled people expect it to be much lower. More on this later.
[2] See, for example, Hartman (2013), Mustanski et al. (2010).

experience of music, visual perception of artworks, etc.). And it's easy to think that the mere-difference view of disability must deny this.[3]

But it's perfectly consistent with the mere-difference view that disability sometimes or even always involves the loss of some goods. It's just that, according to the mere-difference view, disability can't be *merely* a loss or a lack. That disability is merely a loss or a lack of some good is, of course, how people often view it. Take all the goods had by a 'normal' person. Subtract a few. That's disability. But the mere-difference view can maintain that this is an inadequate conception of disability (just as, in section 1.3.2, I argued that the view that disability is merely the loss of an ability is an inadequate view of disability) without denying that some or even all disabilities involve the loss of some goods.

The mere-difference view can maintain that the very same thing that causes you to lose out on some goods (unique to non-disability) allows you to participate in other goods (perhaps unique to disability). For example, the mere-difference view can grant that the ability to hear is an intrinsic good. And it's an intrinsic good that Deaf people lack. But being Deaf is not simply the lack of the ability to hear. There are other goods, perhaps other intrinsic goods—the unique experience of language had by those whose first language is a signed rather than spoken language, the experience of music via vibrations, etc.—experienced by Deaf people and not by hearing people. Deafness can involve the lack of an intrinsic good without being *merely* the lack of an intrinsic good.

To be clear, the claim is not that whenever disabilities involve the absence of some intrinsic goods the lack of those goods is somehow 'compensated for' by other, disability-specific skills or abilities. A defender of the mere-difference view doesn't need to hold a 'Supercrip' view, in which disabled people invariably have heightened senses or special, disability-enhanced skills which 'make up for' their disability. Disabled people are not Daredevil. The claim is, instead, that there can be unique goods associated with living in a disabled body. Those goods don't need to be things we might ordinarily describe as 'abilities' (see section 3.5).

Consider a different case. We might, at least insofar as we think abilities like hearing and walking are intrinsic goods, also think that

---

[3] Cf. Silvers (2003).

the ability to be pregnant and give birth—to grow a new person in your own body!—is an intrinsic good. As abilities go, it is certainly an impressive one. People who are male lack this ability. Nor is there any obvious male-specific ability we can point to that *compensates* men for this lack. Being male is different than being female, and comes with some different abilities and experiences, but it's not as though there's some fantastic ability that only those of the male sex have which 'makes up for' the fact that they cannot have babies. And yet we don't tend to think that people who are male are automatically worse off, overall, than people who are female simply because they lack an ability we might count as an intrinsic good. There are plenty of interesting, valuable, enjoyable things about being male—or so I am told, anyway. None of these in particular are specific abilities which 'make up for' the fact that males can't become pregnant, give birth, lactate, etc. But they make us think that people who are male haven't been given a sorry deal in life.

Likewise, many disabled people assure us that there are plenty of interesting, valuable, enjoyable things about living in a disabled body. There are unique experiences not had by the non-disabled, which disabled people value. (See chapter 3 for discussion and examples.) The mere-difference view needn't deny that disabled people miss out on some intrinsically good abilities or experiences—it's just that they have access to other, different good things.

2.1.3 Social harm and intrinsic harms

An important consequence of the above discussion is that the mere-difference view of disability is not—contra what is sometimes assumed—equivalent to the social model of disability. As discussed in section 1.4, the social model of disability maintains that the bad effects of disability are due *entirely* to social prejudice. To quote the slogan: It is society that disables.[4] Now, this is certainly one way of holding a mere-difference view of disability (or, more carefully, a mere-difference view of the impairments that give rise to disability in our current social circumstances). But as the above discussion highlights, the mere-difference view can also allow that disability—by itself, independent of its social context—involves the loss of intrinsic goods. That disability involves

---

[4] The social model can leave it open that *impairments* have bad effects that are not socially mediated, given the insistence on a disability/impairment distinction.

the loss of intrinsic goods simply doesn't entail that disability is therefore on the whole or all-things-considered bad for you. Indeed, the view of disability that I will defend in chapter 3 is one in which disability can (and perhaps always does) involve, independent of its social context, the loss of intrinsic goods, but is nevertheless neutral with respect to well-being.

2.1.4 Intrinsic bads

So the mere-difference view can't simply be the view that disability doesn't involve the loss of goods, nor the view that disability doesn't in fact reduce well-being. But nor can the mere-difference view be characterized simply as the view that disability is not intrinsically bad for you, or intrinsically something that makes you worse off. Suppose, for example, that your view of well-being is a strong form of hedonism: you think that the only thing that's intrinsically good for you is pleasure, and the only thing that's intrinsically bad for you is pain. Disability doesn't make you *intrinsically* worse off on this view. But suppose you further think that disability always or almost always leads to a net loss of pleasure, and that this loss of pleasure would persist even in the absence of ableism. In that case, your view of disability sounds like a bad-difference view—even though disability isn't something that's *intrinsically* bad for you.

Likewise, suppose you maintain some sort of desire-satisfaction theory of well-being: you think that what is intrinsically good for a person is the satisfaction of their desires (either their actual desires, or their suitably idealized desires), and that what is intrinsically bad for a person is the frustration of their desires. But suppose you also think that disability is strongly correlated with a frustration of desires. That is, not only does disability frustrate desires in the actual world, but it would still frustrate desires in worlds where society was perfectly accepting of disabled people. Again, this looks like a bad-difference view of disability. But it's not a view on which disability is intrinsically bad for you. Disability causes things that are intrinsically bad for you, and does so in the way that's counterfactually stable, but disability *itself* isn't intrinsically bad for you.

2.2 What the Bad-Difference View Might Be

Characterizing the difference between the bad-difference and mere-difference views of disability is thus not as straightforward as it might have originally seemed. In fact, it is not straightforward at all. The bad-difference/mere-difference distinction is best understood as a distinction between claims about the interaction between disability and well-being. According to the bad-difference view, disability has a negative effect on well-being that is counterfactually stable—disability would have such effect even in the absence of ableism. The mere-difference view, in contrast, maintains no such negative connection between disability and well-being.[5]

But there are many different, quite disparate theories of well-being. And there's no clear way of characterizing the mere-difference/bad-difference distinction that cuts across all these different accounts of well-being—or at least, if there is one, I haven't been able to come up with it. With this in mind, I think the best thing to do is to give several different, non-equivalent ways of characterizing the mere-difference/-bad-difference distinction. Hopefully, at least one of them will be adequate, whatever your theory of well-being.

I'm going to offer four candidate accounts of the bad-difference view of disability. None of these are necessary for commitment to a bad-difference view, but accepting any is *sufficient* for commitment to a bad-difference view. In offering these four candidate accounts of the bad-difference view, I don't take myself to be giving an exhaustive account of the bad-difference view—there are doubtless other ways to go about it. I offer these, rather, as illustrative of the kind of thing I have in mind in my usage of 'bad-difference':

(i) Disability is something that is an automatic or intrinsic cost to your well-being.

(ii) Were society fully accepting of disabled people, it would still be the case that for any given disabled person x and any arbitrary non-disabled person y, such that x and y are in relevantly similar personal and socio-economic circumstances, it is *likely* that x has a lower level of well-being than y in virtue of x's disability.

---

[5] As chapter 3 will emphasize, this point needs to be put carefully. It's compatible with the mere-difference view that even in the absence of ableism disability would be bad *for some people*. Even in the absence of ableism, disability might have a negative effect on well-being, depending on what it is combined with. The claim is simply that disability does not by itself or automatically have such a negative effect on well-being.

(iii) For any arbitrary disabled person x, if you could hold x's personal and socio-economic circumstances fixed but remove their disability, you would thereby improve their well-being.

(iv) Consider two possible worlds, w and w*, which are relevantly similar to the actual world except that w contains no ableism and w* contains both no ableism and no disabled people. The overall level of well-being in w* is higher than the overall level of well-being in w, in virtue of the fact that w* contains no disabled people.

They don't exactly trip off the tongue, I'll admit. But hopefully the ensuing discussion will show why this level of complexity is needed. So let's now examine each of (i)–(iv) in turn.

(i) Disability is something that is an automatic or intrinsic cost to your well-being.[6]

Broadly Aristotelian or 'objective list' views of well-being often view disability in a way that supports (i). There is, on these views, some norm of human flourishing from which disability detracts. This is one way of holding a bad-difference view of disability.

Again, as explained in section 2.1.2, the claim that disability always involves the loss of an intrinsic good is *not* sufficient for commitment to a bad-difference view. The claim of (i) is that disability itself automatically or intrinsically makes you worse off. But that's not equivalent to, or entailed by, the claim that disability involves the lack of an intrinsic good (again, consider the male sex).

So, for example, Elizabeth Harman (2007) includes disability among her list of things that count as 'bad states'. According to Harman:

Bad states are understood as states that are in themselves bad, not bad because they are worse than the state the person would otherwise have been in. (If one wants a further account of a bad state, I am willing to offer one: bad states are those states that are worse in some way than the normal healthy state for a member of one's species.) (p. 139)

But it's important to note here that although Aristotelian or objective list views often *in fact* support this characterization of the bad-difference

---

[6] I say automatic or intrinsic, rather than just intrinsic, because I want to leave open that someone could have this kind of view without thinking that disabilities are something intrinsic. The idea behind (i) is simply that the badness of disability isn't mediated by something else (a reduction in satisfied desires, an increase in pain, etc.). Disabilities are just bad simpliciter.

view, they certainly don't have to. Nor does commitment to a mere-difference view in any way involve rejection of objectivist theories of well-being. It's perfectly consistent for an objective list view of well-being to simply leave out non-disability from their list of things that a flourishing life requires. Likewise, it's perfectly consistent for them to maintain that disability always incurs a loss of some objective good, but can also create opportunities for experiencing other, different objective goods—perhaps ones not available to the non-disabled. And so on.

This point is sometimes resisted by disability-positive philosophers. Anita Silvers (2003) and Lawrence Becker (2000), for example, both argue against broadly Aristotelian views of well-being, assuming that the Aristotelian picture cannot be disability-positive. But the disability-negative tenor of most Aristotelian theories of well-being is contingent. It's not well-being-as-flourishing that's the problem, it's flourishing-as-lacking-disability that's the problem.

As mentioned, though, we might want to characterize the bad-difference view in a way that doesn't appeal to the intrinsic badness of disability itself. It might be only the frustration of our (perhaps suitably idealized) desires that is intrinsically bad for us, for example. But if we think disability is the kind of thing that tends to frustrate desires, and would still be that sort of thing even in the absence of ableism, that looks like a bad-difference view of disability, even though it isn't a view on which disability is *intrinsically* bad. Here is a first pass at characterizing such a view, though it's an attempt that I ultimately think is unsuccessful:

> #(ii) Were society fully accepting of disabled people, it would still be the case that for any given disabled person x and any arbitrary non-disabled person y, such that x and y are in relevantly similar personal and socio-economic circumstances, it is *likely*[7] that y has a higher level of well-being than x.

A characteristic commitment of the bad-difference view is that even if we eradicated ableism, disability would still (be very likely to) have a negative impact on well-being. That's not to say that any disabled person would be worse off than any non-disabled person. It might be better to be a rich disabled person than a poor non-disabled person, or it might be

---

[7] I'm understanding talk of 'likelihood' here as objective probability. It is the objective, rather than subjective, probability that seems to matter in this case.

better to be a disabled person with lots of loved ones than a lonely non-disabled person. So the thought is something like this: if you compared two people who were relatively similar in their socio-economic and personal circumstances—they had the same amount of friends, the same amount of money, the same investment in enriching hobbies, etc.—but who differed in whether they were disabled, the disabled person would likely be worse off than the non-disabled person, society's acceptance of their disability notwithstanding.

Why is (ii) phrased in terms of likelihood? Simply because on at least some subjectivist views of well-being it's implausible that disability would *always* have a negative effect on well-being. Suppose, for example, that you hold a non-idealized version of a desire-satisfaction theory of well-being, and further think that disability is strongly correlated with the frustration of desires. Your view of disability wouldn't support (i), because you don't think that disability makes people intrinsically worse off. But your view of disability also does not support the claim that, if two people are in relevantly similar circumstances but one is disabled, the disabled person is *always* or *definitely* worse off. After all, you have to make room for non-standard desires. It's perfectly possible that some disabled people don't desire to be non-disabled, and perfectly possible that some non-disabled people have more frustrated desires (for whatever reason) than some disabled people. What your view of disability does support, however, is the claim expressed in #(ii). You think that, even in the absence of ableism, a disabled person is *more likely* to have unfulfilled desires than a non-disabled person in relatively similar circumstances (because disability *usually* frustrates desires, even if it doesn't always frustrate desires). And so you think a disabled person is likely to be worse off, in comparison to a non-disabled person in relevantly similar circumstances.

But the problem with #(ii) is that it isn't strong enough to capture the basic idea of the bad-difference view. And that's because all it tells us about is the correlation between disability and well-being, and correlation in this case is not enough. To see why, consider a different example. Suppose there were a band, The Overly Emotive Whiners, whose fan base is primarily composed of angst-ridden, dissatisfied adolescents. It seems reasonable to suppose that being an angst-ridden, dissatisfied adolescent is strongly correlated with comparatively low levels of well-being. But if that's the case, then being a fan of The Overly Emotive

Whiners is also strongly correlated with low levels of well-being. Take two people in relevantly similar circumstances, one of whom is a fan of The Overly Emotive Whiners and one of whom is not. It's not implausible that it comes out as likely that the Whiners fan will have a lower level of well-being. But this fact alone doesn't seem to support a bad-difference view of being a fan of The Overly Emotive Whiners. Let's assume their music is not execrable enough to make your life go worse for you simply by exposure to it. The fact that fans of the band are likely to have lower levels of well-being than non-fans is explained by something else—namely, the fact that fans of the band are likely to be angst-ridden adolescents.

A bad-difference view of x seems to require more than a *correlation* between x and comparatively lower levels of well-being. And that's simply because having x and having lower levels of well-being could be correlated for accidental reasons. What we need, I think, is something hyperintensional—something like a notion of *in virtue of*. Mere necessary connection is inadequate, I think, simply because necessary connections just give you necessary correlation, and that still doesn't seem strong enough. For example, someone who thinks nomological possibility is the strongest form of possibility would think that, for humans at least, being human and being mortal are necessarily coextensive. Yet you could plausibly maintain that being mortal is bad-difference, while being human is not.[8] So, for better or worse, it seems that at least certain kinds of subjectivists about well-being may need to use a hyperintensional locution like 'in virtue of' if they are to capture anything like the mere-difference/bad-difference distinction. In place of #(ii) I suggest:

---

[8] It might be tempting to think that we should instead invoke causation—e.g., x is a bad-difference just in case it is likely to cause you to have lower levels of well-being. But causation doesn't obviously solve the problem. It could be the case that being a Whiners fan causes a drop in well-being, because hanging around other maladjusted people makes you maladjusted. And yet it's not *in virtue of* being a fan that your well-being drops, it's in virtue of the maladjustment. Regardless of this point, I think that causation is too committal, and in some cases over-generates. Suppose there were, as a matter of fact, more unhappy people than happy people (or more people with a preponderance of frustrated desires compared to those with a preponderance of fulfilled desires). Being awake is one of the causes of being unhappy (or having frustrated desires). If the world was such as to contain more unhappy/frustrated than happy/unfrustrated people, then being awake would be likely to be a cause of lower levels of well-being. But I seriously doubt that the scenario described is one in which we should adopt a bad-difference view of wakefulness.

(ii) Were society fully accepting of disabled people, it would still be the case that for any given disabled person x and any arbitrary non-disabled person y, such that x and y are in relevantly similar personal and socio-economic circumstances, it is *likely* that x has a lower level of well-being than y in virtue of x's disability.

Option (ii) addresses the thoughts that motivated #(ii), but avoids the problems of mere correlation. It does, however, introduce the added complication of 'in virtue of'.[9] Perhaps, however, interpersonal comparisons of well-being are the wrong way to go to begin with.[10] They might introduce too many variables, or simply fail to get to the heart of the issue. So skeptics about such interpersonal comparisons might be happier with something like:

(iii) For any arbitrary disabled person x, if you could hold x's personal and socio-economic circumstances fixed but remove their disability, you would thereby improve their well-being.

Almost no one—however committed to a bad-difference view of disability she may be—thinks that being disabled *always* makes your life go worse for you, no matter what. Someone might have been a lonely shut-in, with no friends and no community, before she became disabled. She then goes to a rehabilitation center, where she makes a lot of friends, becomes involved in sports or the arts, etc. This person's life has, on balance, gone better for her in a way that's causally related to becoming disabled. But, the skeptic might protest, it hasn't gone better for her *in virtue of* being disabled. It's gone better for her in virtue of the fact that she now gets out of the house more (and though becoming disabled caused that, it isn't becoming disabled itself that's improved her well-being). If she could keep her friends, her interests, and her community but lose her disability most people think she would be better off. There

---

[9] I imagine that some defenders of, for example, desire-satisfaction theories of well-being might want to maintain that the only things in virtue of which your life can be said to be going better or worse for you are desires—your life goes better for you in virtue of having fulfilled desires and worse for you in virtue of having unfulfilled desires. That is, nothing that isn't a desire is such that your life goes better or worse for you in virtue of that thing. If that's the case, nothing like (ii) will work. Someone with this sort of view of well-being needs to adopt a stronger claim, like (iii).

[10] Perhaps interpersonal comparisons of well-being often given rise to *incommensurability*. See Chang (2002).

are caveats, of course. If a person makes her living from disability theater or is a star in the Paralympics, it isn't obvious she'd be better off without her disability. These are plausibly cases where we can't remove her disability without also removing other things she values (her career, etc.). But if we could hold fixed most of her external circumstances— what she does for a living, who her friends are, etc.—but remove her disability, a standard interpretation of the bad-difference view says we've thereby made her better off.[11] And that's the idea (iii) tries to capture.

(iii) is a strong claim, however. So strong, in fact, that there might be good reasons for the defender of the mere-difference view to think it doesn't make any sense. Why think it's possible, for example, to hold fixed someone's personal and social circumstances while removing their disability? Thinking that it is possible seems to rely on an overly medicalized view of a disability. If disability is not just a physical condition—if it's also a social identity— then it's not clear we could, in any meaningful sense, remove a person's disability but hold their important social and personal circumstances fixed.

So it's important that there are other options (like (ii)) that are weaker, but which still count as bad-difference views. For example, the desire-satisfaction theorist could maintain that you don't automatically or always make someone better off if you can hold their circumstances fixed but remove their disability. After all, you have to leave room for odd desires. Still, it's *incredibly likely* that you make someone better off by removing their disability. That claim is weaker than (iii), but still in the spirit of bad-difference views.

Some people, however, are skeptical about counterfactual claims about individual well-being (like (ii) and (iii)), particularly claims about what would happen to a particular person's well-being in different circumstances (like (iii)). For this sort of skeptic, we can formulate a version of the bad-difference view that doesn't appeal to claims about individual well-being:

(iv) Consider two possible worlds, w and w*, which are relevantly similar to the actual world except that w contains no ableism and w*

---

[11] That's not to say that we wouldn't also make her better off if we changed some of her circumstances. Maybe she had always wanted to be a surgeon, but couldn't because her disability impeded fine motor control. Perhaps she'd be better off if she was now able to pursue her dream and become a surgeon. The account offered by (iii) is silent about this— the point of (iii) is that simply in virtue of removing her disability, we would thereby make her better off (even if we changed nothing else).

contains both no ableism and no disabled people. The overall level of well-being in w* is higher than the overall level of well-being in w, in virtue of the fact that w* contains no disabled people.

The thought behind (iv) is this: the bad-difference view maintains that it would be better for there to be not merely an absence of prejudice against disability, but also an absence of disabled people; in contrast, the mere-difference view maintains that an ideal world contains an absence of prejudice against disability, but might well contain plenty of disabled people.[12] The claim being made in (iv) needs to rely heavily on the context-sensitivity of what counts as similar to the actual world in order to get at this idea. We're picking out two worlds—one with no ableism, one with no ableism and no disabled people. Worlds w and w* are—we're assuming—*relatively* similar to the actual world, except that they don't contain ableism.[13] So, for example, it's not the case that the reason w* lacks disabled people is that they have all been systematically exterminated, or have suddenly died, or something like that.

According to the bad-difference view, a world similar to our own but lacking both ableism and disabled people is better than a world merely lacking ableism: w* is preferable to (has a higher overall level of well-being than) w. Disability detracts from well-being, according to (iv), even in worlds in which there is no ableism. (iv), like (iii), needs the concept of 'in virtue of' to say this (for the same reasons that #(ii) was too weak, a version of (iv) which merely compared the well-being of the two worlds would likewise be too weak). It's not just that w* has a higher level of well-being, it's that w* has a higher level of well-being in virtue of the fact that it lacks disability.

There's a further thought that's associated with (iv), and which seems connected to bad-difference views, that's also worth discussing—but which I don't think is ultimately characteristic of a bad-difference view. Suppose that the Disability Fairy comes down from heaven and offers you a choice: Do you want people to continue to be born disabled? She

---

[12] At least on the understanding of disability defended in chapter 1. According to the picture of disability defended by the social model, there would not be any disabled people in such a future utopia, simply because social prejudice is what causes disability. But there would still be people with *impairments*.

[13] So let's assume for the sake of argument that the closest worlds without ableism aren't worlds without people, for example.

assures you that if you say no there won't be any catastrophic, non-disability-related consequences—people will still have just as many babies, it won't institute a new era of genetic perfectionism, etc. All that will happen is that congenital disabilities will no longer exist. A hallmark of most bad-difference views of disability is that you should take the Disability Fairy's deal.

But, importantly, accepting the Disability Fairy's deal is neither necessary nor sufficient for holding a bad-difference view of disability. Someone who accepts a bad-difference view but also accepts a strong form of consequentialism might have reason to reject the deal, for example. If people could still become disabled (even if they can't be born disabled), then taking the Disability Fairy's deal might lead to severely lower levels of well-being for those who become disabled, simply because there will be fewer disabled people, and thus less pressure on society to be accommodating.

Why not just have the Disability Fairy's deal be prevention of all future disabilities, whether congenital or acquired? Because then it seems plausible that many—perhaps even most—defenders of the mere-difference view would accept the deal as well. There are a lot of very bad things that cause people to become disabled—environmental disasters, drug addiction, cancers, car crashes, violence, war, etc. To prevent anyone from *becoming* disabled, you would at least have to radically alter a lot of these things (and perhaps eliminate some entirely). The mere-difference view doesn't deny that many of the things that *cause* disability are bad, even though it denies that disability itself is bad. If the Disability Fairy's deal involved altering, improving, and perhaps even eliminating these bad things, it might easily be worth taking—even if it meant eliminating disability.

But even restricted to congenital disability, it's at least *compatible* with a mere-difference view that you should take the Disability Fairy's deal. Suppose you thought that, as a matter of fact, disabled people tend to have lower levels of well-being than non-disabled people—and that this is because of society's ableism (rather than because of anything about disability itself). But suppose you further thought that ableism is an entrenched part of society—it just isn't going to change, at least for the next few centuries. If you're a consequentialist, you might then think that the thing to do in this case would be to take the Disability Fairy's deal; doing so would, as a matter of fact, have a positive effect on well-being. Taking the deal isn't really in the broader spirit of mere-difference views, but it isn't strictly inconsistent with them either—it doesn't entail that you think disability is *by itself* something that has a negative connection to well-being.

So while the Disability Fairy case is interesting, and is the kind of thing often associated with bad-difference views, I don't think it actually gets a grip on the issue. The question of whether we should prevent disability can come apart from the question of whether disability is, by itself, bad for you.

To sum up: none of (i)–(iv) is necessary for maintaining a bad-difference view. But maintaining any of (i)–(iv) is sufficient for a bad-difference view of disability.[14] The mere-difference view of disability must deny all of (i)–(iv). And it must deny other, relevantly similar claims—(i)–(iv) by no means exhaust the ways we might characterize commitment to a bad-difference view. Instead, I intend (i)–(iv) as examples of the various ways we can explain a negative connection between disability and well-being, which is the characteristic commitment of the bad-difference view.

2.3 What the Mere-Difference View Is

But the mere-difference view is not simply the denial of (i)–(iv) (that is, not simply the denial of the bad-difference view). The mere-difference view must also deny any version of a 'good-difference' view: a view that disability is the kind of thing that by itself or intrinsically makes you *better* off. (I call this the 'Magneto View' of disability.) But I don't know of anyone who's actually defended such a view (except for Magneto, and he's fictional).

Mere-difference views are also typically associated with various positive claims about disability, including:

(a) Disability is analogous to features like sexuality, gender, ethnicity, and race.

(b) Disability is not a defect or departure from 'normal functioning'.

---

[14] Well, not quite. For (iii), you also need to assume some basic things about modal space that rule out funny types of Finkish counterexamples. Suppose that disability is in fact mere-difference, but that there's a malevolent anti-disability demon who will reward anyone whose disability is removed with blessings, gifts, infinite luck, whatever. In that case, if you removed someone's disability, you would make them better off. With the predictability of a broken record, adding 'in virtue of' to (iii) would help here.

(c) Disability is a valuable part of human diversity that should be celebrated and preserved.

(d) A principal source of the bad effects of disability is society's treatment of disabled people, rather than disability itself.

None of (a)–(d) are obviously essential to maintaining a mere-difference view of disability. And I'm going to assume here that denying both bad-difference and good-difference views is sufficient to maintain a mere-difference view. But something along the lines of (a)–(d) is characteristic of the view of disability that at least *most* mere-difference views maintain. Commitment to (d) is of course not unique to mere-difference views; bad-difference views can agree that social prejudice causes harm to disabled people (indeed, they can even agree that it is the principal cause of harm to disabled people). But bad-difference views and mere-difference views often disagree over how much weight they place on (d), and likewise on *to what extent* the bad effects of disability are caused by society, rather than by disability itself.

2.4 Default Views and Common Sense

It's often taken for granted within philosophy that some version of the bad-difference view is the default or common-sense position.[15] And perhaps it's true that the bad-difference view—or some loose gesturing in that direction—is the common-sense view, simply insofar as it does seem to be the view that most people hold, and the view that is standardly assumed. Similarly, it's perhaps true that the mere-difference view has the burden of proof, simply insofar as the mere-difference view is in opposition to what is standardly assumed. But in assuming the bad-difference view as the default position, people often seem to be claiming something stronger: that we're *justified* in assuming the bad-difference view (without comment and without argument) or that the bad-difference view is *obviously* true.

---

[15] This is, to name one prominent example, the unexamined assumption behind Parfit's 'handicapped child case', an assumption which is generally taken for granted in much of the secondary literature on Parfit's case. (Though it's important to note that there are many versions of the non-identity problem discussed in the secondary literature that, unlike the handicapped child case, don't involve disability at all. Parfit's assumptions about the badness of disability seem entirely orthogonal to the interesting issues of the non-identity problem.) For Parfit's original case see Parfit (1984).

But as I hope the above discussion (particularly in section 2.1) illustrates, such assumptions are far too strong. To assume the bad-difference view is to assume a negative connection between disability and well-being. But the judgements that we're making about disability take place in a social context in which disabled people face profound barriers, stigma, and prejudice. For the bad-difference view to be obviously true, it would need to be obviously true that disability would still be bad-difference even in the absence of such prejudice. I am skeptical that anything of the kind is *obvious*—whether or not it is true.

But, it may be protested, it really is just *obvious* that disability is a bad thing. To those for whom such an intuition is steadfast, I have two main things to say—one empirical, the other philosophical. On the empirical front, there is a vast body of evidence that suggests that non-disabled people are extraordinarily bad at predicting the effects of disability on *perceived* well-being. Non-disabled people tend to assume that disability will have substantial negative effects on perceived well-being, and that the perceived well-being of the disabled will be substantially lower than their own. But a substantial amount of research suggests that this is simply not the case.[16] The non-disabled appear to be bad at predicting the impact of disability on the disabled, and tend to systematically overestimate the bad effects of disability on perceived well being and happiness.[17] What this empirical information shows is, of course, up for debate. I don't mean to claim that perceived well-being is well-being simpliciter, or even that there's a tight connection between the two. But the relevant point can be made without taking a stand on the relationship between perceived well-being and actual well-being. We tend to think it's obvious that disability has very bad effects on *perceived* well-being (that is, on how happy, satisfied, or content disabled people believe themselves to be)—but we're wrong about this. And when asked to predict how disabled people will rate their own *perceived* well-being, we likewise get things very wrong. So we're in a position to know that some of what we might have thought is obvious or common sense about disability is just

---

[16] Excellent overviews of the relevant literature can be found in Bagenstos and Schlanger (2007). Bagenstos and Schlanger state in their literature review that a 'massive body of research has demonstrated that people who acquire a range of disabilities typically do not experience much or any permanent reduction in the enjoyment of life' (p. 763).

[17] An excellent summary of the relevant empirical information can be found in Loewenstein and Schkade (1999).

plain wrong, and demonstrably so. Why think we're any better at telling what is obvious about well-being simpliciter, whatever its relationship may be to perceived well-being?

Now for the philosophical point. The claim that it is simply obvious that disability is bad-difference is, I take it, an intuition. More to the point, it's an intuition about something that is a subject of prejudice and stigma. But if we have good reason to believe that disability is the subject of prejudice and stigma, then it seems we also have good reason to think our intuitions about disability aren't going to be particularly reliable, and aren't going to be a good groundwork on which to construct a theory of disability—especially if that means favoring the intuitions of the non-disabled over the testimony of the disabled. We should perhaps take as a caution what Hume thought was obvious about non-white races:

I am apt to suspect the negroes, and in general all the other species of men (for there are four or five different kinds) to be naturally inferior to the whites. There never was a civilized nation of any other complexion than white, nor even any individual eminent either in action or speculation.[18]

and what Kant thought was obvious about women:

[Women] use their books somewhat like a watch, that is, they wear it so it can be noticed that they have one, although it is usually broken or does not show the correct time.

A woman who has a head full of Greek . . . or carries on fundamental controversies about mechanics . . . might as well even have a beard, for that would express more obviously the mien of profundity for which she strives.[19]

Surely remarks such as these should make us wary of thinking that our intuitions are a direct line to pure reason. They are formed in—and informed by—the culture and society in which we find ourselves. And while that might (might!) not matter much when it comes to intuitions about logic or mathematics, it matters a great deal when it comes to intuitions about the well-being of oppressed groups. Methodologically, relying on intuition—without the support of independent argument—in a case where we know there is active prejudice is suspect at best.

And it is particularly suspect when it contravenes the testimony of many members of that disadvantaged group. That is not to say that the

---

[18] Quoted in Palter (1995).   [19] Quoted in Schott (2004).

testimony of disabled people must be sacrosanct. Testimony is never infallible. And there might, furthermore, be complicated, subtle philosophical reasons that would lead you to discount particular forms of testimony. Such reasons will be discussed in chapter 4. But discounting testimony after careful argument is a very different thing from saying it's simply obvious that disability is a bad thing, and so simply obvious that those who say it isn't are somehow misguided or kidding themselves.

Let's leave aside, then, the bare intuition that disability is just *obviously* a bad thing. Perhaps it's something particular about disability—or even something about particular disabilities—that's driving the thought that the bad-difference view should be the default position. Again, it can't simply be that disabilities involve the lack of intrinsic goods or abilities, as that's compatible with the mere-difference view. Yet perhaps the thought is that there are some things often associated with disabilities that are clearly or obviously bad, and which always make your life go worse for you—shortened lifespan or chronic pain, for example. The connection between such features and disability, the thought goes, is enough to make it clear that disability is bad-difference.

But it can't be quite that simple. To begin with, the connection between such features and bad-difference is somewhat more complex than saying that they are obviously bad or obviously make your life go worse for you. Plenty of random things we don't consider bad-difference turn out to have surprising effects on lifespan. Unless we want to end up with a bad-difference theory of maleness, for example, we can't say that shortened lifespan per se obviously entails bad-difference (as males have shorter life expectancy than females, across cultures and at every stage of life).[20] We'd have to say that a *substantially* shortened lifespan is what entails bad-difference. (What counts as substantially shortened? Good question.)

As for pain, the connection between chronic pain and at least *perceived* well-being is much more complicated than many people suppose. It simply isn't the case that more physical pain = worse, no matter the circumstances. For starters, there is research which suggests that perceived experience of pain and tolerance of pain are (perhaps widely) variable across cultures.[21] More significantly, perhaps, research also suggests that first-person experience of the badness of pain doesn't

---

[20] Barford et al. (2006).
[21] See, for example, Morse and Morse (1988); Bates et al. (1993).

track the objective features of the physical complaint or what we might prima facie think of as the 'most painful' conditions. For example, the self-assessed quality of life of patients with fibromyalgia and 'non-specific low back pain' consistently rates much lower than that of people with what seem to be physically more detrimental or objectively painful (if that concept even makes sense) conditions.[22] Likewise, a substantial body of research suggests that the best predictor of well-being in cases of chronic pain isn't objective features of the physical complaint, but is rather one's attitude toward pain.[23] And finally, there are the various ascetic traditions—from religious mysticism[24] to contemporary athleticism[25]—that actively pursue pain and report to value the experience of pain. I don't mean to conclude from any of this, of course, that pain isn't in fact a bad thing. But what seems evident is this: The assumption that physical pain is *neatly and directly* correlated with reduction in well-being is a crude oversimplification.[26]

---

[22] See, for example, Burkhardt et al. (1993); Lamé et al. (2005); Boonen et al. (2005). It's possible, of course, that non-specific low back pain really is among the most painful conditions one can have, but I'll admit to being skeptical about this.

[23] See especially McCracken (1998); Viane et al. (2003). Viane et al. found that 'acceptance of pain predicted mental well-being beyond pain severity and pain catastrophizing, but did not account for physical functioning . . . [I]t was found that acceptance of pain was strongly related to engagement in normal life activities and the recognition that pain may not change. Acceptance . . . was strongly related to a cognitive control over pain.'

[24] As Ariel Glucklich notes in her fascinating *Sacred Pain*, 'the most highly revered religious documents (taken in the broad sense) around the world have often treated pain not as an "unwanted guest" but as a useful and important sensation worthy of understanding and cultivating' (2001, pp. 12–13).

[25] Consider, for example what Haruki Murakami (2009), a dedicated long-distance runner, has to say about running:

'Of course it was painful, and there were times when, emotionally, I just wanted to chuck it all. But pain seems to be a precondition for this kind of sport. If pain weren't involved, who in the world would ever go to the trouble of taking part in sports like the triathlon or the marathon, which demand such an investment of time and energy? It's precisely because of the pain, precisely because we want to overcome that pain, that we can get the feeling, through this process, of really being alive—or at least a partial sense of it' (p. 171).

'You enter the race to enjoy the experience of running twenty-six miles, and you do enjoy it, as you go along. Then it starts to get a little painful, then it becomes seriously painful, and in the end it's that pain that you start to enjoy' (Murakami, *New Yorker* blog, http://www.newyorker.com/online/blogs/books/2013/05/murakami-running-boston-marathon-bombing.html).

[26] NB One needn't reject hedonism about welfare to say this. When hedonists say that well-being is pleasure and the absence of pain, I take it that by 'pain' most hedonists mean something like 'experienced suffering' rather than 'physical pain' (and the point of the above discussion is that these two concepts can and do come apart). Regardless of this

But leaving these complexities aside, let's assume that features like chronic pain or a shortened lifespan are things that are simply bad for you full stop. This doesn't support the idea that the bad-difference view is the default view, simply because it's perfectly compatible with the mere-difference view. The mere-difference view maintains that disability is not bad-difference, not that *no aspect* of disability is bad-difference. We can maintain that disability is mere-difference without maintaining that everything about disability is perfectly fine and shouldn't be ameliorated (more on this in the next chapter).

Mary Wollstonecraft's *A Vindication of the Rights of Woman* can plausibly be read as defending a mere-difference view of both the gender woman and the female sex. But I seriously doubt that Wollstonecraft thereby intended to defend a mere-difference view of *all aspects* of being a female at that time. For example, it seems perfectly consistent for Wollstonecraft to argue that being female is mere-difference, but that the extreme pain, disastrous side-effects (tears, fistulas, etc.), and high mortality rate associated with childbirth at the time were all not them-selves mere-difference. Being a female, according to Wollstonecraft, is no worse than or inferior to being a male. And yet I suspect she would welcome the reproductive advances that have (at least for females in industrialized societies) largely reduced the negative and dangerous aspects of childbirth that were common and largely inescapable in Wollstonecraft's time. Moreover—as we'll discuss extensively in the next chapter—Wollstonecraft's position doesn't seem threatened by the prospect that *some* bad features of being a woman or being female are simply ineliminable; it's consistent with a mere-difference view of being female that there will inevitably be *some* bad things about being female.

Similarly, disability rights activist Laura Hershey can be viewed as a prominent advocate of a mere-difference view of disability. But she was nevertheless an active supporter of medical research that would prolong the lifespan of persons with her own disability (muscular dystrophy). What Hershey strongly objected to, however, was the idea that the goal of such research was ultimately a 'cure' for the disability. What many disabled people want, Hershey argued, is to live with their disabilities

point, however, the hedonist can still accept that there's no neat correlation between physical pain and reduction of well-being precisely because some physical pains can be correlated with pleasures. More on this in section 3.12.

for longer and with better adaptive technology—not to have a magic bullet that turns disabled bodies into non-disabled bodies.[27]

The simple fact that things like chronic pain and shortened lifespan are associated with some disabilities doesn't mean that to defend a mere-difference account of disability is to say that such features are themselves mere-difference. Yes, chronic pain and shortened lifespan are a part of some people's experience of disability, but we needn't assume that they are an essential part of those disabilities—just as Wollstonecraft didn't assume that painful, dangerous childbirth was an essential part of being female.

More strongly, there's no reason to assume that, even if such features were an essential part of a particular disability, such a disability would *itself* thereby be bad-difference. One can maintain a mere-difference view of disability itself while still thinking that *some* features commonly associated with disability are bad-difference, and that disabled people would be better off without such features. Something can be neutral overall, but have aspects which are bad (see section 3.5).

Finally, we might take a brief argument from Jeff McMahan (2005) as support for the idea that bad-difference is the default view. McMahan argues that we can easily see that disability is bad-difference, not mere-difference, because the badness of disability is *aggregative*. The more disabilities you have, the worse off you are. And if some unfortunate individual had many disabilities, they would simply be unable to function.

But McMahan's quick argument doesn't work. Suppose it was true that the badness of disability is always aggregative. It wouldn't follow from this that disability is bad-difference—things can be bad in combination which are not bad in isolation. Moreover, it simply isn't true that the badness of disability is always aggregative. Consider, for example, someone who has congenital patellar dislocation (their knees are malformed and sometimes permanently dislocated). If this person acquires an injury that requires the use of a wheelchair, their experience of using a wheelchair is not going to be any harder than the average experience of using a wheelchair just because they had a previously existing disability. And, indeed, using a wheelchair will eliminate one of the substantial

---

[27] Hershey (1993). We'll return to the issue of 'cures' for disabilities in chapter 5.

difficulties (problems and pain with walking) of their original disability. McMahan's claim is that having two disabilities is obviously worse than having one—the badness of disability 'stacks'. But that just doesn't seem true. Having two disabilities isn't always harder, more difficult, etc. than having one.

There are, of course, complicated and nuanced arguments against the mere-difference view. I'll be examining two of these—the argument that the first-person testimony of disabled people is in an important sense unreliable, and the argument that if the mere-difference view is true it makes it permissible to cause disability and impermissible to cure disability—in chapters 4 and 5, respectively. But for now what I hope to have shown is that the bad-difference view should not be treated as the obvious or default position. It's perhaps true that the bad-difference view is the common-sense position, if 'common sense' just means 'what most people believe'. But hopefully the above discussion illustrates that the question of bad-difference vs. mere-difference is much more complicated than most people realize.

3

The Value-Neutral Model

> Disability is not a brave struggle or 'courage in the face of adversity.'
> Disability is an art. It's an ingenious way to live.
>
> Neil Marcus (1992)

I think the mere-difference view of disability is correct. Having a disability is something that makes you different, but not something that by itself makes you worse off because of that difference. Being disabled is simply something that makes you a minority—it is a way of having a *minority body*.

Nevertheless, as anyone who is disabled can tell you, not everything about disability is a bed of roses. Moreover, I don't find it plausible that—as is sometimes asserted—all, or at least the most substantial, bad effects of disability are socially mediated. Sure, *some* of the bad effects of disability are caused by social attitudes and social prejudices. But at least for many disabilities, there would be things about them that were difficult or unpleasant even in an ideal society. And while many people value and enjoy being disabled, not everyone values and enjoys being disabled. More strongly, I find it plausible that some people wouldn't like being disabled even in an ideal society. And I think such preferences should be listened to and respected—not dismissed as implicitly ableist or obviously caused by social prejudice—just as the preferences of those who value disability should be listened to and respected.

But I think all of this is compatible with the mere-difference view of disability. The mere-difference view isn't committed to the idea that disability is just a big, grand party, nor to the idea that everyone would experience it as such if we could only eliminate social prejudice.[1] So the

---

[1] To be clear, I don't think any sensible disability-positive position actually says this (the social model certainly doesn't say this). But disability-positive positions are often *interpreted* as saying something like this.

goal of this chapter is to develop an account of disability that both counts as a mere-difference view and accommodates the many-splendored, Janus-faced nature of disability.

The account of disability I present here—which I'll call the Value-Neutral Model—aims to show that disability is a *neutral* feature (I'll explain what I mean by 'neutral feature' in subsequent discussion). But its being a neutral feature is compatible with its being—in a restricted sense—something that's bad for you. The same feature, I'll argue, that's bad for you with respect to some aspects of your life can be good for you with respect to other aspects of your life. That can mean you value the feature on the whole, but it doesn't make its bad effects any less real, or any less bad. Crucially, though, I'll argue that this doesn't make disability unique among comparable social categories. Features such as, for example, sex or sexual orientation can likewise be said to be 'mixed bags' with respect to well-being.

3.1 Negative and Positive Effects on Well-being

Let's start by defining some terminology. It's important to note that I'm simply stipulating how I'll be using this terminology *for the purposes here*, rather than trying to make claims about how such terminology should be understood in wider debates. Nothing in the area is uncontroversial, so I'm just going to make some terminological stipulations and proceed from there. (If you don't like these particular definitions, though, I should note that nothing much hangs on defining them exactly as I've done here. I'm giving these definitions mostly for the sake of clarity, and like most definitions in philosophy they are probably subject to funny counterexamples.[2] You should be able to get the gist of the distinctions I'm interested in even if you don't like the particular way I'm drawing the distinctions.) In what follows I am assuming that:

---

[2] For example, you might worry about cases in which intuitively x is bad for you, but the closest world in which you lack x is a world in which you have y, which is even worse. I'm hopeful that context will be enough to pick out a similarity metric on which cases like this aren't a problem, but if you're worried about them you can strengthen the antecedents in the following definitions (to something like 'the closest world in which x lacks Φ and the other factors affecting x's well-being are held fixed').

Φ has a *negative effect* on x's well-being just in case the closest world(s) w in which x lacks Φ is a world in which x has a higher level of well-being than x has in the actual world

Φ has a *positive effect* on x's well-being just in case the closest world(s) w in which x lacks Φ is a world in which x has a lower level of well-being than x has in the actual world

Φ has a *neutral effect* on x's well-being just in case the closest world(s) w in which x lacks Φ is a world in which x's level of well-being is the same as the level of well-being x has in the actual world

Φ is *bad for x* just in case Φ has a negative effect on x's well-being

Φ is *good for x* just in case Φ has a positive effect on x's well-being

Φ is *indifferent for x* just in case Φ has a neutral effect on x's well-being

Again, in defining 'good for' and 'bad for' in this way, I'm not attempting to make any substantial claims in value theory. I'm simply stipulating how I'm going to be using the phrases 'good for' and 'bad for' in this particular context. And the reason I'm using them in this way, in this particular context, is because it's a way that will help me to clarify certain distinctions—as I hope will become clear in subsequent discussion.

3.2 Global Bads and Local Bads

Some things are bad for you *on the whole* or *all things considered*. Other things are bad for you with respect to certain aspects of your life or with respect to certain times. I am assuming here that it makes sense to talk about both your well-being at a particular time and your well-being with respect to certain features, and the difference between these and your overall well-being (your well-being as a person across time). I will give examples of both in the discussion that follows, but I won't attempt to define them further.

Let's call the distinction between things that are bad for you on the whole and things that are bad for you only with respect to particular features or particular times the distinction between *global bads* and *local bads*. I'll characterize this distinction as follows:

Φ is *locally bad* for x iff Φ has a negative effect on x's well-being with respect to some feature *F* or some time *t*

Φ is *globally bad* for x iff Φ has a negative effect on x's overall well-being

Similarly, we can understand a distinction between local and global goods:

Φ is *locally good* for x iff Φ has a positive effect on x's well-being with respect to some feature F or some time t

Φ is *globally good* for x iff Φ has a positive effect on x's overall well-being

Something that is a local bad needn't be a global bad (and vice versa for local and global goods). And we can easily see why. If Φ is locally bad for you but globally good for you, that can simply be because (i) Φ is also locally good for you; (ii) the fact that Φ is locally good for you makes it the case that the closest worlds in which you lack Φ are worlds in which you have a lower level of well-being than you do in the actual world (even though you plausibly lack Φ's local bads in that world).[3]

Crucially, the very same thing that is, in some respects, a local bad can also, in other respects, be a local good. My sister gets up at 6 a.m. almost every day to go running. This habit is a global good to her—it makes her fitter, less stressed, and happier. But there are definitely aspects of her life for which it's a local bad. She *hates* getting out of bed at 6 a.m. The first five minutes she's awake and the first five minutes of her run are always unpleasant. She gets rather nasty blisters. Her running habit incurs local bads, but is a global good. And that's because the very same thing—getting up early to go running—that is a local bad with respect to some features of her life is a local good with respect to others, in such a way that the local goods outweigh the local bads.

Local bads can be understood as local to a particular feature, or local to a particular time. My sister has chronically sore feet because of her running. That's a bad that's local to a particular feature (her feet), but not to a particular time (her feet are pretty much always sore). My sister is also epically miserable for the first five minutes she is awake in the morning. That's local to a particular time (the misery passes quickly once she wakes up a bit), but it's less easily localized to a particular feature (by

---

[3] For an interesting exploration of this type of reasoning see especially Chang (2004).

all accounts her entire conscious experience is one of abject misery— she's really not a morning person). We often trade local bads in either sense for global goods.

Similarly, something can be a global bad while still being a local good. No kid likes getting the flu. When given the choice, most any kid would prefer not getting the flu to getting the flu. But when you get the flu, you don't have to go to school. Not going to school is great—it's the one good thing about getting the flu. Even though on the whole getting the flu makes things go worse for you—it's a global bad—it does have one salient local good, in that it lets you stay home from school. Even if you'd happily trade staying home from school to get rid of the fever, aches, chills, nausea, etc., staying home from school is still—in its own right—a local good.

The child's flu is a global bad because the local bads outweigh the local goods. Staying home from school is great, but it's not worth feeling so miserable. My sister's running is a global good because the local goods outweigh the local bads. Sore feet are unpleasant, but they're worth it for the fitness and stress relief she gets from running. The point here is an utterly simple one: Things can have good effects, even if they are all-things-considered bad for you, and things can have bad effects even if they are all-things-considered good for you.

3.3 Instrumental and Non-Instrumental Value

Sometimes, people give surprising testimony about what they count as a global good. They never realized what truly mattered in their life until they got cancer. They had a terrible work–life balance until a painful divorce showed them that something had to change. They were never really willing to stand up for themselves and demand to be treated with respect until they were bullied. And so on.

But there's an important difference between the cancer survivor with a new perspective on life and my sister the early morning runner. My sister values running for instrumental reasons—she likes that it keeps her fit and relieves stress. But she also enjoys running for its own sake. That is, she values her experience of running each morning, in addition to valuing the indirect benefits she gets from running each morning. That doesn't mean she values everything about the experience of running, of course. She hates the first half mile. She doesn't like sore feet or blistered heels. She's not a big fan of sweating. But on the whole she enjoys running, in addition to enjoying the good effects (like fitness and stress relief) of running.

In contrast, the newly wise cancer patient doesn't—I'd assume—enjoy having cancer. She doesn't value her experience of having cancer for its own sake. She may value changes in her life that have been caused, at least in part, by her having cancer. She may even think that those changes wouldn't—perhaps couldn't—have come about unless she had been faced with a potentially terminal illness. But the cancer and the epiphany are at least in principle separable. She can imagine reaping the benefits without having had cancer. And if she could get the benefits without the cancer, that would be great.

My sister can't imagine getting all the benefits of running without the running itself. And that's because part of what she values is *the running itself*. She values her experience of running directly, not just the independent goods that running has brought her. She values running in a way that the cancer patient doesn't value cancer.

Here is what my sister and the grateful cancer survivor have in common: they are both such that they value their experiences (the running and the cancer, respectively). But my sister values running for both instrumental and non-instrumental reasons, whereas the cancer survivor values cancer only for instrumental reasons.

For the purposes here, we need a finer-grained distinction than simply the good for/bad for x distinction that I've employed above. Plausibly, something might be *good for x* (in the sense of 'good for' that I'm using) despite being something that's bad or negative simpliciter. Getting cancer might be something bad or negative simpliciter, even if it is on the whole *good for* the grateful cancer survivor. In the next section, I'll attempt to outline such a finer-grained distinction.

There are, of course, those who won't be moved by these considerations, because they're skeptical about the distinction between instrumental and non-instrumental value (or perhaps skeptical that we non-instrumentally value anything other than pleasure or happiness). It's worth noting, though, that if you're a skeptic about the instrumental/-non-instrumental distinction, the case for a mere-difference view of disability is much easier to make, simply because one obvious objection ('oh sure, people value being disabled, but they only value it instrumentally') isn't available. In allowing for the instrumental/non-instrumental distinction, I'm intentionally making things more difficult for myself.

Whether or not it's well-motivated, the instrumental/non-instrumental distinction is important for some (especially objectivist) theories of well-being, and part of what I want to show is that my account of disability is fully compatible with these stronger theories of well-being. In theories of well-being where the instrumental/non-instrumental distinction is unimportant—or where the only non-instrumental value is pleasure—my account (and mere-difference views more generally) are much easier to motivate. I discuss these issues in more detail in sections 3.11 and 3.12.

3.4   Good, Bad, and Neutral Simpliciter

Some things are *good simpliciter* with respect to well-being. These things enrich your life. You'd be missing something if you didn't have them. Other things are *bad simpliciter* with respect to well-being. They detract from your life. They make your life worse. And yet many more things are *neutral simpliciter* with respect to well-being—their presence doesn't, by itself, make you better or worse off than people without such things.[4]

But, as I hope the above discussion has illustrated, net effect on well-being isn't sufficient to capture the difference between things that are good, bad, or neutral simpliciter. Perhaps there may be *some* things that always, or nearly always, have a net positive effect on well-being (are always good *for you* in the sense laid out in section 3.1). Similarly, there might be things that always, or almost always, have a net negative effect on well-being, no matter the circumstances.

But I take it that such things, if they exist at all, are rare—and they don't exhaust what we'd like to categorize as good, bad, and neutral simpliciter. To make that characterization, we need to go beyond net effect on well-being. And that's simply because sometimes something

---

[4] In saying all of this, I'm trying to be as neutral as possible with respect to theories of well-being (though the claim is in tension with the strongest versions of subjectivism, such as hedonism). The point here needn't be that there are some things that are intrinsically good, and which make up an essential part of the good life (though that's one way of interpreting it). It could simply be that there are some things that are strongly correlated with a satisfaction of desires, or which a suitably idealized agent would desire to desire, etc.

that is itself bad can have an overall or all-things-considered positive effect on well-being. And likewise, mutatis mutandis, some things that are themselves good can have an overall negative effect on well-being. Maybe getting cancer is bad simpliciter. Maybe going through a bitter divorce is bad simpliciter. But we can imagine circumstances in which *on the whole* your life goes better for you because of such experiences. Things that seem paradigmatically negative (like cancer) can sometimes have an overall positive effect on well-being (be a global good, in the terminology of section 3.2). That doesn't mean the experiences are themselves good or valuable. It just means that sometimes bad things can have good consequences, such that overall the good effects outweigh the bad.

In contrast, many—perhaps most—traits are *neutral* with respect to well-being. They are not *by themselves* good or bad simpliciter, insofar as you aren't missing something if you lack them or worse off in virtue of having them. But such traits can still, of course, make your life go better or worse for you, depending on what they are combined with.

Having red hair is neutral with respect to well-being. Having red hair is not by itself good or bad, it does not by itself make your life go better or worse for you. But having red hair in a society with strong anti-ginger prejudice may well make your life go worse for you. In this case though, it's not having red hair simpliciter that makes your life go worse for you—it's having red hair in a context of anti-ginger prejudice. This is a case in which a neutral feature combines with something extrinsic—social prejudice—for a negative net effect on well-being.

Being naturally inflexible is neutral with respect to well-being. Being naturally inflexible does not by itself make your life go better or worse for you. But it might well make your life go worse for you if your greatest dream has always been to be a ballet dancer. Again, though, in this case it's not being inflexible simpliciter that's bad for you—it's being inflexible in combination with a desire to be a ballet dancer (so this time in combination with something intrinsic) that makes your life go worse for you.

But, of course, both the above traits, although they can be bad for you, can also be good for you. In the Wildlings culture described by George R. R. Martin in the *A Song of Ice and Fire* series, having red hair is considered a sign of luck and courage—red-headed people are 'kissed by fire'. In such a culture, having red hair could easily make your life go better for you, as those with red hair are singled out for special privileges and generally looked up to. Likewise, being naturally inflexible may be bad for you if you want to be a ballet dancer, but it could also be good for you if instead you want to be a distance runner (there's a lot of evidence suggesting that those who are naturally less flexible have better running economy).[5]

According to the sense of 'good for' stipulated in section 3.1, Φ is good for x just in case the presence of Φ increases x's well-being (that is, the closest possible worlds in which x lacks Φ are worlds in which x has a lower level of well-being than x has in the actual world). Likewise, Φ is bad for x just in case the presence of Φ decreases x's well-being. The point above is simply this: Some trait Φ which is itself neutral with respect to well-being can be nevertheless good (or bad) *for x*. Inflexibility is itself neutral. But it can be *bad for* the would-be dancer, *good for* the would-be distance runner. Whether Φ is good/bad for x is not merely a function of whether Φ is itself good or bad simpliciter with respect to well-being. Whether Φ is good/bad for x is also—and in large part—a matter of what else (both intrinsic and extrinsic) it is combined with. Again, what this emphasizes is that we need some way of getting at the distinction between good, bad, and neutral simpliciter traits other than the overall causal effect they have on well-being.

So here is what I propose:

Φ is *good simpliciter* just in case for any person x who has Φ x has a higher level of well-being in virtue of having Φ than they would have had if they lacked Φ.

Φ is *bad simpliciter* just in case for any person x who has Φ x has a lower level of well-being in virtue of having Φ than they would have had if they lacked Φ.

Φ is *neutral simpliciter* just in case Φ is neither bad simpliciter nor good simpliciter.

Perhaps having people that love you, having fulfilling projects, or being kind are good simpliciter—your life goes better in virtue of including those kind of things, and would go worse in virtue of lacking them. That needn't mean, however, that having such features always leads to a net increase in well-being. There could be strange circumstances in

---

[5] Saunders et al. (2004).

which such features are *bad for* (as defined in section 3.1) particular individuals.

Likewise, perhaps experiences like going through a bitter divorce, being bullied, or having cancer are bad simpliciter—your life goes worse in virtue of those experiences, and would have gone better in virtue of lacking them. But, as discussed, this doesn't mean that their presence leads to a net decrease in well-being. Sometimes things that are themselves bad can lead to a net increase in well-being—for example, you re-evaluate your priorities and have a renewed sense of determination to achieve your goals after surviving cancer, you finally learn to stand up for yourself after being bullied, etc.

The thought here is that if something is bad simpliciter, your life goes worse *in virtue of it specifically*, even if its overall causal effects on your well-being ultimately make you better off. Even if you end up learning how to stand up for yourself after being bullied, you aren't better off in virtue of being bullied. Being bullied is just the cause of some other thing—a greater sense of strength or self-esteem, perhaps—and that other thing is something that makes you better off. And likewise, mutatis mutandis, for things which are good simpliciter. Perhaps you're always better off in virtue of having fulfilling projects or being happy, even if there are cases in which the overall net effect on your well-being of such features could be negative.

Having red hair, in contrast, is neutral simpliciter—your life doesn't go better or worse in virtue of your hair being any particular color. But that's compatible with having red hair being good for you, or bad for you. Having red hair can have a positive or negative net effect on well-being, depending on what it's combined with, even though it's a neutral feature.

Notice, though, the way I'm using 'good simpliciter' and 'bad simpliciter' is very strong, such that many things we often think of as good don't turn out to be good simpliciter (and are, instead, neutral simpliciter).[6] Take, for example, having children. I take parents at their word when they tell me that having children is something wonderful, enriching, special, etc. But as someone who is happily child-free, I don't think my life is missing anything simply because I don't have kids.

---

[6] Similar terms are typically used in a much weaker way in the literature on well-being. See, for example, Campbell (2016). Again, I'm simply defining how I'm using the terms for the purposes here.

Having kids can be great—if you want them, if you have full reproductive choice in whether or not to have them, if you have the resources to support them, etc. That is, having kids can be great in the right circumstances. But not having kids can be great—equally, differently great—too.

Again, there will be those skeptical that there is any such distinction between the good, bad, and neutral simpliciter. There's just the effect that things have on well-being, and that's it. But again, such skeptics should be far less resistant to a mere-difference view of disability in the first place. What my characterization of disability aims to show is that even granting a lot of strong assumptions (of the sort often favored by objectivists), we can give a plausible account of disability as mere-difference.

3.5 The Value-Neutral Model

With these distinctions in place, I can now present my view of disability, which I'm calling the Value-Neutral Model. Disability is neutral simpliciter.[7] It can sometimes be bad for you—depending on what (intrinsic or extrinsic) factors it is combined with. But it can also, in different combinations, be good for you. And all of that is compatible with disability sometimes—perhaps always—being *locally* bad for you (that is, bad for you with respect to particular things or particular times).

The specifics of this view will depend on your favored theory of well-being. I'll explore a few options for how the details can be spelled out in sections 3.10–3.12. But what I want to focus on in the following sections is an epistemic argument. My claim is that we have good evidence—whatever our particular commitments about well-being—to think something like the Value-Neutral Model is true.

To begin with, consider gayness instead of disability. As I've defined it, I suspect most people would agree that being gay is neutral simpliciter (as is being straight). You aren't better off simply in virtue of being gay, but neither are you worse off. Being gay does, however, make many people's lives go worse for them, because of what it is combined with: most saliently, social prejudice and discrimination against gay people. Even in the face of homophobia, however, there are many gay people whose lives go *better* (or at least not worse) for them because they are gay—there

---

[7] Cf. Anita Silvers's influential work on a 'neutral framework' for understanding disability. Silvers (2003), (2001).

are unique, valuable aspects to their experience of gayness that mean a great deal to them, which enrich their lives, and which they would not trade for the somewhat easier life of your average straight person. Given the social context, however, I doubt that there are any gay people for whom gayness is not bad for them in some respect or other. No matter how much you value your overall experience of being gay, it's still bad to be discriminated against, it was still bad to be bullied in high school, it's still bad to have to be cautious about when and where you can enjoy even the mildest public displays of affection with a partner, etc. But the very same feature that is bad for you with respect to some features or some times (that is, a local bad) can also be good for you with respect to other features or other times (that is, a local good), such that *on the whole* it is good for you (that is, a global good). Being gay can be a global good, but I suspect that in today's social context it is always or nearly always also a local bad.

Importantly, though, this pattern of interaction between being gay and well-being does not depend entirely on social attitudes toward gayness (though it is obviously heavily influenced by them). Even if we lived in a society free of homophobia, there might still be local bads associated with being gay. And more strongly, there might still be people for whom being gay was (globally) bad *for them*. If you are gay (and you and your partner are cis), you cannot biologically reproduce with your partner. Even in an idealized society, there might be gay people who have a deep, long-standing desire to have the biological child of their partner.[8] For such a person—depending on how profound the desire is—it might be the case that being gay is bad *for them*, even though being gay is not itself negative. And even if the desire to biologically reproduce with their partner was not strong enough to make it the case that being gay was globally bad for them, it could still be bad for them qua person who desires to biologically reproduce with their partner. That is, being gay could still be a local bad, even if it was not a global bad—and for reasons independent of social prejudice or stigma.

---

[8] It's possible, of course, that genetic technology will one day allow same-sex reproduction. But the point here is simply that there could be, for some people, downsides to being gay that aren't wholly determined by social prejudice, not that those downsides are necessarily ineliminable. The same point applies to the subsequent discussion of male reproduction.

Likewise for having biological features associated with male sex.[9] For many people, having such features is an advantage—it's something that marks you out for social privilege, given the way society currently works. But for some people, having these characteristics is a definite disadvantage. Some trans women, for example, are women who have biological features associated with male sex. As a result, these women often go undergo years of social stigma, persecution, and in some cases medical treatment. It's plausible that having male-associated sex characteristics is bad for *some* (not all, but some) trans women, even though it is not bad simpliciter. Moreover, having male-associated sex characteristics could plausibly still be bad for *some* trans women even in a society free of transphobia. So, for example, some people could desire very deeply not to have those particular sex characteristics, and also desire not to undergo the hassle of any procedures to alter them. Male-associated sex characteristics could be bad for such a person, even though they are neutral simpliciter.

More generally, being male could be bad for some people independently of how society views maleness, and despite the fact that being male is neutral simpliciter. Suppose someone with male sex organs had a deep desire to be pregnant, give birth, and breastfeed (as some males do). Regardless of social attitudes, being male might be bad *for them*, even though it is not bad simpliciter. Similarly, even if their life was such that being male was not a global bad, their desire to be pregnant could still be enough (again, regardless of social context) to make it a local bad.

What I am going to argue—throughout the rest of this chapter—is that the testimony of disabled people gives us good reason to think that disability functions like gayness and maleness with respect to wellbeing. It is, by itself, neutral. But it can be a global good or a global bad, depending on what else (internal or external) it is combined with. And circumstances in which it is a global good or globally indifferent can, of course, still be ones in which it is a local bad.

---

[9] Importantly the claims here are about male sex and male-associated sex characteristics, not about the gender man. On at least some theories of gender, being gendered as a man is always good for you, because of the privileges it brings. And, more importantly, on some theories of gender an idealized society wouldn't contain people gendered as men (or as women)—though it would still contain people of the male sex. See, e.g., Haslanger (2000). In the discussion that follows, I'm assuming that there is a sex/gender distinction, and that sex is—or perhaps more carefully, sex-associated characteristics are—biologically based, although I note that this assumption is controversial.

As we've already discussed, disabled people frequently self-report good quality of life. But such reports are, of course, consistent with disability being bad simpliciter, and merely offset by other goods. And this is the narrative of disability that we're most familiar with—the positive aspects of disability have to do with 'overcoming' disability. But many disabled people reject this narrative of disability, and describe their own experiences in ways that support the view that disability is neutral. I'll discuss a few examples below, but readers should note that other representative examples of disability-positive testimony are interspersed throughout the book.

To begin with a historical example, Dostoevsky dealt with severe epilepsy his entire adult life. The unpredictability and intensity of his seizures was a great difficulty for him. And yet here is what he had to say about his experience of epileptic seizures:

For several instants I experience a happiness that is impossible in an ordinary state, and of which other people have no conception. I feel full harmony in myself and in the whole world, and the feeling is so strong and sweet that for a few seconds of such bliss one could give up ten years of life, perhaps all of life.

I felt that heaven descended to earth and swallowed me. I really attained God and was imbued with him. All of you healthy people don't even suspect what happiness is, that happiness that we epileptics experience for a second before an attack.[10]

Dostoevsky's epilepsy was doubtless a *local* bad for him in many respects. But his experience of epilepsy was such that he describes it as being a global good (not the least because it had a profound impact on his writing). Nor is there any sense in which Dostoevsky's epilepsy was a global good only because of what non-disability-related things it caused, or only because he was able to 'overcome' it.

That's not to say that Dostoevsky's experience is representative. Disability is certainly—given the actual circumstances—a global bad for many disabled people. That is, many disabled people are such that in the nearest possible world where they lack their disability, they are better off. But, of course, we can't infer that a trait that is often a global bad in its current social context would often be a global bad in different (better) social contexts.

---

[10] Quoted in Tammet (2007), p. 43. It is believed by some that Dostoevsky had temporal lobe epilepsy. See especially Baumann et al. (2005).

More importantly, though, many disabled people claim that disability is not bad for them, even in their actual, present circumstances. For some, this claim is similar to that of the grateful cancer survivor—they claim their lives have on the whole gone better because of disability, but they do not value their experience of disability itself. Perhaps their disability has taught them valuable lessons in perseverance, perhaps it has made them stronger, etc. But others claim to value their experience of disability itself and strongly reject narratives of 'overcoming' disability. It's not just that disability happened to have some nice consequences which they valued enough to not mind the disability, but rather that *being disabled* is something valuable. This idea is the bedrock of the disability pride movement.

So, for example, here is writer Sarah Eyre describing her experience of MS in her essay 'A Few Awesome Things About Being Disabled' (2012):

I . . . have all these tiny strange bits of joy. There are all these unexpected lovely things that are awesome about being me, Sarah-Who-Has-MS. They are (well, now, were) secret, and they only come with this specific life—my life as a disabled person. They are mine, and they are wonderful, and I can't imagine not having them . . .

Look, I'm not going to talk about parking. Yes, I have a parking placard, and it isn't awesome, exactly; it's more just something I need to use.

What is awesome, though—although it might not sound that way at first—is having a lesion on my brain stem that makes me hear music that isn't there. Once my neurologist confirmed that auditory hallucinations were 'normal' for my condition and that I wasn't actually losing my grip on reality, I started to really enjoy them. The music itself is haunting and distant, like listening to a song being played in the house next door, maybe; something familiar that I can almost make out, but can't quite hear clearly. I can spend an hour just lying on my bed, listening: it's beautiful. It isn't always there, but when it is there it's as though I have my own personal soundtrack, and I love it.

Also awesome: euphoria. For as long as I can remember, I've had these sudden surges of random joy, moments when everything seemed a hundred times more beautiful than it had five minutes before, moments when I am quietly but fully in love with the world. This isn't mania: I don't do anything in these moments, or make any life-changing decisions. The actual, scientific term for it is euphoria, and it's pretty great.

Similarly, here is an excerpt from playwright Neil Marcus's *Storm Reading*. Marcus has generalized dystonia, which he prefers to call 'flourishing dystonia':

[Marcus speaks]
For years I've been under the medical microscope. I've been called: twisted, paralyzed, tortured, afflicted, horribly disabled, disfigured, unintelligible and confined to a wheelchair. No one asked me what I thought. Now it's time for the world to hear my story, in my terms . . .

[Another actor begins to read]
'Playwright Neil Marcus has flourishing dystonia, a neurological condition which allows him to leap and soar and twist and turn constantly in public, thus challenging stereotypes of every sort and making him very interesting to watch and sit next to during lunch hour. It rides him like a roller coaster at times.'[11]

Again, such positive experiences are by no means universal—many disabled people are worse off as a result of being disabled. (Though again it's important to again emphasize that non-disabled people tend to wildly overestimate the negative effects of disability on at least *perceived* well-being.[12]) Yet, as the disability rights community is quick to point out, they are made worse off by disability in a social context laden with prejudice and stigma against the disabled. It is no wonder, the thought goes, that people suffer from disabilities when they routinely face barriers to access and accommodation, when they are pitied and marginalized, when they are constantly told that to be disabled is to endure a great misfortune. (I'll discuss the connection between the stigmatization of disability and positive views of disability more in chapter 6.) We should be no more puzzled that disabled people in today's society are often made worse off by their disabilities than we are that gay people in the 1950s were often made worse off by their sexuality.

But here we come to the great point of resistance. While most readers will, I hope, agree that society is in many ways prejudiced against the disabled, it nevertheless seems to many that being disabled is bad in a way that's independent of such prejudice. Some popular mere-difference views of disability—most notably some versions of the social model of disability—ascribe all the bad effects of disability to social prejudice (indeed, on at least some readings of the social model, disability itself

---

[11] Video of a performance of the play is available here: https://vimeo.com/26988933.
[12] As a reminder, a substantial body of research suggests that disabled people do not rate themselves as being in general less happy or satisfied with life than do non-disabled people. An excellent overview of much of the relevant research can be found in Frederick and Loewenstein (1999).

entirely consists in social prejudice).[13] But this strikes many as incredible. If you are Deaf, you cannot enjoy the auditory experience of music. No amount of social change will alter that. The auditory experience of music is a good thing. So there are good things you will miss out on, if you are Deaf, even in an idealized society. Likewise, if you are blind, you cannot visually appreciate artwork, or the faces of your loved ones. No amount of social change will alter that. Visually appreciating artwork, or the faces of your loved ones, are good things. So there are good things you will miss out on, if you are blind, even in an idealized society.

The crucial point about the Value-Neutral Model of disability is that—unlike some other versions of the mere-difference view—it can allow for this. Yes, it's a good thing to be able to visually appreciate the faces of your loved ones, and yes, you miss out on that if you're blind, and yes, no amount of social change will alter that fact. But it simply doesn't follow from that that blindness is something bad. Missing out on the visual appreciation of loved ones' faces may well be a local bad. That is, a blind person—even in an ideal society—may be worse off qua person who would like to visually appreciate the faces of their loved ones. I say 'may' here because I am reluctant to say that features like this are *always* or *automatically* even local bads. The non-blind among us are, of course, inclined to value the visual appreciation of our loved ones' faces highly, and think that it would be a great loss not to have that ability. But I worry about the inference from 'this ability is something we value' or 'this ability is something good' to 'those without this ability are worse off—at least with respect to that ability'. Ostensibly, many women who elect to have children value their ability to do so highly. And when it comes to abilities, gestating new life in your own body surely ranks among the impressive and profound. But we don't think that those who lack this ability are automatically worse off, even if we think that the ability itself is

---

[13] It's a vexed question exactly what the social model ascribes to disability, and what it ascribes to 'impairments'. It is sometimes taken as analytic that *all* the bad effects of disability are socially mediated, simply because disability just is social discrimination against people with impairments. (For example, the British Council of Disabled People defines disability as 'the disadvantage or restriction of activity caused by a society which takes little or no account of people who have impairments and thus excludes them from mainstream activity'.) But that, of course, leaves it open that impairments themselves have lots of bad things associated with them that are not socially mediated—that is, it leaves open a bad-difference view of impairment. The social model is often combined with the view that impairments are, by themselves, little more than a mild nuisance. See section 1.4.1.

valuable, good, whatever. We're not inclined to say that the lack of this ability is automatically even a *local* bad for most people who are male, for example, or (I would hope) for the female who both cannot become pregnant *and* has no desire to do so. Lacking this ability may well be a local bad for some, but not for all. I worry that our inclination to think that lack of abilities to do with vision/hearing/mobility/etc. would always be (at least a local) bad has more to do with norms and normalcy. More than half the population lacks the ability to get pregnant, and yet seems to be doing just fine. We're everyday greeted with examples of people who don't seem in any way worse off for lacking that ability (that is, they're not even worse off *with respect to that ability*), and lacking that ability seems perfectly normal. Whereas lacking the ability to see, to hear, to walk, etc.—that's something we see as entirely abnormal, and we're much less comfortable with the idea that people could possibly lack such abilities and not be worse off as a result. Yet it's not clear why this is the case. We're perfectly happy with the idea that an ability can be valuable without those that lack it being thereby worse off in any way. Likewise we're perfectly happy with the idea that an experience—becoming a parent, getting married, etc.—can be valuable without those who don't have such experiences thereby being worse off in any way.

But suppose, for the sake of argument, that not being able to visually appreciate the faces of your loved ones is always a local bad (and perhaps even bad simpliciter). It doesn't follow that being blind is bad simpliciter, or *bad for* those who are blind. And that's because the very same thing—blindness—that's a local bad with respect to your ability to visually appreciate the faces of your loved ones can also be a local good for you with respect to other things you care about. For example, storyteller and activist Kim Kilpatrick talks a lot in her online journal 'Great Things About Being Blind' about her inability to stereotype or judge people based on how they look and her complete lack of self-consciousness or vanity about her visual appearance—two things she values highly, and which are part of her experience of blindness.[14] And then, of course, there is the body of empirical research demonstrating the sensory uniqueness of the congenitally blind.[15] Blindness could be bad for you

---

[14] 'Great Things About Being Blind' can be found at http://kimgia3.blogspot.com/
[15] See, for example, Sathian (2000); Ptito and Kupers (2005).

with respect to some features, but good for you with respect to other features, such that *on the whole* blindness isn't bad for you.

It's worth being very clear about what is being said here. I'm not endorsing what I call the 'X-Men view' of disability—where the local bads of disability are 'compensated for' by special enhanced abilities had only by the disabled. Unless we adopt a very fine-grained notion of abilities, the account I'm offering is saying something much more subtle than that. Disability can offer unique, valuable experiences—things that count as local goods—without producing things we'd usually classify as extra abilities. Disability can make it—as in Kim Kilpatrick's case—harder to feel certain kinds of self-consciousness or engage in certain types of prejudice, disability can offer a sense of liberation from cultural norms about how your body should look or behave, disability can help you develop an appreciation for a different pace of life or give you a new and different aesthetic appreciation for the varieties of the human body. Many disabled people even find great value in some of the things non-disabled people assume are the worst aspects of disability—including, as Eva Kittay has discussed at length, dependence on others.[16] The potential goods of disability are by no means limited to extra, disability-specific abilities. This is not the X-Men view. Yes, sometimes disabilities do come with specific abilities—ones we tend to overlook. But disability can also be—as Rosemarie Garland Thomson puts it—an 'epistemic resource' and a 'narrative resource': it can expand the scope of what we can know and what we can experience, in ways that disabled people often find very valuable.[17]

Of course, even in an idealized society, there might be people such that blindness is bad *for them*. Depending on an individual's hopes, dreams, desires, and plans, being blind might be globally bad for them even in a society without ableism. (Just as, for similar reasons, being gay could still be globally bad for someone in a world without homophobia, and being male could still be bad for someone in a world without sex-related prejudice.) But being blind can be bad for some individuals without being bad simpliciter. The fact that it is sometimes bad for some individuals doesn't license the conclusion that it's bad simpliciter.

And cutting against the idea that disability is bad simpliciter is the simple fact that many people value their experience of disability. It's

---

[16] Kittay (forthcoming).   [17] Thomson (2012).

something that means a lot to them, something they celebrate. The question, of course, is whether they are making some sort of mistake in doing so. Is the disability-positive person more like the marshall at the gay pride parade, or more like the battered woman who values her abusive relationship? I will address this question in detail in chapter 4, examining the argument that the first-person testimony of disabled people who claim to value being disabled can be dismissed as a type of *adaptive preference*. But the basic position I want to defend here is this: The burden of proof is on the person who wants to say that valuing disability is *unlike* valuing gayness. Both are instances of a person valuing (and celebrating) their membership in a particular social category. In the absence of compelling argument that it is somehow mistaken for disabled people to value disability in this way—that is, that valuing disability and valuing gayness are importantly different—we should assume these cases are on a par. I'm going to assume for the sake of argument, in what follows, that these cases are in fact analogous, and that there is nothing aberrant about valuing disability. I'll then defend that assumption in subsequent chapters.

Let's return now to the case of blindness. Even in an ableism-free society, being blind might still constitute a local bad. And for some people, being blind might also constitute a global bad. Being blind might be bad *for them*. But there are others who don't (even in our own, ableism-ridden society) feel the same way. While blindness is almost invariably a local bad, many blind people report that it is not a global bad. In fact, they suggest that they value their experience of blindness, just as those of us who are sighted value our experience of being sighted. This, for example, is what writer and activist Rebecca Atkinson (who lost her sight gradually as an adult) had to say when she was presented with a potential 'cure' for her blindness, and found herself conflicted about whether to take it: 'If this experiment of going blind has taught me anything, it's that what you lose in one place you gain elsewhere, and while a blind life is different than a sighted life, it is not lesser.'[18]

And we see this pattern replicated across a wide range of disabilities. Yes, they can be and often are local bads. Yes, for many people they are global bads. Yes, they could be global bads even in the absence of

---

[18] Atkinson (2007).

ableism—they could be bad *for some people* even in the absence of ableism. But that doesn't mean they are bad simpliciter. Even in our actual, ableist society many disabled people report that their disabilities are not global bads. And, more strongly, even in our actual, ableist society many disabled people report that they value their experience of disability non-instrumentally. As Tom Shakespeare writes, 'the celebration of disability pride is the celebration of difference, and the acceptance of difference: it is about subverting negative valuation and reclaiming disability.'[19] Disability thus displays the pattern of a *neutral* feature. It may be good for you, it may be bad for you, it may be utterly indifferent for you—depending on what it is combined with. But disability—at least if we take the testimony of many disabled people at face value—isn't itself something that's bad. It is, like many other minority features, *neutral* with respect to well-being.

3.6 The Value-Neutral Model as Mere-Difference

I've presented the Value-Neutral Model as a type of mere-difference view of disability. What I'll argue in this section is that the same things that support the Value-Neutral Model itself—namely, the testimony of disabled people and the particular social context in which that testimony occurs—also support the rejection of bad-difference claims about disability.

Clearly, according to the Value-Neutral Model disability is not an automatic or intrinsic cost to well-being. But things get more complicated with some of the more nuanced versions of the bad-difference view. Recall:

(ii) Were society fully accepting of disabled people, it would still be the case that for any given disabled person x and any arbitrary non-disabled person y, such that x and y are in relevantly similar personal and socio-economic circumstances, it is *likely* that x has a lower level of well-being than y in virtue of x's disability.

Perhaps, one might argue, the disability-positive testimony of disabled people doesn't give us reason to reject a bad-difference view like (ii), even

---

[19] Shakespeare (1996).

if it gives us reason to think that disability is neutral simpliciter and sometimes a global good. That could all be compatible with disability being strongly counterfactually correlated with reduction in well-being. Those who experience disability as something positive could be curious outliers—cases that are interesting anomalies, but not ones that undermine a bad-difference view.

Despite the fact that disabled and non-disabled people report similar levels of happiness and life satisfaction, there might still be good reason to think that in our actual, present circumstances disability is at least *likely* to make people worse off. Disabled people are substantially more likely to be unemployed, poor, victims of abuse and hate crimes, etc.[20] That doesn't mean, of course, that, in the actual circumstances, we should think an arbitrary disabled person is likely to have a lower level of well-being than a non-disabled person in relevantly similar socio-economic circumstances. But let's grant for the sake of argument that we should. It still wouldn't give us any reason to endorse (ii).

For that, we'd need good reason to think that people are likely to be worse off *in virtue of being disabled* in all closest worlds in which disabled people aren't disadvantaged by social prejudice. It's important to note that such a world is radically different from the world we actually inhabit, which will limit what we can say about it. Recall #(ii)—which as you perhaps don't remember, is just (ii) without the 'in virtue of'. Unlike (ii)—which I think is false—I think we should be agnostic about #(ii). To have reason to accept (or reject) #(ii), we'd need to have good reason to believe that the overall distribution of well-being in a fairly distant possibility is some particular way. And I don't see how we could get evidence for that kind of claim.

Consider, analogously, the case of sex. For all I know, in the nearest world free of sex-based prejudice, those who are female are somewhat more likely to have a higher level of well-being than those who are male. But equally, for all I know in such a world those who are male are the ones more likely to have a higher level of well-being. The two key points here are these. I am in no position, given my current epistemic state (inhabiting, as I do, a world so imbued with sex-based prejudice), to make a judgement about what, if any, difference there would be between

---

[20] See Fleischer and Zames (2011).

the well-being of males and females in such a world. Counterfactual judgements are tricky at the best of times—they seem close to impossible in a case like this. And more to the point, even if I were in a position to make such a judgement, it doesn't seem that facts of this kind are particularly significant. If the Well-being Oracle told me that in the closest possible world that is free of sex-based prejudice it just so happens that an arbitrary female is likely to have a slightly higher level of well-being than an arbitrary male in similar circumstances, that doesn't by itself support a bad-difference view of the male sex. There could be all sorts of accidental reasons for why such distributional facts about well-being obtained.

This just further shows why something like #(ii) is too weak to serve as a sufficient condition for a bad-difference view of disability. So let's return our focus to (ii). Unlike #(ii)—where I think we should be agnostic—I think the same considerations that support the Value-Neutral Model should lead us to think that (ii) is false. Even in our actual, very non-ideal world, disabled people routinely report high levels of life satisfaction and it is increasingly common—especially within the burgeoning disability pride movement—for disabled people to say that their disabilities are something they value and would not change about themselves. Moreover, there's substantial evidence that social factors like family support, social integration, and accessible employment are more strongly correlated than 'severity' of disability to at least perceived well-being in disabled people (more on this in section 3.7). Given that all of this evidence is available to us, even in a context in which disabled people face substantial prejudice and stigma, I suggest we have good reason to think that (ii) is false.

That's not, of course, to deny that even in a world without ableism disability could sometimes be bad *for an individual* (and, likewise, sometimes be good for an individual). What I'm arguing is that whether a disability is bad (or good, or indifferent) for you depends on what else it is combined with. Some personalities, some plans, some hopes and dreams, etc. will be frustrated by disability. Others will be aided and enriched. If you have a deep desire to be a ballet dancer, but you don't have 'good feet' (for example, your arches are too flat, your feet are too wide, etc.) then your foot shape can reasonably be said to be bad *for you*. But your life doesn't go worse for you simply in virtue of your foot shape. Your foot shape is part of the explanation, but it is certainly not the whole explanation. Things go badly for you because of a combination of things: an entrenched desire to be a ballet dancer, norms about how ballet dancers' feet should look, and the shape of your feet. It is, at most, partly in virtue of your foot shape that things go badly for you. Conversely, if you are lonely or bitter your life is worse for you *in virtue of* being lonely or bitter. The position of the Value-Neutral Model is that having a disability is more like foot shape in a ballet dancer than it is like being lonely.

For similar reasons, motivations for accepting the Value-Neutral Model are also motivations for rejecting:

> (iii) For any arbitrary disabled person x, if you could hold x's personal and socio-economic circumstances fixed but remove their disability, you would thereby improve their well-being.

Disability-positive testimony—unless we adopt wholesale skepticism about it—gives us good evidence that removing someone's disability (provided you can hold fixed other circumstances) doesn't thereby make that person better off. It would make some people better off, it would make some people worse off, and for some it would have little impact whatsoever.

Finally, the same sort of considerations apply to:

> (iv) Consider two possible worlds, w and w*, which are relevantly similar to the actual world except that w contains no ableism and w* contains both no ableism and no disabled people. The overall level of well-being in w* is higher than the overall level of well-being in w, in virtue of the fact that w* contains no disabled people.

Whatever the comparative facts about overall well-being between such worlds might be—and, as per the discussion of (ii), I'm skeptical that we're in any sort of position to make judgements about that—the complex range of evidence we have about people's actual experiences of disability makes (iv) implausible.

3.7 Particular Disabilities and Bad-Difference

It's worth noting, however, that everything I've said so far is about disability per se, rather than about particular disabilities. But as discussed in chapter 1, *disability* as a kind is socially constructed—it's not a natural kind, it doesn't carve at the joints. It's perfectly compatible with the Value-Neutral Model that some specific traits that we class as disabilities are not themselves neutral. That is, it's perfectly compatible with the Value-Neutral Model that there are particular disabilities that are bad simpliciter. Being bad-difference is not *characteristic* of the things we classify as disabilities, according to the Value-Neutral Model, but that's consistent with some specific disabilities in fact being bad-difference.

That being said, I don't think we can have warrant for thinking of a particular disability that *that* particular disability is bad simpliciter. To have warrant for such a claim, we would need to have good reason to think that the disability would be bad even in the absence of ableism. Such judgements are fragile at best. As discussed previously, a world without ableism is a very, very different world from our own. Evidence that a particular disability would be bad simpliciter even in such a world doesn't look easy to come by. More importantly, we have no reason to think that which (if any) individual disabilities are bad (rather than neutral) tracks out intuitive judgements about the 'severity' of the disability. Personal testimony of disabled people who report a positive experience of disability, even in our actual, non-ideal social context, is found along a wide spectrum of what some might call the 'severity' of disability.

Similarly, empirical studies about *perceived* well-being indicate that at least self-assessed or perceived well-being doesn't track what your average non-disabled person would assume it tracks. For example, what we would call the more 'severe' disabilities don't seem to have a substantially worse impact on perceived well-being than what we would consider comparatively 'minor' disabilities, even in our current social context.[21] Likewise, for particular disabilities that can vary in their 'severity', what we would classify as the objective severity of the condition isn't a particularly good predictor of perceived well-being.[22]

---

[21] See, for example, Stensman (1985), in which surveys discovered no statistically significant difference between the self-assessed quality of life of patients with 'severe' mobility disabilities and non-disabled controls and Bruno et al. (2011), in which researchers found that most—74 percent—locked-in syndrome patients rated themselves as happy, and those who rated themselves as unhappy often attributed their unhappiness to factors that could be improved—such as daily activities and assistance—rather than their objective physical state.

[22] For example, Lobentanz et al. (2004). Researchers found that the best predictor of quality of life in MS patients was depressive mood, rather than degree of physical impairment, and that depressive mood was not well correlated to degree of physical impairment. Similarly,

So even if we allow—as the Value-Neutral Model does—that some individual disabilities are bad-difference rather than mere-difference, we must exercise extreme caution in saying of a particular disability that *that disability* is bad-difference. Intuitions (particularly of the non-disabled) about what is bad for the disabled and what is *in fact* bad for the disabled come apart.

As an illustrative example of what I'm talking about, Marc Mauer (2010), chairman of the National Federation of the Blind, complains:

Whether they have sufficient honesty to admit it or not, many of the professionals dealing with blindness believe that [if you are sight-impaired] the more you can see the better off you are. They create a hierarchy of sight. Those only 'mildly visually afflicted' are at the top; the 'stone blind' are at the bottom.

But this, Mauer argues, is simply not the case. It is often the experience of the visually impaired—especially those who go blind gradually—that being entirely without sight is actually an easier situation to navigate than being only partially without sight. It is a misapprehension—and perhaps a prejudice—of the non-blind to believe that, for those with substantial vision loss, the more sight you have the better (or the less 'severe' your sight loss is the better).[23]

So the Value-Neutral Model leaves it open that individual disabilities are in fact bad-difference. And I think that's a virtue of the account. But it's hard to see how we could get warrant for making de re claims about the bad-difference of a particular disability—particularly given the body of evidence suggesting that the badness (or otherwise) of disability doesn't track what most people would expect it to track. Moreover, the range of testimony we have from disabled people who value disability—across a wide variety of disabilities and encompassing what we might consider the most 'severe' and the most painful disabilities—is enough to suggest that *most* disabilities are mere-difference.

Benito-Leon et al. (2003) conclude that 'the strongest correlations with health-related quality of life appear to be patient rated emotional adjustment to illness and patient rated handicap' (where 'patient rated handicap' is the patient's own perception of their limitations—often mediated by social and emotional factors—rather than the objective disease state).

[23] Interestingly, there's empirical support for Mauer's observations. Roy and MacKay (2002) found that those with 'low vision' experienced more frustration and less contentment than those we would call 'totally blind'.

3.8 Difference and Degrees

I've presented a model of disability according to which disability is neutral. It is often, perhaps even always, locally bad. But it is also often locally good. Whether it is globally good or globally bad depends on what it is combined with. In this respect, it is not unique. Features like sex and sexual orientation can also be both local bads and local goods, global bads or global goods.

But I suspect that one major point of resistance will be this. I've given a model in which it's *consistent* that disability is neutral, even if it always or nearly always involves local bads. But consistency does not entail plausibility. Given the amount and scale of local bads plausibly incurred from most disabilities, the thought goes, it's implausible that disability is neutral. In this respect, disability is unlike sex and sexual orientation. Granted, sex and sexual orientation might sometimes incur local bads not mediated by social stigma (and might even occasionally be global bads even in stigma-free societies). But most of these local bads incurred by sex and sexual orientation are minor, and the occasions on which they might be global bads are rare. This makes sex and sexual orientation very different from disability.

This objection is an objection based on degrees. Yes, the thought goes, sex and sexual orientation can sometimes be locally bad (perhaps even globally bad). But they are locally bad to a lesser degree—locally bad with respect to fewer aspects of life, and with respect to aspects of life which are less central, important, etc.

It's far from obvious, however, that this degree-based claim is correct. That is, it's not obvious that disability would (in an idealized society) incur local bads in greater number or greater severity than would sex or sexual orientation. I worry that assuming the degree-based claim both underestimates the extent to which many bad effects of disability are socially mediated and underestimates just how serious the local bad effects of sex and sexual orientation might be for some people.

Perhaps the claim is instead that the local bad effects of disability would be more common. Even if, for example, some trans women incur many local bads from having male-associated sex characteristics, and males with a strong desire to be pregnant incur some very substantial local bads from being male, *most* people who are male incur no such costs. Whereas that's not the case for disability—most people who are blind incur local bads from being blind, most people who are wheelchair users incur local bads from being wheelchair users, and so on.

Notice that's it's not clear why we should think that even this much weaker claim is true. There are many things that we typically think of as neutral which almost always involve (fairly substantial) local bads. For example, consider being female. Being female is not worse than being male. And yet for most people who are female there are *some aspects* of having a female body that are unpleasant, complicated, painful, etc.[24] (Ask basically any female you know.) It doesn't follow that being female is bad simpliciter or worse than being male, even though these local bads are incredibly common and often quite significant.

But the main point to make against a degree-based objection is simply this: Even if it's correct, it doesn't seem like it gives any reason to think that disability isn't neutral. The degree-based objection says that disability is unlike sex or sexual orientation because it incurs *many more* local bads or *more substantial* local bads. The extent of these local bads makes it implausible that disability is a neutral trait. But even if we grant that disability does involve a greater degree of local bads, this gives us no good reason to think that disability is bad simpliciter, given what we know about the actual first-person testimony of disabled people. We're comfortable with the basic idea that a feature that is bad with respect to certain aspects of your life can nevertheless be good with respect to other aspects of your life, such that *on the whole* it doesn't make you worse off. The degree-based objection says, however, that it's implausible that disability works like this.[25] It's implausible that something that involves that many local bads or that much local badness isn't a negative trait. But in reply to the degree-based objection we can simply point to the actual reported experiences of disabled people—the plays and novels celebrating disability and disability culture, the disability pride parades, the relatively high percentage of disability rights activists who say they value being disabled and would not want to be 'cured' (even if a magic pill was available that cured their disability with no risks and no side effects).[26] Why, exactly, is

---

[24] And, of course, the female body has historically been pathologized as broken or defective in much the same way as the disabled body is currently pathologized.

[25] Or more carefully: says that it's implausible that disability works like this in any way other than the grateful cancer survivor model.

[26] Hahn and Belt (2004).

it meant to be implausible, given this body of evidence, that disability is neutral, even granting the degree of local bads incurred?

To make the degree objection convincing you'd again need some good reason to discount the testimony of actual disabled people. You'd need good reason to think that disability pride parades are not like gay pride parades, that disabled people who say they value being disabled and would not want to be 'cured' are not like gay people who say they value being gay and would not want to be 'cured', and so on. That is, you'd need a reason to think that in some important sense disability activists are confused or unreliable about their own well-being. It's this issue that we'll turn to in the next chapter.

3.9 Valuing Disability

I imagine that, at this point, some readers will be wondering, 'Yes, but *what does it mean* to value disability?' Perhaps we can readily imagine valuing particular aspects—'symptoms'—of disability. We can understand, for example, what it means for Dostoevsky to value pre-seizure auras or for a blind person to value not being self-conscious about their appearance. But perhaps it's a difficult move from that to understanding what it means for a person to value *being disabled.*

My suspicion is that this line of thought relies—implicitly or otherwise—on an overly medicalized view of disability, where disability is nothing more than a collection of physical traits and symptoms. Thinking about disability that way, it would be understandably hard to grasp what it means to value disability, rather than just valuing particular symptoms or particular traits.

Unless we accept a very reductive view on which the only thing we really value is pleasure or happiness—more on this in section 3.10—it makes good sense to think that we can value experiences over and above our valuing of their component parts or their effects. My sister values running. She doesn't just value its effects on her fitness and stress levels. There are other perfectly good forms of exercise (cycling, rowing) that she could employ for those same effects, but which she doesn't enjoy as much as running. Nor can her enjoyment of running easily be broken down into her enjoyment of particular foot-on-pavement patterns of movement or biomechanics. She values her experience of running—of *being a runner*—and all that it encompasses. She likes how running makes her feel. She likes waving to the other runners she sees out early in the morning. She likes picking out running shoes. She likes all the complex, multifaceted aspects of her experience of being a runner.

It's even easier to understand what it means for people to value things that are part of their social identity or sense of self. If someone says they value being gay, we don't—again, the reductionists aside—typically think that what they mean by that is that they value specific sex acts or instances of sexual desire. When, for example, Apple CEO Tim Cook says, 'So let me be clear: I'm proud to be gay, and I consider being gay among the greatest gifts God has given me'[27] we don't interpret him as simply talking about his enjoyment of specific sex acts. Being gay is something more than that—it's about identity, culture, and an overall set of experiences, both social and personal, related to having a particular sexual orientation.

Being disabled is—at least for many disabled people—something that profoundly affects social identity and sense of self in much the same way.[28] One's overall experience of being disabled is much more than the experience of specific physical symptoms. Rather, it's the complex, multi-faceted experience of inhabiting a body that doesn't meet the social norms for what bodies should be like. When people value disability, they value this unique, complex experience.

3.10 Objective List Theories

So far, I've argued that we have good reason to believe that some version of the Value-Neutral Model is correct. But the details of what it is for a trait to be neutral will depend in part on your background theory of well-being. In the remainder of this chapter I'll show how the basics of the Value-Neutral Model can be articulated within the frameworks of different theories of well-being. Obviously, I can't show how things will play out for every theory of well-being out there. What I'll do is look at some relatively generic versions of some of the most popular theories of well-being, and show how the Value-Neutral Model can be articulated within those theories. Hopefully what I say for these cases will be illustrative of a

---

[27] http://www.bloomberg.com/news/articles/2014-10-30/tim-cook-speaks-up.
[28] Indeed, being disabled can be understood as a 'transformative experience'—see Paul (2014) and Howard (2015).

more general schema for how to adapt the Value-Neutral Model to suit specific theories of well-being.

According to objectivism about well-being, there are some features your life can contain that are objectively valuable or good, and which objectively make your life go well, regardless of the attitudes that you have to those features. Objective list theories of well-being are those that lay out a list of objective goods (either de re, by naming the goods specifically, or de dicto, by saying that there is such a list, even though we may not be in a position to know what's on it) and maintain that well-being consists in participation in these goods. Overall well-being, according to objective list theories, is determined by participation in these individual goods (regardless of pro-attitudes toward them). *How* overall well-being is determined by participation in individual goods remains a vexed question. Do you have to have some measure of all of the goods to lead a flourishing life? Or can you lead a flourishing life just so long as your life is filled with enough objective goods? Are all goods equal, or are some more central or important than others? And so on. I'm going to do my best to sidestep these questions here. It's not my interest to defend an objective list account of well-being, but simply to show that an objective list account of well-being and the Value-Neutral Model of disability are compatible.

Obviously, the Value-Neutral Model won't be compatible with every version of an objective list view. If you hold a version that says that an individual must have *all* the goods on your list in order to flourish, and then stipulate that being non-disabled is on your list, the Value-Neutral Model is trivially false on your view. But I take the arguments from the preceding sections to be, in part, arguments that being non-disabled (or something extensionally equivalent) shouldn't be something the objectivist simply stipulates is on the list of objective goods. Specifically disability-negative views notwithstanding, there will be plenty of articulations of the objective list view that are compatible with the Value-Neutral Model. Let's take the example list of goods offered in Heathwood (2013):

enjoyment
freedom
happiness
being respected

knowledge
health
achieving one's goals
friendship
getting what one wants
being a good person
being in love
creative activity
contemplating important questions
aesthetic appreciation
excelling at worthwhile activities.[29]

The claim of the Value-Neutral Model is that disability can be locally bad for you while also being locally good for you, such that it is on the whole good for you. Disability itself is neutral—your life doesn't go better or worse for you in virtue of being disabled, and disability is something it's permissible (but not required) to value non-instrumentally.

Now consider again the case of Dostoevsky. Dostoevsky's epilepsy had an adverse affect on his health[30]—it represented a reduction in a specific objective good, which is what a local bad amounts to for the objective list theory. But his epilepsy—the very same thing that negatively affected his health—also had profoundly positive effects on his creative activity and his happiness (recall that he claims that 'all of you healthy people don't even suspect what happiness is'). So the very same feature that is a local bad is also a local good, such that on the whole it's plausible that Dostoevsky's epilepsy is good *for him*; it increases the overall amount of objective good that he participates in.

I think we can all agree, though, that temporal lobe epilepsy in one of history's greatest novelists isn't a generally representative case of disability. In particular, Dostoevsky gets something special—seizure auras—from his disability that are part of what make his disability so valuable to him. Again, I want to be very clear that I am not championing an X-Men

---

[29] NB Heathwood doesn't endorse this list! He offers it simply as an illustrative example of the sorts of things that might go on an objective list theory.

[30] NB Dostoevsky's particular disability had an adverse affect on his health, but it's important not to confuse disability in general with poor health. Some people have health problems as a result of their disability, and sometimes disability can result from a health problem, but that's certainly not the case for all disabilities. There are many extremely healthy disabled people. See Wendell (2001).

theory of disability, where disability isn't bad because it always brings with it extra, special abilities. Disability can be a good and valuable aspect of people's lives without imbuing them with any special talents, sensory experiences, etc.

Consider, instead, how Simi Linton (2006) describes her experience of disability. Linton is a disability rights activist (as well as leading figure in disability studies) who claims—like many disability rights activists—to value and enjoy her experience of disability. Let's now consider a single dimension of the objective list we're looking at: freedom. There are certainly ways in which Linton's disability might be said to negatively affect her freedom. As a wheelchair user, there are some places she simply cannot go, for example (in some cases because they have not been built accessibly, but in other cases just because of what the natural world is like). But there are other senses of 'freedom', and other things you can be free *from*. Linton describes her experience of becoming disabled as liberating—she no longer feels constrained by the (sometimes crushing) weight of social expectation about what women's bodies should look like, about how 'normal' people should behave, etc. Her disability allows her freedom from expectations about being normal or being an ideal woman. In describing her experience working in sex education with disabled people, for example, she remarks that:

Over time, I came to understand that linking disability to a robust sexual life is one of the more radical ideas one can put forth. It is radical because it debunks the myth of the long suffering disabled person, but it is even more disruptive because it challenges accepted ideals of sexual prowess... If disabled people can invent new definitions of sexual ability, the cultural norm is called into question. (p. 83)

On the whole, she describes disability as something that's increased her sense of personal freedom, even if there are some aspects of her life in which she is less free because of her disability. The important point here is that the local bad/global good structure can be replicated even within the confines of a particular good (it needn't always be swapping loss of good *a* for gains in good *b*). So even if you had a view according to which you have to have *all* the goods on the list—and have them in some sufficient amount—to lead a flourishing life, the Value-Neutral Model can still show how a disabled life can be a flourishing life. And that's still compatible with the idea that disability is often or always a local bad.

Roughly similar things can be said, however, for a grateful cancer survivor (let's call him Joe). Joe took a massive hit to one item on the list—health—when he developed cancer, and doubtless to several others as well (happiness, enjoyment, etc.). But now that he's been through chemotherapy and is in remission, Joe has a new outlook on life. It's plausible that his participation in many of the objective goods is increased: being a good person, contemplating important questions, excelling at worthwhile activities. Maybe Joe is even happier now than he was before cancer, and gets more enjoyment out of life.

The objectivist can allow that things that are themselves bad (for individuals or simpliciter) can causally contribute to flourishing. Even if getting cancer is bad simpliciter, its net effects might sometimes, in some cases, be good enough that one's overall well-being increased as a result. But the difference between Joe and Simi Linton or Dostoevsky is that Joe's illness is only indirectly connected to an increase in well-being. Getting cancer was part of a causal chain that led to acquiring some objective goods, but the experience of having cancer wasn't itself something that brought with it objective goods. In contrast, for both Linton and Dostoevsky, it is the experience of being disabled that is itself constitutive of some of the goods in their lives. Similarly, while Joe may value his cancer instrumentally (he's grateful for his new outlook on life), he doesn't value it non-instrumentally. He doesn't value *having cancer*, even if he values some of cancer's long-term effects on his life. Linton and Dostoevsky, in contrast, ostensibly value *being disabled*. Their experiences of having disabled bodies, rather than simply, say, life lessons about perseverance or courage or what have you, are of value to them. (This point remains basically the same for the case of desire satisfaction accounts, so I won't discuss it again in section 3.11. We'll return to it in section 3.12.)

As discussed in section 3.9, I can imagine someone objecting, at this point, that Linton and Dostoevsky don't *really* value being disabled. Dostoevsky values euphoric auras and Linton values social liberation, but both of those are in principle separable from their disabilities. What they really value are felt experiences only contingently associated with being disabled, not disability itself. The first thing to say about this objection is that, followed to its natural course, it leads to a form of hedonism: The only things we really value are pleasurable experiences. But for this form of hedonism, as I'll discuss in section 3.11, the distinction between the disability activist and Joe isn't significant. Secondly—and perhaps more importantly—this objection betrays a kind of skepticism to first-person testimony about value claims that we don't typically deploy. So, again, we don't usually tell gay people, when they say they value being gay, that all they *really* value are specific kinds of sex acts. We usually take them at their word. Disability activists often say they value being disabled. They hold disability pride parades. They make art that celebrates disability. And so on. It seems an odd sort of skepticism to try to find alternative explanations for the value claims they're making.

Again, though, while some people value being disabled (and others simply don't mind it), not everyone does—nor is it plausible that everyone would, if we lived in a society without ableism. So, instead of Dostoevsky, consider Beethoven. Deafness is something that's valuable to many people, but it was devastating for Beethoven (causing him to withdraw from most social interaction, stop performing, and even consider suicide). Deafness caused a considerable reduction, for Beethoven, in many of the goods on our list: getting what one wants, excelling at worthwhile activities, creative activity, happiness, enjoyment, etc. But it wasn't that deafness *by itself* caused such a severe reduction in well-being. It was deafness combined with a career as a composer and a conductor, a love of the auditory experience of music above almost anything else, and an intense creative drive to compose music that was devastating. Deafness by itself doesn't entail a reduction in well-being. Whether being Deaf reduces, enhances, or has little effect on your overall well-being—that is, whether being Deaf reduces, increases, or doesn't change the amount of goods you have—will depend on what else it's combined with.

3.11 Desire Satisfaction Theories

There are various hybrid views of well-being that attempt to steer a middle ground between objective list views and fully subjective desire satisfaction accounts—accounts in which, for example, well-being consists in having desires or projects directed toward certain objectively good or valuable things, and then having those desires satisfied or those projects succeed.[31] I'm going to skip over these in-between options,

---

[31] See Woodward (2016) for an excellent overview.

THE VALUE-NEUTRAL MODEL 113

as the way that the Value-Neutral Model can be articulated within them is—unsurprisingly—something of a combination of the way it's articulated in objective list views and the way it's articulated in subjectivist versions of the desire satisfaction account.

So let's proceed to a subjectivist version of desire satisfaction accounts of well-being: Your life goes well for you insofar as your desires are satisfied and badly for you insofar as your desires are frustrated. It's good for you to get what you want, and bad for you to fail to get what you want.[32] The Value-Neutral Model, articulated within a desire satisfaction framework, says that whether disability leads to an overall increase in frustrated desires depends on what else it is combined with. Disability by itself isn't the sort of thing that leads to an overall increase in frustrated desires. But that's compatible with disability being the sort of thing that sometimes or always frustrates *some* desires.

Ben Mattlin is a writer and disability activist with spinal muscular atrophy (SMA), a condition similar to muscular dystrophy—his experiences with which he chronicles in his book *Miracle Boy Grows Up: How the Disability Rights Movement Saved My Sanity*. He's never been able to walk or stand, and for the last decade he's been unable to use his hands. But Mattlin describes himself as being someone who's gotten pretty much everything he wanted in life: a degree from Harvard, a wife he loves deeply, two daughters, and a successful career as a freelance writer, editor, and NPR correspondent. And he maintains that 'something is lost if you don't see SMA as part of the normal variety/diversity of human life.'[33] Like his friend Laura Hershey, he was an active campaigner against the Jerry Lewis telethon, finding its depiction of disabled people demeaning and its focus on cures unhelpful. Like Hershey, he's a fan of the concept of disability pride.

Yes, there are a lot of things Mattlin can't do because of his disability. But for many of them, it's simply the case that he has no particular desire to do them. He's been able to get what he really wants—a

---

[32] I'm going to gloss over questions of whether the best way to articulate the desire satisfaction theory is via actual desires, higher-order desires, suitably idealized desires, etc., as these complexities don't really matter for my purposes here. See Heathwood (2016) for an excellent summary and Bradley (2007) and Arneson (1999) for critical overviews.

[33] From Mattlin's blog 'Adventures in Modern Life', http://www.benmattlin.blogspot.co.uk/2013/06/a-post-conference-post.html.

fulfilling career, an engaging intellectual life, a loving family—without needing to do things like walk. He openly acknowledges that his sort of body might have been a burden for someone who wanted different things—someone who really wanted to be a firefighter or an athlete, for example—but for what he wants out of life, his body hasn't been an impediment.

Recall the case of inflexibility. For an aspiring ballet dancer, it's devastating. But for most people, it's no big deal. According to the desire satisfaction theory, whether having an inflexible body is bad for you depends on what you want, and on whether being inflexible stops you from getting what you want. For the dancer, it does. And the same goes for SMA. Whether having a body with SMA is bad for you, according to the desire satisfaction account, depends on what you want. For some people, having SMA would stop them from getting what they want, but for Mattlin, it hasn't.

Arguably, many of Mattlin's preferences are adaptive—at least in some sense of 'adaptive'. That is, it's plausible that in some places he's tailored his preferences to suit his capabilities. We'll discuss the issue of adaptive preference in detail in the next chapter, but in a nutshell what I'll argue is that preferences like Mattlin's are adaptive in a way that's innocuous and universal (in a way that we all adapt our preferences to what's available to us and to what we can do). As a child, I stopped wanting to be an acrobat when I realized I was extremely uncoordinated and stopped wanting to be a wizard when I realized that wizards aren't actually real (that was a sad day). Mattlin's preference adaptation, I'll argue, is more like that than the preference adaptation of someone with Stockholm syndrome.

There are, of course, some desires that SMA frustrates, even for Mattlin (some socially mediated, some not). And that's what it is, on the desire satisfaction account, for disability to be a local bad. But there are also other desires that SMA helps fulfill. For example, Mattlin thinks that his experience of SMA has helped to make him a better writer (not to mention opening up unique writing opportunities for him) and deepened his relationship with his wife. That's what it is, on the desire satisfaction account, for disability to be a local good. The same thing—Mattlin's SMA—that frustrates some desires helps to fulfill others. Mattlin's experience of SMA is that on the whole his life hasn't been better or worse because of SMA—just different.

3.12 Hedonism

Hedonism is, roughly, the view according to which well-being is constituted by pleasure and the absence of pain. The best life is the one that
combines the most pleasure with the least pain. (There are, of course,
tricky questions about whether, for example, you should aim for max-
min or min-max, but we'll leave those to the side.) Some versions of
hedonism are objectivist.[34] Pain is just objectively bad for you. The sado-
masochist's life is going badly for her, whether or not she enjoys the pain
(if she gets genuinely pleasurable sensations from the pain, then that's
good, but it would be better if she could seek out those pleasurable
sensations without associated pain). But I'll be focusing here on subjectivist versions of hedonism—those that equate pleasure with (very
roughly) experiences that you enjoy and wish to continue, and pain
with experiences that you dislike and wish to cease.[35]

It's tempting to think that it's simply analytic that *painful* disabilities
can't be neutral if hedonism is correct. But that's too quick. For the
example in this section I'll specifically use the case of a painful disability
in order to illustrate this.

Nadina LaSpina is a disability rights activist and educator who
contracted polio as a young child, and now has post-polio syndrome.
Growing up, she endured seventeen surgeries and numerous broken
bones in a failed attempt to restore her ability to walk, an effort that
ultimately led to the amputation of both her legs below the knee. As
an adult, LaSpina is in chronic pain, and likely will be for the rest of
her life:

Pain is part of her disability, says LaSpina; it comes with the territory. She says
she's happy with herself 'as a person with a disability—with whatever pain there
is. That's part of it.'
It's like being Italian, she goes on. 'I'm proud of being Italian. There are things
I'm ashamed of, like the existence of the Mafia—but these things do not stop me
from embracing my Italian-ness. I love being a woman, but I hate going through
menopause. But I wouldn't want a sex-change operation just because of menopause. Certainly the pain . . . of disability [is] not wonderful, yet that identity is
who I am. And I am proud of it.'[36]

---

[34] See Bradley (2013).   [35] See, e.g., Crisp (2006) and Heathwood (2007).
[36] Johnson (1998).

With respect to being a person who dislikes physical pain—who prefers physically painful sensations to cease—LaSpina's disability is bad for her. And that's what it is for disability to be a local bad according to hedonism: It's a net increase in pain and net decrease in pleasure with respect to a given feature or given time. But there are other aspects of her life in which disability involves a net increase in pleasure and a net decrease in pain (which is what it is to be a local good, for the hedonist). Disability has given her a strong sense of empowerment, a feeling of community with other disabled people, and has involved her in the unique artistic community of disability culture.

LaSpina strongly rejects the idea of a 'cure' for her disability. She is proud of her disability, and describes it as a positive experience. Her experience of disability is something that she wants to continue, even though there are aspects of it that she dislikes and would prefer to cease. According to the basic model of hedonism, her disability is good for her, even though there are respects in which it is locally bad for her.

There are, of course, many other people who would have different reactions to disability. Many disabled people would prefer not to be disabled, and doubtless there are disabled people who would prefer not to be disabled even in the absence of ableism. But being disabled—even painfully disabled—doesn't by itself represent a reduction of well-being for the hedonist.

It's worth noting, at this point, that the Value-Neutral Model can be articulated—even for painful disabilities—even on the stronger, objectivist version of hedonism, which maintains that physical pain is simply objectively bad for you (regardless of how you feel about it). On such a version of hedonism, physically painful disabilities would be bad for you insofar as they are painful. But it's perfectly plausible that some physically painful experiences are systematically connected to pleasurable experiences. If that's the case, then objectivist hedonism doesn't rule out that flourishing lives can involve substantial amounts of pain—it's just that those pains need to be correlated with pleasures (whether bodily or otherwise) in a way that the overall pleasure/pain balance is maximized. And that's the experience LaSpina seems to be describing. Her experience of pain is directly correlated with many of her greatest pleasures (disability community, disability culture, etc.): They are all aspects of her disability. Just as an athlete's experience of pain from athletic training is correlated with many of the things she values—competition, success, hard work, etc.—about being an athlete, LaSpina's experience of pain is correlated with many of the things she values about being a disabled person. Hedonism says the best life is the one that maximizes the pain/pleasure balance—but that isn't obviously achievable *only* by minimizing pain.

Another important thing to note about this form of objective hedonism, as mentioned in section 3.10, is that the distinction between disability activists who value being disabled and cases like Joe the grateful cancer survivor largely breaks down. That's because, for this sort of hedonist, the only thing it makes sense to value non-instrumentally is pleasure, and the only thing your life goes better in virtue of is pleasure. The net total pleasure in some disabled people's lives has been increased because they are disabled. But the net total pleasure in some cancer patients' lives has been increased because they had cancer. So far, they're on a par. (Note that the same doesn't seem to be true for the weaker, subjectivist version of hedonism. Joe values a lot that he's gotten out of his experience of cancer, but ostensibly he doesn't want his cancer to continue, whereas many disabled people report not only that they value the effects of being disabled, but also that they want their experience of disability to continue—they would not want to be 'cured'.) The distinction between positive, neutral, and negative traits (understood independently from the actual effect they have on net levels of pleasure and pain) doesn't seem to make sense on this strong version of hedonism—there are just things that increase your total amount of pleasure, things that don't, and that's the end of it.

So there's a sense in which the Value-Neutral Model can't be fully articulated within this strong version of hedonism. But this is unsurprising—it's simply much easier to hold a mere-difference view of disability if you adopt this version of hedonism, at least insofar as you think a mere-difference/bad-difference distinction even makes sense. The positive/neutral/negative distinction that I employ in developing the neutrality is appealed to specifically to defend against a certain kind of objection. Namely: Why shouldn't we think that people value disability only in the way that people sometimes value the important lessons of bad experiences? But this sort of objection shouldn't trouble anyone persuaded by this strong form of hedonism. The only 'bad experiences' are the ones that lead to a net loss of pleasure, and the only 'good experiences' are the ones that lead to a net increase in pleasure. If Joe's cancer really has led to a net increase in pleasure, then Joe's cancer isn't a bad experience.

I'm not even sure this (again, very strong) version of hedonism should be interested in the question of bad-difference/mere-difference distinctions for general features like 'disability'. What should matter is the actual effects of individual features on individual lives—and the only salient question should be: Did that feature actually lead to a net increase in pleasure? There are further pragmatic questions that might guide action, of course. Is disability the sort of thing that *tends to* or *is likely to* lead to a net loss in pleasure? And here there might be genuine differences between the happy disabled person and Joe. There's a large body of evidence that disability doesn't—in the long run—have a substantial negative effect on perceived well-being. People march in disability pride parades, but they don't march in cancer pride parades. And so on. This sort of thing is, I'd imagine, the kind of thing that would weigh into decision-making for the hedonist. I'll admit that I find the epistemological questions here formidable—but I think that's a problem for this version of hedonism, not for mere-difference/bad-difference distinctions. It's hard to know of *any* particular feature whether that particular feature will actually lead to a net increase in pleasure, given how complicated and unpredictable the world is.

4

Taking Their Word for It

> If disabled people were truly heard, an explosion of knowledge of
> the human body and psyche would take place.
>
> Susan Wendell (1989)

Thus far, I have been making appeals to the testimony of disabled people
about their own experiences of disability. More specifically, I have been
drawing heavily on the breadth of disability-positive testimony that can
be found within the disability rights movement. There are many disabled
people who claim to value their experience of disability—who say that
they like being disabled and would not prefer to be non-disabled.[1] And
there is more than just these first-person reports of well-being. There is
art, there is theater, there is dance, there is film, there are parades—all
celebrating disability as a valuable form of diversity.

I've been appealing to disability-positive testimony—and to disability-
positive culture—to argue for the plausibility of a mere-difference view of
disability more generally (chapter 2) and for the plausibility of my own
favored version of a mere-difference view, the Value-Neutral Model
(chapter 3). But appeals to this kind of testimony—and to disability
culture more broadly—are only in good standing if the testimony is
reliable. It doesn't need to be infallible, of course. Testimony never is.
It just needs to not be systematically misleading. And yet some argue that
the testimony of disabled people about their experience of disability *is*
systematically misleading. This chapter examines such arguments, primarily the argument that such testimony is unreliable because it involves
adaptive preferences. Borrowing from the work of Miranda Fricker,

---

[1] Hahn and Belt (2004). The strongest anti-'cure' statement I know of comes from
Nancy Eiesland (1994). Eiesland—a disabled theologian—believed in the resurrection of the
physical body, and argued that she would be disabled in heaven.

I argue that skepticism about the testimony of disabled people who claim to value being disabled is a type of testimonial injustice.

4.1 Knowing What It's Like

Before addressing the main worry about disability-positive testimony from disabled people—that it is adaptive preference—it's worth considering some other common (but to my mind less challenging) reasons for doubting such testimony.

To begin with, we might be skeptical about disability-positive testimony because we worry that disabled people simply do not 'know what they're missing'. The blind person may be perfectly content in their blindness—and think that being blind is a very good way to be—but that's because they don't know what it's like to see. The Deaf person may be perfectly content in their Deafness—and think that being Deaf is a very good way to be—but that's because they don't know what it's like to hear. And so on.

But such objections to disability-positive testimony are ineffective. To begin with, we don't generally require that a person know 'what it's like' to be not-Φ in order to give positive testimony about the value of being Φ. We don't dismiss the testimony of women who claim to value being women because they don't know what it's like to be men. We don't dismiss the testimony of gay people who claim to value being gay because they don't know what it's like to be straight. And so on.[2]

The move is perhaps tempting in the case of disability because we often conceive of disability as *mere lack*. Being a woman is not merely the lack of male gender. Being gay is not merely the lack of heterosexual desire. But disability is often conceived of as a mere lack of a relevant ability. If you are Deaf you lack the ability to hear, if you are blind you lack the ability to see, etc. And furthermore, lacking an ability is *what it is* to be disabled. But as already discussed, this conception of disability is deeply inadequate.

---

[2] And, as Laurie Paul (2014) persuasively argues, we perhaps overestimate the extent to which we can know 'what it's like' to be in circumstances other than our own. Non-disabled people often seem to think they can imagine what it's like to be disabled, without addressing the extent to which being or becoming disabled is a transformative experience.

Moreover, it's simply false that all disabled people who express disability-positive views—including the view that they wouldn't want to become non-disabled—don't know what it's like to be non-disabled. And that's because such views are expressed by those with *acquired* disabilities as well as those with *congenital* disabilities. That is, people who become disabled—including those who have become disabled as adults—and who thus know what it's like to be non-disabled also express disability-positive views. These views are rarely expressed in the first few years after acquiring disability, as it (unsurprisingly) takes time to adjust to being disabled. But disability-positive testimony isn't exclusive to those who were born disabled.

4.2 'I'll Be Glad I Did It' Reasoning

Elizabeth Harman (2009) has argued that at least some disability-positive testimony results from mistaken application of a form of 'I'll be glad I did it' reasoning. Being disabled can be identity-determining in important ways. For many disabled people, it's the case that had they never been disabled, they would in some relevant sense not be 'the same person'. And it's this identity-determination, Harman argues, that's ultimately a source of much confusion in disability-positive testimony.

It's perfectly acceptable and rational, according to Harman, for people to value and prefer that they be the people they in fact are. And so, insofar as disability is a part of making many disabled people the people they are, it makes sense for those people to value disability, and even prefer disability to non-disability. The problem, Harman argues, is when disabled people project these preferences beyond their own situation—when they claim that disability is in general to be valued (just because they value it) or that disability ought not to be removed from infants (just because they are glad that their own disabilities weren't removed as infants), and so on.

The problem for such testimony arises when we consider that sometimes it makes sense for us to prefer that bad, or at least suboptimal, things happen. We can value disability, according to Harman, insofar as we value the unique experiences and perspectives of disabled people. But that doesn't mean we ought to value disability simpliciter. Sometimes unique perspectives and experiences are shaped by things that are bad, or at least suboptimal. We can value the unique perspectives and experiences without thereby thinking that what shaped them isn't bad, or at least suboptimal. The mistaken inference in the testimony of many disabled people, Harman argues, is the move from valuing their own experiences of disability to claiming that disability is valuable simpliciter. We can be glad that disabled people are the people they are, and not prefer that they have been different. But this doesn't license being glad that there are disabilities.

On Harman's picture, then, disability-positive testimony is similar to the testimony of the grateful cancer survivor. The grateful cancer survivor is, in some sense, glad that she got cancer—she wouldn't be the person she is today if she hadn't had cancer, and she's glad she's the person she is today. But the simple fact that the grateful cancer survivor is glad she's the person she is today (and she wouldn't be that person without cancer) doesn't give us reason to value cancer.

The main problem for Harman's model when applied to disability, though, is that vast swaths of disability-positive testimony seem very different from the kind of testimony we get from the grateful cancer survivor.[3] Disabled people aren't simply claiming to value 'who they are' as people. They are claiming to value disability. Valuing disability is the crux of the entire disability pride movement—with all its parades and its festivals and its culture.

We can and do distinguish between things we value merely because of how they've shaped us, and things we value for their own sake. Much disability-positive testimony expresses—very consciously and explicitly—the latter type of sentiment. And so if Harman is right, many disabled people are deeply confused. They are failing to tease apart two fairly basic ways in which we could value things. To make this plausible, we need some sort of explanation about why otherwise rational people are making this kind of systematic mistake. In the next section, I explore exactly such an explanation—the claim that disabled people's testimony is systematically mistaken due to *adaptive preference*.[4]

---

[3] For a more detailed discussion of Harman's view and its application to disability see Howard (2015).

[4] The claim that disability-positive testimony is (irrational) adaptive preference has many similarities to the claim that it is an irrational form of status quo bias. My main response—based on the idea of testimonial injustice—is the same for both criticisms, so I won't discuss status quo bias in any detail. But see Dorsey (2010) and Nebel (2015). And see Campbell and Wahlert (2015) for specific discussion of disability and status quo bias.

4.3 Adaptive Preference—the Basics

Appeal to adaptive preferences as a way of undermining testimony about well-being arises primarily from the capabilities approach to welfare, popularized by Amartya Sen and Martha Nussbaum. Importantly, the picture of adaptive preference that Nussbaum and Sen develop doesn't depend on commitment to the capabilities approach, and can make sense in isolation from it. But I'll briefly explain the capabilities approach, as doing so will help explain what adaptive preference is meant to be.

The capabilities approach conceives of human welfare in terms of certain basic and essential goods, which are construed as capabilities.[5] In order to thrive, according to Sen and Nussbaum, a person must be able to participate in these fundamental goods (i.e., have the capability to access them). If any are lacking, then that person cannot truly flourish. Likewise, in order to be considered just, a society must ensure (as far as possible) that all of its citizens have access to these basic goods.

There is, of course, an obvious worry about such an account of well-being: Not all people or cultures value all the capabilities that Sen and Nussbaum have in mind. But the capabilities approach famously develops a response to this problem via an appeal to adaptive preferences. The adaptive preference model purports to give a compelling explanation of why a person might alter their preferences toward something that is suboptimal. Once this explanation is in place, the thought goes, there is then no reason to take a person's preference for a life without one or more of the basic goods as evidence that a life without one or more of the basic goods can in fact be just as optimal as a life with them all. As we'll see, though, the adaptive preference model adopted by Sen and Nussbaum doesn't hang on any of the particularities of the capabilities approach, and could easily be incorporated by other theories of well-being.

Sen's and Nussbaum's discussion of adaptive preference draws heavily on the work of Jon Elster. Elster (1983) describes adaptive preferences as

---

[5] The distinctive feature of the capabilities approach is the focus on what a person can *do*, not on what she has. Having a certain amount of resources may be vital to ensuring basic capabilities, but those resources are important only insofar as they facilitate basic capabilities. Likewise, according to the capabilities approach we should aim, not toward equality of resources, but rather toward equality of capability. There is a set of fundamental capabilities that are understood as together comprising the basic threshold for human flourishing. See Nussbaum (1993), (2001a), (2001b) and Sen (1985), (1990), (1993).

the phenomenon familiar from the La Fontaine fable of the fox and the grapes. The fox desires to eat a bunch of grapes hanging from a tree, but eventually realizes that they are too high up for him to reach. Having discovered that he cannot get the grapes, he decides that he didn't really want them anyway—grapes are too sour for foxes.

What has happened in this situation? According to Elster, the fox originally encounters a scenario where he believes his set of options includes getting and eating the grapes. In this scenario, he prefers to eat the grapes. But then things change: The fox finds that his set of viable options has contracted, and eating the grapes is no longer a part of it. Faced with this situation of contracted options, the fox no longer prefers to eat the grapes. For Elster, this change in preference is fundamentally irrational because it is not autonomous—it is mere adaptation. The fox does not decide to alter his preferences to suit his new situation. He simply experiences a preference change (likely from an unconscious need to avoid disappointment and frustration). The hallmark of rationality, for Elster, is autonomy—conscious decisions made in light of considered options—so preference changes that are adaptive in this respect he deems irrational.

This does not mean, however, that all preference changes in response to diminished options must be irrational. Elster distinguishes changes in preference that are adaptive from those that he calls 'character-planning'. Imagine an alternative fable that goes like this. The fox loves grapes, but is traveling to a country where no grapes grow, but where another sort of summer fruit is abundant. The fox decides to cultivate a taste for this new fruit, so that he will still have something tasty to eat. This new fruit is much sweeter than grapes, but after several tries and a lot of con-centration, the fox realizes that this increased sweetness is in fact very pleasant—he now really does prefer the new fruit over grapes, and so could say without any hesitation that grapes are a little too sour for foxes. Elster argues that this sort of preference change—though it has the same end result and also arises from a contraction of viable options—is rational because it is the result of a conscious decision. The fox does not simply realize that he now finds grapes too sour; rather, he has made a concerted effort to cultivate a taste for a new fruit, and as a result he prefers the new fruit to grapes.

The difference between the two cases, according to Elster, is that the first change in preference arises merely from an 'affective drive'—a basic, subconscious need not to face frustrated or unmet desire. The second change, in contrast, arises from a meta-desire—a desire to change one's desires in light of new circumstances. The latter can result in autonomous, considered actions, whereas the former cannot (it is mere adaptation). So the latter can be rational whereas the former cannot.

Many philosophers, however, find Elster's emphasis on autonomous deliberation to be somewhat misplaced. To use an example given by Nussbaum (2001a), imagine that as a child you desire to be a famous opera singer, though you later learn that you aren't much of a singer and thus being a famous opera singer isn't really within your feasible career options. It seems that it's perfectly rational for your preferences to change in light of this—for you now to no longer prefer to be an opera singer, and perhaps think that you would prefer to be, say, a philosopher (which happens to be what you are) rather than an opera singer no matter what your singing ability—even if you did not, when you were eight, consciously set about altering your preferences through the application of a meta-desire. The simple point here is that all of us adapt—in some sense of adaptation—our preferences based on our limitations and our circumstances. There doesn't seem to be anything irrational about such preference changes. (If anything, not adapting your preferences in this way seems irrational—it would be bizarre, to say the least, to never change your preferences in light of your circumstances.)

In response to such concerns, Luc Bovens (1992) gives an alternative way of distinguishing sour grapes-type preference changes from perfectly acceptable preference changes. Both kinds of preference change Bovens envisages can be considered 'adaptive', but one is rational while the other is not. An agent's adaptation of preferences in light of a contracted options set is rational just in case it coheres with the rest of the agent's beliefs and desires.[6]

Consider the second fox fable. This fox doesn't merely come to believe that grapes are too sour for foxes. He also comes to believe that things that are much sweeter than grapes are delicious, that anything that is the same level of sweetness as grapes is too sour for

---

[6] For a more detailed discussion of the differences between Elster's and Boven's views see Bruckner (2009). Bruckner argues for the rationality of an even wider range of adaptive preferences than does Bovens, though both are in agreement that Elster's constraints on rationality are far too narrow.

foxes, etc. That is, in adapting his preference toward the new fruit, he's not just changed his preferences about grapes, he's changed all his related taste preferences such that they cohere with his new-found preference for the new fruit.

Contrast this to the original fable. The fox hasn't altered his other preferences about tastiness when he decides that grapes are too sour for foxes. He likely doesn't suddenly crave things that are much sweeter than grapes, and he wouldn't turn his nose up at an alternative tasty treat that came his way, even if it was just as sour as the grapes he claims not to want. For this reason, Bovens argues, the fox in the classic fable looks to be doing something objectionable and irrational, whereas the fox in the alternative version of the fable does not. One fox has simply altered his preferences about grapes, which ends up in tension with many others of his beliefs, desires, and preferences. The other, in response to lack of grapes, has altered his entire preference set about tastiness. But notice that it's no part of the fox's ending up, after adapting his preferences, with a fully coherent set of taste preferences that he consciously *decided* to change his preferences. He could end up in the very same situation from having undergone a subconscious preference change, and would still be counted as having fully rational preferences. Again, Nussbaum's opera-dreamer child likely didn't one day willfully decide to change her preference in order to fit her options. Nevertheless, assuming that as an adult she has a set of preferences that are fully coherent with her preferring to be a philosopher rather than an opera singer, those preferences can be seen as fully rational.

Nussbaum, though, thinks internally coherent preferences aren't enough to make it the case that your preferences aren't problematically adaptive. And that's because she thinks you can have a coherent set of preferences for things that aren't good for you. And so, in contrast to Bovens, Nussbaum construes the issue of whether changes in preference are problematically adaptive as more deeply normative.[7] A change in one's preferences in response to a contraction of viable options is objectionable primarily (or perhaps only) in those cases where the change leaves one preferring something that is somehow less good or less optimal. That is, the change in preferences is problematic insofar as it

---

[7] See especially the discussion in Nussbaum (2001a).

leads to a preference for something that one *should not*, ceteris paribus, prefer. A change in preference is adaptive, in Nussbaum's sense, just in case it represents a change in (or formation of) preferences in response to diminished options toward something suboptimal.

Here are two paradigm examples, the first a case of adaptive preference change and the second a case of adaptive preference formation. Firstly, in the phenomenon known as Stockholm syndrome, victims of kidnapping or hostage-taking come to prefer being kidnapped—they come to believe that their kidnapper is really on a noble mission, and has rescued them, and that their kidnapping is thus of great benefit to them, etc. It's fairly easy to see how beliefs and preferences such as this could arise. The kidnap victim is put in a traumatic situation from which they see no possibility of escape, so simply in order to cope they (subconsciously or otherwise) lose the desire to escape. Such coping mechanisms may well be an admirable facet of human psychology, but we'd be very reluctant to say that the preferences of a person with Stockholm syndrome are rational, or serve as evidence that being a kidnap victim is a good way to live. Rather, according to Nussbaum, we should simply say that such preferences are adaptive.

Secondly, a woman who grows up in a deeply patriarchal society may well form preferences for submissive gender roles—shunning educa-tion, taking orders, and in some cases even accepting abuse. It's likely, though, that in her upbringing she did not consider alternatives to these—if she was even able to consider them at all—as viable options. Thus her set of viable options is limited from the start. As a result, she may well adapt her preferences to suit her situation. Again, says Nuss-baum, this might be an admirable coping mechanism, but we'd hesitate to say that her preferences for submissive gender roles are rational,[8] formed as they were by the deeply patriarchal system she was placed in, and from which she sees no escape. Thus the presence of her preference for submissive gender roles does not by itself give us any evidence that a life that coheres to submissive gender roles is just as good as a life that does not. Because her preferences are adaptive—formed toward some-thing suboptimal in light of a severely diminished set of options—they cannot serve as such evidence.

---

[8] Though for arguments that at least some such preferences are, see Bruckner (2009).

Again, a diagnosis of adaptive preference is warranted in the above cases because they involve *both* a change in preference due to a constraint of options *and* a change in preferences toward something suboptimal. Neither condition is, by itself, sufficient for a change in preference to be adaptive in the normatively laden sense that Nussbaum describes. To illustrate, here are two examples of preference change that *do not* constitute adaptive preference.

The first example, already discussed above, involves a change in preference due to a limited range of options. Nussbaum recalls, when she was younger, dreaming of being an opera singer—but quickly discovering she didn't have the voice of a professional opera singer. And so her preferences adapted. She came to prefer being an academic to being an opera singer. Nussbaum's options were constrained—being a professional opera singer wasn't really a viable career path for her. And it's very likely that this constraint on her options affected the formation of her preferences. But there's nothing irrational or misleading about the resulting preferences. Indeed, it would be somewhat perverse to refuse to adapt your preferences in this very ordinary way—to insist on clinging to your implausible and unobtainable dream, come what may. The difference between this sort of preference change and a genuine adaptive preference, Nussbaum argues, is that while both are in some sense the result of constrained options, adaptive preferences are specifically those cases in which constrained options create preferences specifically for something that is somehow suboptimal. Being a philosopher is just as worthy a life choice as being an opera singer, and so this case isn't a case of adaptive preference in the normatively laden sense that Nussbaum and Sen describe.

The second example involves a change of preferences toward the suboptimal. In the beginning of *A Christmas Carol*, Ebenezer Scrooge is portrayed as someone who has developed, over time, increasing preferences for miserliness and isolation. These preferences are clearly preferences for the suboptimal—they aren't good for Scrooge. But they aren't caused by constraints in options. The more wealthy and successful he becomes, the more options Scrooge has. And yet it's precisely as his options expand that Scrooge's miserliness increases. His preferences aren't adaptive, then, because although they're preferences for the suboptimal, they aren't caused by constraints in options.

4.4 Adaptive Preference and Preference for Disability

The version of adaptive preferences most suited to skepticism about disability-positive testimony is the Nussbaum–Sen model. Clearly, disabled people's preferences are adaptive *in some sense*, insofar as disabled people's preferences are shaped by their disabilities (and likely would have been different had these people not been disabled). But I take it that such adaptation isn't epistemically problematic; all of us—disabled or otherwise—have had our preferences shaped by our circumstances, our particular skills, and our particular limitations. So to be skeptical about any testimony based on adaptive preference in this broad sense would be to embrace a pretty general form of skepticism. I take it that skeptics about disability-positive testimony want something more specific.

Elster's version of adaptive preferences won't give them that, since as Nussbaum rightly notes, most of our preferences—including ones that seem perfectly rational—weren't the result of deliberate character-planning. So if we dismiss disability-positive testimony as adaptive in Elster's sense, we'll also dismiss lots of other testimony, including testimony we aren't typically skeptical about. Bovens's version of adaptive preferences won't yield the right sort of skepticism either, simply because most disability-positive preference won't count as adaptive in Bovens's sense. Disabled people don't seem to betray the kind of internal inconsistency of the fox in the original fable (who claims that grapes are too sour, but likes plenty of things of equal sourness). Their preferences seem perfectly consistent, even if they strike the non-disabled as unusual.

The Nussbaum–Sen model, in contrast, does allow us to say that disability-positive preferences are adaptive in a way that most other personal preferences are not. If—and this is the big 'if'—we can say that preferences for disability are preferences for something suboptimal (in a way that preferences for being an academic instead of an opera singer are not), then the Nussbaum–Sen model can allow us to say that disability-positive preferences are adaptive in a way that most preferences are not. For this reason, I'm going to discuss the Nussbaum–Sen model specifically in what follows, and it's Nussbaum–Sen-style adaptive preferences that I'll mean by 'adaptive preference'.

Many disabled people claim that their well-being is not diminished by their disability—they lead lives that are as full, rich, and rewarding as those led by non-disabled people. Some disabled people even claim that, for them, being disabled is preferable to being non-disabled. They value being disabled and have no desire for their disability to be removed (in more pejorative terms, they have no desire for 'a cure'). And I have been appealing to this kind of testimony when arguing that disability is mere-difference rather than bad-difference.

Yet it's easy to see how such preferences might be explained away as problematically adaptive in the Nussbaum–Sen sense. Disability constrains your options. This constraint is often permanent. It's perhaps an admirable psychological trait—evidence of human adaptability and perseverance, maybe—that, when confronted with such severe constraints, we can adapt our preferences such that we end up feeling fairly satisfied with our lives. But precisely because such preferences are adaptive, they're no evidence that disability isn't bad-difference.

Like the woman who is raised in a deeply patriarchal culture, someone who is born disabled grows up with a limited range of viable options and choices. She may well form preferences that align with what she can do. If she's blind, she likely won't grow up wanting to be a photographer. If she's Deaf, she likely won't grow up wanting to be a sound technician. If she has cerebral palsy that affects her hands, she likely won't grow up wanting to be a vascular surgeon. And so on. She may wind up perfectly content, with most of her preferences satisfied. But her preferences were formed in response to a severely constrained set of options. That she is perfectly satisfied with her life—that she wouldn't prefer to be non-disabled, even—doesn't by itself tell us anything about whether her life is just as optimal as a non-disabled life, or about whether her preferences are rational.

Like the kidnap victim who comes to love her kidnapper or the abused wife who stays with her husband because she believes the relationship is good for her, someone who *becomes* disabled has their options suddenly and severely constrained (in a way that seems inescapable). In order to cope with such an extreme life change, she may well adapt her preferences. If she becomes a wheelchair user, she may develop an interest in wheelchair sports. If she develops a chronic illness, she may claim that the slower, more contemplative pace of life she is forced to adopt actually suits her better. And so on. Again, she may wind up perfectly content, with most of her (altered) preferences satisfied. But that she ultimately ends up just as satisfied with her disabled life as she was with her non-disabled life—that she wouldn't prefer to return to her non-disabled life, even—doesn't by itself tell us anything about whether her life with a disability is just as optimal as her life without one, or about whether her (altered) preferences are rational.

Again, the main point is this. The preferences of disabled people can be diagnosed as (problematically or irrationally) adaptive. If the preferences of disabled people are adaptive in this way, then they cannot be appealed to as evidence for any sort of mere-difference of disability. Disabled people may often give testimony that seems as though it supports a mere-difference view, but if their preferences are adaptive this testimony is systematically misleading.

4.5 Overgeneralization of the Adaptive Preference Model

The diagnosis of adaptive preference can easily explain why the pro-disability testimony of disabled people is unreliable. But a major worry is that the explanation it offers is not simply easy, it is *too easy*. If the adaptive preference story works in the case of disability, it ought to work in other, relevantly similar cases. But if it does, the net result is problematic overgeneralization.

The following reasoning sounds like parody. Many people who are male claim that their well-being is not diminished by their sex. In fact, some males even report that they value being male and would not prefer to be female. And yet being male severely and permanently constricts a person's options. There are profound, centrally important aspects of the human experience that they simply cannot participate in. They cannot become pregnant. They cannot give birth. They cannot lactate. And so on. Faced with this limited option set, males may well adapt their preferences, and may wind up perfectly content with most of their preferences satisfied. That males can do this may well be an admirable psychological coping mechanism. But their preferences don't by themselves give us any evidence that being male is just as good as being female.

The above reasoning sounds like parody, but this reasoning sounds (or ought to sound) unnervingly familiar. Many gay people claim that their well-being is not diminished by their sexuality. In fact, some gay people even report that they value being gay and would not prefer to be straight. And yet being gay severely and permanently constrains a person's options. They cannot conceive a child with a same-sex partner. They do not experience heterosexual desire and attraction. They do not enjoy heteronormative relationships. And so on. Faced with this constrained set of options and experiences, gay people may well adapt their preferences, and may ultimately end up perfectly content with most of their preferences satisfied. But their preferences don't by themselves give us any evidence that being gay is just as good as being straight.

The first line of reasoning sounds like parody because we don't doubt the testimony of males about being male. The simple fact that males are limited in some respects when compared to some other group (females) doesn't change this. The second line of reasoning sounds familiar because we *have* doubted the testimony of gay people about being gay. But both cases should make us question the adaptive preference model's application to disability.

Disabled people are constrained and limited by their bodies. And so, the story goes, they adapt their preferences in suboptimal ways in order to get by. This adaptive process helps them cope, but it also means their testimony about their own well-being is unreliable in important respects. But this story looks prone to gross overgeneralization, given how common it is to adapt preferences in light of bodily limitation. The simple fact is that, disabled or non-disabled, we are *all* limited and constrained by our bodies. To have a body that is any particular way is to have a body that is limited and constrained in some respects and in comparison to other kinds of bodies. That's just part of what it is to have a body. Some of us are male, some of us are female. Some of us are tall, some of us are short. Some of us are flexible, some of us are stiff. Some of us are stocky, some of us are willowy. There are all sorts of ways that bodies can be. And each way a body can be comes with some limitations and constraints.

We all adapt our preferences due in part to the limitations of our bodies—that's an utterly ordinary thing to do. It would be a severe overgeneralization to characterize all such adaptation as adaptive preference in the Nussbaum–Sen sense. And it would lead to skepticism about huge amounts of first-person testimony about well-being. Recall, though, that preferences are adaptive in the Nussbaum–Sen sense just in case they are preferences that result from a constraint on options for something *suboptimal*. So to block the worry of overgeneralization, there needs to be a principled reason why we ought to say that pro-disability, but not pro-gay or pro-male or pro-whatever else, preferences are preferences tailored toward something *less good*.

4.6 Which Preferences are Suboptimal?

Preferences are adaptive, in the Nussbaum–Sen sense, when they are preferences *for something suboptimal* formed in response to constraints on options. And so, the thought goes, diagnosing the preferences of some males for a male body as adaptive is illegitimate, because the limitations of the male body aren't bad. Diagnosing the preference of some abuse victims to remain with their abusers as adaptive *is* legitimate, in contrast, because being in an abusive relationship is bad or suboptimal (when compared to not being in one). Likewise, diagnosing the pro-disability preferences of some disabled people as adaptive is legitimate, because being disabled is bad or suboptimal when compared to not being disabled. Pro-disability preferences are problematically adaptive because they are preferences for something that's bad.

But this brings us to the second major worry for the adaptive preference model: It fails to overgeneralize only by making an unwarranted assumption. To diagnose the pro-disability preferences of some disabled people as adaptive, we need to assume that being disabled is somehow bad or suboptimal. Yet whether being disabled is somehow bad or suboptimal is precisely what's up for debate—and precisely what many disabled people deny. And they take their own first-person experiences as evidence for their position. If the diagnosis of adaptive preference is correct, then those first-person experiences aren't in fact good evidence. But, conversely, if the pro-disability view held by many disabled people is correct, then their preferences aren't adaptive.

The adaptive preference model is incredibly powerful. If we diagnose someone's (or an entire group's) preferences as adaptive, we are discounting their testimony about their own well-being. We are saying, in effect, that the non-disabled—the majority—are in a better position than the disabled—the minority—to evaluate disabled people's well-being. That's a serious claim. And it's the type of claim that has an unhappy history. To illustrate this, it's worth considering how the adaptive model might have been applied in times when we had somewhat different opinions about what counts as suboptimal.

In the preceding section, we discussed the limitations of the male body. But consider, instead of the male body, the female body. Through many centuries of European history the female body was pathologized in much the same way that the disabled body is currently pathologized. The female body was 'the weaker vessel' (1 Peter 3:7). The female body was the body of 'the frail sex'. The female body was, in the Aristotelian tradition that dominated European thought in the Middle Ages, quite literally a *deformed* male body.[9] Given this devaluing of the female body, people at the time would have had—by their own lights—every reason to diagnose the preferences of some females for their female bodies as adaptive. If you *preferred* to be female, the best explanation was that your preferences had adapted toward something less good in response to the severe restrictions of the female body (including, of course, the lack of rationality that went along with being female).

Or, in much more recent memory, consider common attitudes toward being gay. In the mid-twentieth century, it was standardly assumed that being gay was a type of psychological disorder. And in this case, something very much like the adaptive preference model was employed to extremely pernicious effect. If you were gay and you didn't seek out 'help'—if you preferred to stay the way you were and didn't want to be 'cured'—this was often taken as yet further evidence of psychological disorder. Your sexual preferences were so disturbed that you didn't even realize you needed help. Claiming that there was nothing bad or suboptimal about being gay was, in this case, interpreted as expressing a preference for something that was *clearly* suboptimal.

It's fair to say that most people today think it's 'common sense' that being disabled is less good than being non-disabled (even if, as discussed in section 2.4, it's not clear what the justification for that claim is supposed to be). But most people in the 1950s thought it was 'common sense' that being gay was less good than being straight. And Europeans in

---

[9] Aristotle argues in *Generation of Animals* that bodies are male by default. Female bodies lack sufficient heat, which explains their different—inferior—physical status. This view was taken to further extremes by some scholastics. Thirteenth-century philosopher Albertus Magnus argued, for example, that 'the female's imperfect state naturally desired perfection through union with the more perfect male.' See MacLehose (2006).

the 1200s probably would have thought it was 'common sense' that being female was less good than being male.

The point here is a simple one. A diagnosis of adaptive preferences is licensed only when preferences are directed toward something suboptimal. We don't, however, make decisions about what is suboptimal from Plato's heaven (or from our armchair). We observe, we evaluate, and—crucially—we listen to testimony. The problem with the adaptive preference model is that it allows us to dismiss certain kinds of testimony as irrational or misleading. And so the adaptive preference model can quickly become a way of defending the moral status quo.

4.7 Testimonial Injustice

In her groundbreaking book *Epistemic Injustice*, Miranda Fricker characterizes ways in which prejudice can cause uniquely epistemic types of harm. One of the main such forms of harm she highlights is *testimonial injustice*. In cases of testimonial injustice, a speaker is not believed or given due credence (where others would be) specifically because they are a member of a group that is the subject of stigma.

And so, for example, Fricker discusses the case of Marge in *The Talented Mr. Ripley*, the 1955 novel by Patricia Highsmith. In the novel, Marge's fiancée Dickie is murdered by Tom Ripley, who then assumes his identity. Marge begins to suspect the truth, and tries to convince Dickie's father—who is searching for his missing son—of what has happened. But the 1950s stereotypes of women's reliability work against her. Dickie's father believes she is hysterical in the wake of Dickie's death. He also believes she's naive and unwilling to accept that Dickie may simply have left her, or may have killed himself. He gently explains, 'Marge, there's female intuitions and then there are facts.'[10]

Of course, Dickie's father should be paying very close attention to Marge's testimony. She's in a better epistemic position than he—or anyone else investigating—is with respect to Dickie's disappearance. She was the last person to see Dickie before he disappeared, she was living with Dickie at the time, and because of her relationship with Dickie she's better able to evaluate the significance of various pieces of evidence

---

[10] Quoted in Fricker (2007), p. 14.

(such as the fact that Ripley is in possession of Dickie's rings, which he claims were a gift, but which Marge knows Dickie would not have given away).

Yet Dickie's father dismisses Marge's testimony. In doing so, he engages in what Fricker labels *identity prejudice*—he judges Marge to be the kind of person who is not reliable. His beliefs about young women—the prevailing beliefs about young women at the time—are that they are often hysterical, that they are naive, and that they make judgements based on emotional responses rather than rational deliberation. And so Dickie's father devalues Marge's testimony—he treats her as an unreliable source when she in fact has better access to relevant evidence than he (or anyone else involved) does. And he does so because she's a woman. This, according to Fricker, is a classic case of *testimonial injustice*. A structural prejudice about a specific group (in this case, that women are overly emotional and irrational) causes the testimony of a particular member of that group to be discounted when it shouldn't be, and when similar testimony given from those outside the group would be believed.

Here, then, is the crux of the worry raised in section 4.6: The adaptive preference model is easily misapplied in a way that leads to testimonial injustice. Generally, we treat people as good sources of evidence about their own well-being. But the adaptive preference model gives us an easy way to discount such testimony—testimony we would otherwise believe—in cases where we have an underlying identity prejudice.

Consider again the case of a gay person in the mid-twentieth century who expresses preferences related to her sexuality. This is someone that we should have believed. We could witness her being in a loving relationship. We could observe her being happy, healthy, and thriving. And everything we observe could then be corroborated by testimony about a topic for which we generally take people to have unique first-person authority: her own happiness and her own preferences.

But we didn't believe her. Because of identity prejudice—gay people are sick, gay people are perverted, etc.—we decided that she was unreliable. In a case where we should have believed her, and where we should have taken her to have epistemic authority, we instead discounted her testimony. That's testimonial injustice.

And the worry is that the adaptive preference model affords us an easy way of justifying and perpetuating our disbelief in cases like this. That is, the adaptive preference model allows us to justify and perpetuate testimonial injustice. The adaptive preference model tells us that we should diagnose preferences as adaptive only in those cases where preferences are formed in response to limited options toward something that is *bad* or *suboptimal*. But, crucially, we don't decide—or don't always decide—what's bad or suboptimal by the lights of pure a priori reflection alone. We can be influenced by bias, stereotypes, and prejudices.

To combat these systematic prejudices, we need to re-evaluate our beliefs. But again, we don't (or shouldn't) do this by abstract reflection. We look at people's lives. We consider people's experiences. And, crucially, we listen to people's testimony. That's how we gain new and interesting information about what kinds of lives can be good lives.

Insofar as it justifies us in discounting first-person testimony, the adaptive preference model can be a way of preventing this kind of progress. Misapplied, the adaptive preference model can simply entrench pre-existing biases.

4.8 Testimonial Injustice and Disability

The disability rights activist Harriet McBryde Johnson wrote the following in her now famous *New York Times* essay 'Unspeakable Conversations':

Two or three times in my life—I recall particularly one largely crip, largely lesbian cookout halfway across the continent—I have been looked at as a rare kind of beauty . . . But most often the reactions are decidedly negative. Strangers on the street are moved to comment:

I admire you for being out; most people would give up.

God bless you! I'll pray for you.

You don't let the pain hold you back, do you?

If I had to live like you, I think I'd kill myself.

I used to try to explain that in fact I enjoy my life, that it's a great sensual pleasure to zoom by power chair on these delicious muggy streets, that I have no more reason to kill myself than most people. But it gets tedious . . .

[T]hey don't want to know. They think they know everything there is to know, just by looking at me. That's how stereotypes work. They don't know that they're confused, that they're really expressing the discombobulation that comes in my wake.

She continues by describing a conversation with Peter Singer:

Are we [disabled people] 'worse off'? I don't think so. Not in any meaningful sense. There are too many variables. For those of us with congenital conditions, disability shapes all we are. Those disabled later in life adapt. We take constraints that no one would choose and build rich and satisfying lives within them. We enjoy pleasures other people enjoy, and pleasures peculiarly our own. We have something the world needs.

Pressing me to admit a negative correlation between disability and happiness, Singer presents a situation: imagine a disabled child on the beach, watching the other children play.

It's right out of the [Jerry Lewis] telethon. I expected something more sophisticated from a professional thinker. I respond: 'As a little girl playing on the beach, I was already aware that some people felt sorry for me, that I wasn't frolicking with the same level of frenzy as other children. This annoyed me, and still does.' I take the time to write a detailed description of how I, in fact, had fun playing on the beach, without the need of standing, walking or running. But, really, I've had enough. I suggest to Singer that we have exhausted our topic.

McBryde Johnson is vividly describing her experiences of—and her frustration with—not being believed by non-disabled people when she describes her own well-being. She feels a sense of futility in even trying to make such descriptions, because she predicts that she won't be believed—that the non-disabled already think they 'know everything there is to know.'[11] And she is right. When McBryde Johnson died in 2008, the *Times* published an obituary, written by Singer. They titled it 'Happy Nevertheless.' McBryde went to great lengths—including her famous essay in the same paper that published the obituary—during her life to explain that she was not happy *nevertheless*. She was just happy, like so many other flourishing disabled people. But she wasn't believed, just as she predicted—in the very same paper—she wouldn't be believed and just as she had so often been disbelieved in the past.

McBryde Johnson's experiences reflect a common theme for those in the disability rights community. They make claims, repeatedly, about the value of disability and about their own well-being. And yet those claims can't seem to get past the stereotypes and presuppositions that people have about disability. And this, I contend, is a classic example of testimonial injustice. We stereotype disabled people as being unfortunate, as

---

[11] Kristie Dotson (2011) discusses this unique form of testimonial injustice, which she labels 'testimonial smothering'. In some cases, members of marginalized groups simply do not bother to give testimony, because they know they will be misunderstood if they do. As Dotson describes it, 'testimonial smothering, ultimately, is the truncating of one's own testimony in order to insure that the testimony contains only content for which one's audience demonstrates testimonial competence' (p. 244).

being long-suffering, as being brave, as being tragic overcomers. When a disabled person says that they are happy—not happy in spite of being disabled, just happy—it doesn't match our view of what disabled lives are like. Likewise, when a disabled person says that they value being disabled, or that being disabled can be just as good as being non-disabled, it doesn't match our view of disability as a misfortune. And so we reinterpret what disabled people are saying. They're so brave that they don't even think of themselves as facing hardship. They've had to overcome so much that they don't even realize what they're missing. And so on. In short, we don't take them at their word, because of our stereotypes of what disability and disabled people are like.

We have identity prejudices about disabled people, just as we had (and no doubt still have) identity prejudices about gay people. We assume that disabled people are unfortunate, the victims of bad circumstances and bad luck, making the best of a bad lot in life. These identity prejudices mean we don't take disabled people at their word in cases where we should, and where we otherwise would. And that's testimonial injustice.

4.9 Evidence and Testimony

For the adaptive preference model to apply to the testimony of disabled people, we need to assume disability is something bad or suboptimal. But that's something we shouldn't assume. Whether disability is bad or suboptimal is exactly the issue under discussion, and disabled people take their testimony about their own experiences to be part of the evidence we ought to consider when evaluating this issue. Absent some compelling independent argument that disability is bad or suboptimal, a diagnosis of adaptive preference looks unjustified.

Moreover, a diagnosis of adaptive preference has the potential to be morally as well as epistemically unjustified. It tells us not to trust testimony in cases where that testimony reports valuing something *we think* is suboptimal. In doing so, it lets us defer to our pre-existing stereotypes of what people's lives are like in order to discount their testimony, rather than *listening* to their testimony in order to re-evaluate our stereotypes. The adaptive preference model, as a result, has the unhappy potential to uphold such stereotypes—including prejudicial stereotypes—rather than allowing testimony to challenge them.

This is not to say that application of the Nussbaum–Sen adaptive preference model is *never* justified. The preferences of gay people or women are cases where applying the adaptive preference model is clearly a mistake. But, likewise, there might be cases—battered women who prefer to stay with their abusers, for example—where it is clearly justified. I don't want to take a view here on whether and to what extent the Nussbaum–Sen model might sometimes be justified, since it's enough for my purposes to argue that it isn't justified in the case of disability-positive testimony. But here is a suggestion for how we *might* understand the difference between good applications of the adaptive preference story and bad ones.

In the good cases, there is a clear disconnect between the testimony (and the preferences the testimony conveys) and the rest of the person's life—including, importantly, other pieces of their testimony.[12] So, for example, in the case of a battered woman who says she stays with her abuser because it's what she wants, we have to consider that testimony in light of other things about her life. If she says she wants to stay in the relationship and the relationship is good for her, but she experiences high levels of stress, anxiety, fear, and depression, her testimony about the relationship may strike us as discordant with the rest of the facts. Moreover, her testimony about her preferences for the relationship may not cohere with the rest of her testimony about the relationship—she may report fear, anxiety, and distress in association with the very same relationship she says she prefers. What are we to make of this? As charitable interpreters, we want to take as much of her testimony as we can at face value. But we can't do that when different parts of her testimony conflict, or when parts of her testimony seem in clear conflict with other pieces of evidence. In a case like this, the adaptive preference model allows us to interpret her testimony in a way that makes overall good sense, without thinking that she is lying or delusional.

In contrast, there isn't this kind of discordance for the disability-positive testimony of many disabled people. They say they value

---

[12] Recall the version of adaptive preference given by Luc Bovens. The fox's claim that grapes are too sour is problematically adaptive, according to Bovens, if it's inconsistent with other preferences—if the fox still enjoys other things that are just as sour as grapes. I'm suggesting something slightly broader than Bovens, insofar as I think not just tension between preferences, but also tension between what people say is good for them and what produces things like anxiety, fear, and antipathy in their lives, might be evidence for preferences being problematically adaptive.

disability. They also say they are happy and satisfied with life, and don't seem to be stressed or anxious to any unusual degree. They have successful careers, loving families, worthwhile hobbies. And while they acknowledge that there are bad things about being disabled, they also emphasize that many of these bad things are due to the way society treats disabled people, and that there can be good things about being disabled too. The overall picture of their testimony is consistent, and it coheres with the evidence from the rest of their lives.

A skeptic might reply, though, that there is a very simple way in which their testimony is in fact in tension with the rest of the evidence about their life: Namely, their life involves a substantially bad thing—namely, their disability—but their testimony does not register this thing as bad. But this is, once again, to make an assumption about disability that, in the absence of independent argument, just isn't warranted. In the battered spouse case, we can point to a lot of things independent of being a battered spouse that we think are bad—stress, fear, anxiety, financial instability, etc.—about the woman's situation, as well as being able to point to internal tensions in her testimony. We would need to be able to do something similar in the disability case—we would need to be able to point to things beyond our basic assumption that disability is bad in order to say that there is a disconnect or tension in the person's testimony. And my claim is that we can't do that.[13]

It's also important to note that in discounting the disability-positive view, we would be discounting more than just bare testimony. Disabled people don't merely say that they value disability. They go on disability pride marches. They create disability-centric art, dance, and literature. They actively celebrate disability in myriad ways. So to simply assume that disability is somehow bad or suboptimal—to assume that disability is the kind of thing we can apply the adaptive preference model to—is to discount not just disability-positive testimony, but the entirety of disability-

---

[13] It's also sometimes suggested that disabled people's pro-disability preferences are inconsistent because, while they might value the disability they have, they still seek to avoid acquiring other disabilities. But it would be absurd to ascribe any inconsistency to this. Plenty of things can be good and valuable in moderation, but not in excess. Plenty of things are such that it makes sense to value the amount you have, but avoid acquiring any more. We don't think someone is being fundamentally irrational, for example, if she values and cherishes the one child she has but actively avoids conceiving another.

positive culture. And discounting an entire civil rights movement because of a pre-existing intuition strikes me as suspect, to say the least.

4.10 Summing Up

For most of this chapter, I've been discussing the particulars of a certain kind of skepticism about the disability-positive testimony of disabled people. The reason I've focused on (one version of) the adaptive preference model is that I think it makes the clearest and best case for discounting that testimony. But abstracting away from the particulars of the adaptive preference story, there is a much more general point here about testimonial injustice.

People—including philosophers—often reflexively doubt the disability-positive testimony of disabled people. Perhaps, they think, such testimony is just 'wishful thinking'. Perhaps it is a strange instance of status quo bias. Perhaps disabled people are kidding themselves. Perhaps they have read too much about the power of positive thinking. Perhaps they aren't really serious, but are just saying these things because they are politically effective. And so on.

And this tendency toward skepticism is typically rooted in—often knee-jerk, unreflective—stereotypes about what disabled lives are like. *Of course* such testimony should be dismissed, given how *obviously* bad it is to be disabled. Disabled people, plucky little overcomers that they are, might be inclined to say otherwise. But that doesn't mean we should believe them.

The general point I am making here is that dismissing wholesale the testimony of disabled people in this way—whether via a story about adaptive preference or something else—is testimonial injustice. Other things being equal, we ought to take disabled people as very good sources of evidence about what it's like to be disabled. Or at least we ought to take them as *better* sources of evidence than the beliefs of the non-disabled about what is common sense. Instead, we tend to dismiss the testimony of disabled people about what it's like to be disabled when that testimony conflicts with our assumptions and expectations about disability. In short, we have identity prejudices about disabled people. We think they are unfortunate, unlucky, clearly worse off than the non-disabled, and so on, and we often think this without much reflection. Those identity prejudices lead us to discount certain kinds of testimony. And to discount testimony in this way is, paradigmatically, testimonial injustice.

5

Causing Disability

I think 'cure' is actually a rather loaded term in relation to my disability, because to cure something implies that you are returning the body to its normal state. My disability *is* my normal state. To cure me in accordance with the medical definition of the word would not only give me new abilities, but also essentially transform me into a whole new person . . . I've embraced my disability as a huge facet of my identity, and I take pride in it. While I don't define myself solely by my disability, having a disability has undeniably shaped who I am. Without my lived experiences as a disabled person, I would be a completely different Emily. And as tough as certain aspects of my life have been, and though I know I will continue to face disability-related challenges throughout my life, I wouldn't trade my life for a minute. My disability has given me a place in a community and a culture; it has been the reason why I've had amazing adventures and unforgettable experiences. To walk freely up and down stairs . . . would never measure up to the things I've done because I have a disability.

Emily Ladau (2013)

In the previous chapter, I looked at one major objection to mere-difference views—including my own—of disability: that they rely on inherently unreliable testimony. In this chapter, I examine a second major objection (or rather, pair of objections) based on what the consequences of a mere-difference would be. Suppose we grant that there isn't anything systematically misleading about the disability-positive testimony of disabled people. We should still be skeptical of mere-difference views of disability, the thought goes, because they have extreme, unacceptable implications. It's often suggested, for example, that if a mere-difference view of disability were correct it would be permissible to cause disability. On the flipside, it's also sometimes suggested that if a mere-difference view were correct it would be *im*permissible to remove disability (or 'cure' disability, to use the value-laden term). In this chapter, I'm going to argue that neither of these twin objections succeeds.

But first, an important caveat. The objection to the mere-difference view from causing disability is based on a presumed entailment. If disability were mere-difference, that would entail the permissibility of causing disability. This is typically discussed via abstracted examples—person x causes disability y in person z—without much in the way of detail or background context. In what follows, I discuss similar abstract examples to show that this entailment doesn't hold. We can't infer that it's permissible to cause some feature x (even in a baby, even in your own baby) simply from the fact that we think x is mere-difference. But that doesn't tell us very much about what we should actually do. What we should actually do could depend on all sorts of factors—the availability of health insurance or the financial resources to provide the care a disabled child will need, the ability to provide access to education and job training, the fact that caregiving responsibilities fall disproportionally on women in our society, etc.[1] The real world is messy, and I don't intend here to—presumptuously—take a view on what actual parents ought to do in actual, messy circumstances. I do, however, intend to offer considerations about how a lot of our reasoning on these matters might, in ordinary situations, be confused and biased.

5.1 A Problem for the Mere-Difference View?

As previously discussed in section 2.4, some version of a bad-difference view of disability is generally taken to be the 'common-sense' or 'intuitive' view of disability. Likewise, many philosophers react to mere-difference views with incredulity. But as we've seen, the situation is incredibly complex, and simply *assuming* a bad-difference view doesn't look warranted. Likewise, as discussed in sections 4.6–4.8, dismissals of disability-positive testimony seem to rely on an unwarranted assumption that disability is bad-difference.

Instead of relying on the *obviousness* of her position the defender of the bad-difference view needs arguments. She needs independent reason—something that doesn't just rely on the assumption that disability is

---

[1] See especially Stramondo (2011).

bad—to support her view. Here is one such argument: If disability were mere-difference rather than bad-difference, it would be permissible to cause disability; it is obviously *im*permissible to cause disability; therefore, disability is not mere-difference; it is bad-difference.[2]

For example, John Harris (2001) writes:

Many people critical of my position talk as if the disabled are simply differently-abled and not harmed in any way. Deafness is often taken as a test case here. In so far as it is plausible to believe that deafness is simply a different way of experiencing the world, but by no means a harm or disadvantage, then of course the deaf are not suffering... But is it plausible to believe any such thing?... Would the following statement be plausible—would it be anything but a sick joke? 'I have just accidentally deafened your child, it was quite painless and no harm was done so you needn't be concerned or upset!' Or suppose a hospital were to say to a pregnant mother: 'Unless we give you a drug your fetus will become deaf. Since the drug costs £5 and there is no harm in being deaf we see no reason to fund this treatment.' (p. 384)

And along similar lines Peter Singer (2004) remarks:

Consider what we would have to give up if we were unequivocally to reject the idea that it is a bad thing for a child to have a serious disability... If serious disability has no tendency to make one's life worse, there would be no reason to fund research into preventing, or overcoming, disability. That would save governments all over the world significant sums of money. Doctors could forget about advising women who are considering pregnancy to take folic acid to prevent spina bifida and anencephaly, as these conditions would not, on this view, disadvantage their children... Pregnant women could feel entirely free to drink as much as they wished, secure in the knowledge that there was no reason to believe that any of the conditions that the Surgeon General calls 'defects' would be likely to make their children worse off... Pharmaceutical manufacturers would not have to test new drugs to see if they produced fetal abnormalities. Doctors could once again prescribe thalidomide as a useful sleeping aid, even for pregnant women. (p. 133)

And here is Guy Kahane (2009):

Now it seems that those who reject [that disabilities such as deafness are a harm] must also reject [that it is morally wrong to turn a hearing child into a Deaf one]. If deafness is not a harm, then either it makes no difference to well-being in comparison with hearing (one needn't hold that it leads to identical well-being, just well-being on a par), in which case it wouldn't matter if one becomes deaf, or it

---

[2] Variations of this argument are given in, inter alia, McMahan (2005), Harris (2001), Kahane (2009), and Singer (2004).

tends to improve well-being, in which case there is positive reason to turn hearing people deaf. So it seems that those who reject [that deafness is a harm] . . . must hold that . . . [p]arents are morally permitted (or even ought to) turn a hearing child deaf. (pp. 211–12)

It's also argued—for parallel reasons—that the mere-difference view is implausible because it would make it *im*permissible to remove disability. Here, for example, is Buchanan, Brock, Daniels, and Winkler (2000):

What is striking about the radical disability advocates' critique, then, is that . . . [it] condemns any effort to eliminate disabilities through medical interventions . . . For if taken literally, the slogan 'change society, not individuals' does not merely insist that we try to make the social world more accessible . . . it would require accommodating those with impairments rather than using medical science to prevent or correct impairments. (p. 265)

Notice that these objections, as they are actually presented, are primarily leveled at straw versions of the mere-difference view. The slide from disability being mere-difference to disability not being, in the actual circumstances, a disadvantage, any sort of harm, etc. is, as we've discussed at length, completely misguided.[3] But let's set this aside, since the basics of the arguments don't hinge on these mistakes.

It's worth emphasizing the importance of such arguments. As we've seen, a bad-difference conception of disability is often assumed as obvious rather than argued for. But taking this as obvious is a mistake. The bad-difference view is a characterization of disability that is *not* obvious to many disabled people. There are many complexities involved (chapter 2), and the disability-positive testimony of disabled people should be taken seriously (chapter 4).

The causation-based objections are an attempt to do more than say that some version of a bad-difference view is obvious. They are an attempt to get some independent traction on the mere-difference/bad-difference debate. To do this, they try to show that the mere-difference view has implausible, impermissible consequences, *even by the lights of its defenders*. In what follows, I argue that these causation-based objections do not succeed: They do not in fact give this sort of independent traction on the mere-difference/bad-difference debate.

---

[3] It's also worth noting that ancephaly and other severe neural tube defects arguably aren't, contra Singer, disabilities at all. Most any social constructionist account of disability would have this result.

5.2 Causing a Non-Disabled Person to Become Disabled

There are many different ways one can cause disability. In what follows, I certainly don't take myself to be giving an exhaustive account of causing disability; but I think the cases I consider are illustrative more generally of the *kinds* of things mere-difference views can say about causing disability. For some cases, treating disability as mere-difference rather than bad-difference does not entail the permissibility of causing disability. For other cases, it plausibly does allow such permissions, but in ways that are unobjectionable. Either way, the issue of causing disability is not one that undermines mere-difference views.

Let's begin by considering perhaps the most straightforward case of causing disability:

> (i) An autonomous agent, Amy, causes another autonomous agent, Ben, to become disabled without Ben's consent. Let's assume Amy does this without malice, but also without the intent to achieve some greater good (i.e., Amy doesn't cut off Ben's leg to prevent the spread of gangrene).

In response to a case like (i), I'll wager that most of us would think that Amy has done something wrong, and perhaps more strongly that she has *wronged Ben.* Moreover, many of us would persist in these reactions regardless of how Ben ultimately reacts to his disability. Even if Ben becomes a happy, well-adjusted disabled person who is proud of his disability, Amy's conduct still seems bad. Does the view that disability is mere-difference rather than bad-difference have a problem justifying this reaction? No. And it's easy to see why not.

The first and most obvious thing to say about a case like (i) is simply that it involves unjustified interference in another person's life. Most of us think you shouldn't go around making substantial changes to people's lives without their consent (even if those changes don't, on balance, make them worse off). We'd be inclined to say that Amy does something wrong if she carelessly (and permanently) turns Ben from a blonde into a brunette, if she carelessly (and permanently) changes Ben's height by a few inches, etc. Such changes aren't particularly substantial, and aren't likely to make Ben worse off in the long run. But we have a basic reaction that Amy shouldn't alter Ben in any of these ways without his consent—regardless the overall effect of such alterations on Ben's well-being. Amy shouldn't mess with people like that.

Unjustified interference is not, however, the only thing wrong with Amy's treatment of Ben. Advocates of the mere-difference view don't think that being disabled is something bad or harmful. But there's a big difference between *being disabled* and *becoming disabled*. Many people find being disabled a rewarding and good thing. But there is an almost universal experience for those who acquire disability—variously called adaptive process or transition costs—of great pain and difficulty associated with becoming disabled. However happy and well-adjusted a disabled person ends up, the process of *becoming disabled* is almost always a difficult one.

The advocate of mere-difference can appeal to transition costs to explain why Amy's causing Ben's disability is wrong—and, indeed, why Amy has done something wrong and harmful to Ben.[4] Let's assume that Ben is a perfectly happy, well-adjusted non-disabled person. If Amy leaves him alone, Ben will continue his happy, well-adjusted life without incident or interruption. If Amy causes Ben to become disabled, Ben's happiness, his lifestyle, and perhaps even his self-conception will be radically, drastically interrupted. He will have to reshape his life around his new disability. If Ben is like most people, this will be a deeply painful process. It may be a deeply painful process that ends with Ben as a perfectly happy, well-adjusted disabled person. But even if Ben adapts perfectly well to his disability, he can justifiably say that what Amy did was wrong. Amy—carelessly, thoughtlessly—caused him great pain. On most any theory of morality, that's wrong.

So it simply does not follow from holding a mere-difference view that it's permissible to cause someone to become disabled in a case like Amy and Ben's. Even if being disabled is not a bad-difference, *becoming* disabled is still a difficult and painful process—a process that the mere-difference view can happily say is wrong to inflict on someone against their will.

5.3 Causing a Non-Disabled Person to Become Disabled without Transition Costs

Not all cases of causing disability, however, involve transition costs. The most obvious such case is where the person who becomes disabled is an

---

[4] Similar points will allow the mere-difference view to uphold the idea that becoming disabled is a misfortune and a harm, even if being disabled is—by itself—neither.

infant (or even a fetus, if you think there's personal identity between a late-stage fetus and the child it becomes). Consider this case: (ii) a woman, Cara, painlessly causes her month-old baby Daisy—who would otherwise grow up to be non-disabled—to become disabled.

Just as in (i), in a case like (ii) most people will judge that Cara has done something wrong. And more specifically, they will judge that she has *wronged Daisy*. But here the wrongness can't be explained by transition costs. Daisy won't suffer a painful transition as she adjusts to disability, because all her formative experiences will include her disability. (She won't even remember being non-disabled.)

Again, the mere-difference view has no difficulty accommodating this. And again, the easiest way to see this is to consider relevant analogies. Suppose, for the sake of argument, a strong biological view of sexuality according to which sexuality is wholly or largely determined by genetics. Further suppose that a procedure was developed that allowed us to alter the genes that determine sexuality in an infant. That is, suppose it was possible to genetically alter a child who would otherwise grow up to be gay such that that child would instead grow up to be straight (and vice versa). Now replace disability in the case above with sexuality: (ii)* Cara painlessly causes her month-old baby Daisy—who would otherwise grow up to be straight—to grow up to be gay.

Most of us, I think, would be inclined to say that Cara does something wrong in a case like (ii)*—that she shouldn't put Daisy through such a procedure. Moreover, we don't think that we're thereby committed to saying it's worse to be gay than to be straight. (It might be equally wrong for Cara to alter Daisy's genes such that Daisy grows up straight rather than gay.) And the same holds if we replace sexuality with sex—even if it were possible to painlessly and harmlessly perform a sex-alteration procedure on an infant, I suspect most of us would think this is something we shouldn't do—not because one sex is superior to the other, but simply because we're uncomfortable with the idea of making such drastic changes to a child's life.

We again seem guided, in such cases, by strong *non-interference* principles. Ceteris paribus, we tend to think you should refrain from drastically altering a child's physical development. (Perhaps this is just an instance of a wider phenomenon—just as, in (i), we tend to think you should refrain from drastically altering a person's body without their consent.) Our reaction to (ii) can be explained as a species of these non-interference principles, rather than anything specific to disability.

It's difficult, of course, to say what these sorts of non-interference principles amount to. We think it's perfectly permissible—indeed, we think it's morally required—for parents to interfere with their children's development, including their physical development. Parents make choices about education, diet, health care—all sorts of things that have dramatic effect on a child's development. And we think that they're perfectly justified in doing so. Indeed, parenthood can seem like one long series of interferences. So perhaps our non-interference judgements in cases like (ii) are simply unprincipled. Or perhaps, more sympathetically, our non-interference judgements are tracking something like a distinction between traits that are *identity-determining*[5] and those that are not. To choose where your child goes to school, what they eat, where they live, etc. is to make decisions about how that person grows up. But to choose to make your straight child gay or your male child female is to, in a sense, make it the case that your child grows up to be *a different person* than they would otherwise have been. And it may be that we find the former sort of interferences acceptable, but not the latter.[6]

Let me be clear: I'm not attempting to give an account of what these non-interference judgements are, nor am I arguing that they are justified. What I'm arguing is that, absent further argument, commitment to the impermissibility of causing feature x doesn't by itself entail—or even suggest—that x is somehow bad or suboptimal. And it doesn't entail—or even suggest—this even in the absence of transition costs. There are plenty of cases in which we think it's impermissible to *cause* some feature x in another person (even a baby, even your own baby), although we by no means think it's suboptimal to *be* x. We think that causing another person (even a baby, even your own baby) to be x would somehow amount to unjustified interference. Whether or not we're right about this, and whatever such non-interference principles ultimately consist in, the distance between thinking some feature x is a perfectly good way to be and thinking it's permissible to cause another person (even a baby, even your own baby) to be x is enough to show that there's no obvious

---

[5] In the looser, ethicist sense of 'identity' (traits that determine self-conception) rather than in the stricter, metaphysician sense of 'identity' (traits that determine numerical identity).

[6] If this is the case, then to make the analogy to gayness or femaleness the mere-difference view would need to maintain that disability is similarly identity-determining. But this tends to be what advocates of the mere-difference view think in any case.

entailment from a mere-difference view of disability to the permissibility of causing another person (even a baby, even your own baby) to be disabled.

But the advocate of the bad-difference view can try to press a disanalogy here. It's wrong for Cara to cause her non-disabled infant to become disabled. But suppose the case was reversed, and Daisy was born disabled. Consider: (iii) Cara painlessly causes her month-old baby Daisy—who would otherwise grow up to be disabled—to become non-disabled.

Most of us would think that Cara does something good in a case like (iii). It would *not* be wrong, most people assume, for Cara to cause Daisy to become non-disabled. (It might even be morally obligatory.) That there is such a discrepancy supports a bad-difference view of disability, rather than a mere-difference view.[7]

In response to this proposed disanalogy, two main lines of response are open to the defender of the mere-difference view: She can agree that there is such a discrepancy between cases of causing disability and causing non-disability, but argue that this discrepancy does not undermine the mere-difference view; or she can deny that there is any such discrepancy, and try to explain away intuitions to the contrary. I'll explain the former response, because I think it's important to note that adopting a mere-difference view of disability does not entail a specific stance on the cause/remove discrepancy. But I ultimately think this milder response doesn't work. The defender of a mere-difference view, I'll argue, should maintain that causing and removing disability are, in the absence of transition costs, on a par.

Suppose that the defender of a mere-difference view wanted to say that causing non-disability in an infant is permissible, but causing disability is not. How might such a discrepancy be maintained if disability is no worse than non-disability? The best foundation for any such discrepancy seems to be the idea of *potential risk*.

If Cara causes Daisy to be disabled, Daisy may well grow up to be a happy, well-adjusted disabled person. But she may not. She may resent her disability, wish to be non-disabled, and be unhappy as a result. Conversely, if Cara causes Daisy to be non-disabled, Daisy is unlikely to grow up resenting her lack of disability or wishing to be disabled. And

---

[7] Versions of this argument are explored in, for example, Edwards (2004) and Harman (2009).

if Cara refrains from causing Daisy to be non-disabled, Daisy may well resent that choice. Causing Daisy to be disabled is *riskier* than causing Daisy to be non-disabled (though, again, we can't assume a priori that causing Daisy to be non-disabled is without risk).[8]

The thinking here is simple. Suppose that the disability in question is blindness, for example. It's unlikely that Daisy, if she grows up sighted, will be frustrated by her sight and wish to be blind. It's not unlikely that Daisy, if she grows up blind, will be frustrated by her blindness and wish to be sighted. Many blind people are perfectly happy with their blindness, but not all of them are. Sight is much less likely to make Daisy unhappy than blindness, given the way the world is now. And so on, mutatis mutandis, for other, relevantly similar examples of disability. It's hard to think of a disability that—given the way the world is now—is *more likely* to have a positive effect on a person's well-being than is the absence of that disability.

But it can't be quite that simple. Being gay is, arguably, a greater risk to well-being than being straight. There are more people who regret being gay or suffer from being gay than (at least consciously) regret or suffer from being straight.[9] But again, consider the case in which we can alter a child's sexuality: (iii)* Cara painlessly causes her month-old baby Daisy—who would otherwise grow up to be gay—to grow up to be straight.

Most of us would balk at the idea that it's permissible to change a child in this way. (Indeed, making such a change strikes many of us as homophobic.) We tend to think such alteration is impermissible, regardless of whether being gay is in some sense *riskier* than being straight.

Perhaps the mere-difference view of disability can press a disanalogy here. Perhaps it would be wrong to cause a child to become straight (instead of gay) because such an action would always communicate homophobia. But in the relevantly similar case of causing someone to be non-disabled, you might argue that the action doesn't always

---

[8] This line of argument is explored—for the case of 'procreative beneficence'—in Kahane and Savulescu (2009).

[9] The most telling evidence for this is the suicide rate among gay teens. A recent meta-analysis of nineteen studies of suicide in gay teens showed that gay teens are three times more likely than heterosexual teens to report a history of suicidal thoughts, plans, or intent. See Moran (2011).

communicate ableism—though the explanation of *why* it doesn't com-municate ableism would need to be spelled out.[10]

Or perhaps the issue is one of *degree* of risk. Any gay person will have to deal with homophobia, and any disabled person will have to deal with ableism. But the parents of a gay child can make proactive efforts to mediate the bad effects of homophobia. They can make choices about what they say, where they live, where they send their child to school, etc.—to make sure their children grew up in an environment that was as gay-friendly as possible. The parents of a disabled child can make similar efforts, of course. But it's not clear that those efforts can have as much effect—since in the case of disabilities the issues facing their child will be access to basic services and navigation of basic social interaction.[11] Our society is very unaccepting of disabled people.[12] And there is a limited amount that individual parents can do to mediate this. They can tell their child that she's valued just the way she is, but they can't make buildings accessible and they can't make people less awkward around her.

So perhaps there's a case to be made that, given the way the world currently is, it is in many cases *riskier* to have a disabled child than to have a gay child—at least in some contexts and environments. And that elevated risk is why there's a discrepancy between (ii) and (iii), whereas there's no such discrepancy between (ii)* and (iii)*. Such discrepancies, however, are highly contingent and circumstantial. If we lived in a society that was more accommodating and accepting of disabled people,

---

[10] It's not obvious why it wouldn't, or why the case is importantly different from that of sexuality. Many disability rights activists argue that cases like (iii) are exactly the sorts of cases that communicate ableism. See, for example, Davis (1995).

[11] The effects of social ostracism on persons with visible disabilities are often profound. There's a vast literature on the topic, but one of the most telling examples is the effect of service dogs for people in wheelchairs. Service dogs perform many helpful assistive tasks, but their owners often report that the most substantial effect of the dog's presence is a mediation of social exclusion. Research shows that strangers will smile or speak to a person in a wheelchair if that person is accompanied by a dog, whereas people in wheelchairs tend to receive little or no social acknowledgement (eye contact, smiles, etc.). See, for example, Mader and Hart (1989) and Hart et al. (1987).

[12] For example, according to the 2011 World Health Organization Report on Disability, disabled people are more than three times more likely than their non-disabled peers to report lack of access to healthcare; in 'developed' countries the employment rate for disabled people is 44 percent (compared to around 75 percent for non-disabled people); disabled children are significantly more likely than non-disabled children to drop out of school (http://www.who.int/disabilities/world_report/2011/report/en/index.html).

the discrepancy could easily disappear.[13] Likewise, if we lived in a society where gay people were even more heavily discriminated against (as they are in some eastern European and African countries, for example), a similar discrepancy might be created.

I present the above line of thought as an avenue that could be explored by the defender of a mere-difference view who wants to maintain that there is a discrepancy between causing disability and causing non-disability, but I ultimately don't think it's what a defender of a mere-difference view should say. I worry that comparing amount and severity of risk (and thus, by proxy, amount and severity of prejudice) is a shaky foundation on which to motivate any such discrepancy. It would be difficult to say how much of a difference in risk would be enough. And, more importantly, it would be difficult to argue that disabled people are somehow *more disadvantaged* than gay people.[14]

I think the defender of a mere-difference view should instead say that, in fact, there is no discrepancy between the cases of causing an infant to be disabled and causing an infant to be non-disabled. This response is not entailed by commitment to a mere-difference view—as the availability of the above line of response shows. But I think it's both more plausible and less extreme than it may appear on the surface.

In order to argue this point, the mere-difference advocate needs to say—contra the response just discussed—that the potential risk associated with disability isn't enough to warrant interfering with the development of a child who would otherwise be disabled in order to make them non-disabled. That is, if non-interference principles are a good guide to action in the case of causing disability, they should likewise be a good guide to action in the case of causing non-disability. (The general issue of causing vs. curing will be discussed further in section 5.5.)

We wouldn't want to cause a child who would otherwise grow up to be gay to instead grow up to be straight (as in (ii)*). Doing so would be unjustified interference, and could reasonably be said to communicate homophobia. That the child is *more likely* to regret being gay than being

---

[13] It might also, of course, vary from disability to disability and vary based on the <disability, context> pair.

[14] There are good reasons to be skeptical of such comparative judgements, both because of concerns about intersectionality (gay and disabled are not exclusive categories) but also because they require us to somehow quantify amounts of severity of social disadvantage. See especially Collins (1990).

straight, and *more likely* to suffer from being gay than from being straight doesn't affect this. Likewise, we shouldn't cause a child who would otherwise grow up to be disabled to instead grow up to be non-disabled. Doing so would be unjustified interference, and could reasonably be said to communicate ableism. That the child is *more likely* to regret being disabled than being non-disabled and *more likely* to suffer from being disabled than being non-disabled doesn't affect this.

A similar, real-world case is that of children who are born intersex. Standard procedure has been to perform sex-assignment operations on these children when they are very young (procedures that are often invasive, painful, and have long-term side effects). The justification is that the best outcomes for such procedures require them to be performed on infants and young children—so if the procedures aren't done when the children are very young, those children might grow up to regret the lost opportunity of having 'normal' sex characteristics or sex assignments. And that's no doubt true—many people probably would regret it if the procedures weren't performed. Yet there are a growing number of intersex advocates who feel that they were wronged by having been subjected to these procedures without consent. They strongly identify as intersex and feel that their sex characteristics have been unacceptably interfered with in order to meet social standards of normalcy. Likewise, there are a growing number of intersex people who did not have their sex characteristics changed, and who are speaking out for intersex awareness and acceptance. These people argue that work needs to be done to change society's assumptions about sex binaries, rather than changing children who are born intersex.[15]

If the defender of the mere-difference view claims that causing disability and causing non-disability are on a par, she takes a position that conflicts with common intuitions about such cases (and with common practice). And critics of the mere-difference view might argue that this is enough to create a problem for it. But this sort of conflict is exactly what should be expected if much of our reasoning about disability is clouded by a poor understanding of the lives of disabled people. Yes, many people will balk at the idea that there might be something morally objectionable about *removing* disability from an infant. But then, most people have a lot of

---

[15] The fascinating BBC documentary *Me, My Sex, and I* (2011) profiles some of these pro-intersex campaigners. See especially Meyer-Bahlburg et al. (2004).

confused assumptions about both disability and the lives of disabled people. We should expect the mere-difference view to end up saying some counterintuitive things in these cases, simply because we should *expect* that our intuitions (which are no doubt shaped by an inadequate understanding of disability) simply aren't a very good guide to thinking about disability.

This point is a simple and familiar one: The intuitions of the (privileged) majority don't have a particularly good track record as reliable guides to how we should think about the minority, especially when the minority is a victim of stigma and prejudice. Just consider how common it was, historically, to find it intuitive that homosexuality was some sort of perversion or aberration, to find it intuitive that non-white races were innately inferior, to find it intuitive that women were less rational than men. The mere-difference view claims that what most people find to be 'common sense' or intuitive about disability (some version of a bad-difference view) is incorrect. We should thus expect such a view to challenge the received wisdom about disability, and to make some claims that most people find 'counterintuitive'. That doesn't mean that the mere-difference view is utterly unconstrained. When its commitments are counterintuitive, it needs to be able to show how those commitments are nevertheless principled and consistent. Conflict with standard intuition in cases like (iii) isn't a problem for the mere-difference view, so long as it's a principled and explicable conflict. And I think the analogy to relevantly similar cases shows that it is both.[16]

Insistence on a cause/remove discrepancy is doubtless motivated by the simple fact that most people assume it's worse, ceteris paribus, to be disabled than to be non-disabled. But the mere-difference view rejects

---

[16] But wait—haven't I been appealing to intuition (especially certain 'non-interference' intuitions)? Yes, I have. But I haven't been appealing to intuition *about disability*. The argument structure has gone like this: (i) if the mere-difference view is correct, then disability is analogous to features like sexuality and gender; (ii) think about how we reason (sometimes based on intuition) about cases involving sexuality and gender; (iii) absent further argument to the contrary, if the mere-difference view is correct then it predicts we should reason about disability in similar ways. Much of what the mere-difference view says about disability is *counterintuitive*—and intentionally so. But the upshot is not skepticism about moral intuition. It's instead the admission that moral intuition can be affected by prejudice and false belief, and that *in cases where we have good reason to think our intuitions are unreliable*, we should look for principled ways of revising and reconsidering that aren't based purely on intuitions.

this assumption outright. What more can be said, then, to support the claim that there is obviously a cause/remove discrepancy? Perhaps the discrepancy has to do with available options. In (ii), Daisy's options are permanently restricted. Again, suppose the disability in question is blindness. If Daisy is blind, she will never be able to see colors, experience visual art, visually perceive the faces of her loved ones, etc. There are goods and experiences that being blind permanently prevents Daisy from participating in. But, mutatis mutandis, there are goods and experiences that Daisy will permanently miss out on in (iii). She will never have the auditory or sensory experiences unique to those who have been blind from infancy, for example. It would be a mistake, furthermore, to think that the only potential good effects of blindness come from the (well-documented) sensory uniqueness of the blind. Consider again Kim Kilpatrick's discussion of the positive everyday experiences associated with her blindness. Her list includes: not being able to judge people based on what they look like, having no sense of self-consciousness about personal appearance and no temptation to 'check the mirror', a love of and facility with Braille, and the deep, profound relationship she has formed with her guide dog.[17]

The mundane point here is that, as discussed in the previous chapter, constraints on options are not unique to disability. *Everyone* is constrained by the way their bodies work. Again, consider males and pregnancy. Now suppose it was possible—as it may someday be—to change a child's sex in infancy; that is, suppose it was possible to turn a male baby into a female baby, and vice versa. It wouldn't follow that someone wrongs a male baby—in virtue of constraining its options—if they fail to perform a sex reassignment operation on it when it's a baby. Similarly, it doesn't follow from the fact that disabilities constrain options that it's wrong not to remove disabilities. Being non-disabled *also* constrains options. (Indeed, having a physical body that is any specific way a body can be constrains options.) It's simply that being non-disabled constrains options in a way we're more comfortable and

[17] http://kimgia3.blogspot.com. Consider also the mission statement from the National Federation of the Blind: 'The mission of the National Federation of the Blind is to achieve widespread emotional acceptance and intellectual understanding that the real problem of blindness is not the loss of eyesight but the misconceptions and lack of information which exist': https://nfb.org/mission-statement.

familiar with. To support the claim that there's an obvious cause/remove discrepancy, you'd need the further claim that the constraints imposed by disability are somehow *worse* than those imposed by non-disability. And that's precisely the claim that the mere-difference view rejects.

Again, though, it's important to stress just how little similarity the kinds of abstract, idealized cases I discuss above bear to most real world cases of causing, preventing, and removing disability. For example, contra Peter Singer's hyperbolic rhetoric, these kinds of cases have—whatever your view on them—very little relevance to whether pregnant women should take folic acid supplements or drink alcohol while pregnant. Women aren't advised to take folic acid simply to prevent a specific disability (spina bifida). Rather, they are advised to take folic acid to prevent a range of neural tube defects, many of which are fatal within a few hours or days of birth. Likewise, advising against alcohol consumption in pregnancy isn't merely to prevent physical disabilities—it's to prevent a complex range of biopsychosocial problems associated with fetal exposure to alcohol. And it is, of course, no part of a mere-difference view of disability that you're also committed to a mere-difference view of all neural tube defects, or of the complex biopsychosocial consequences of fetal exposure to alcohol.

5.4 Causing a Disabled Person to Exist Instead of a Non-Disabled Person

Perhaps the most familiar discussion of causing disability in the literature, however, is not a case in which a single person is caused to become disabled, but rather a case in which a disabled person is caused to exist instead of (in some sense) a non-disabled person. This is, for example, the structure of Derek Parfit's famous 'handicapped child case':[18]

---

[18] Parfit (1984). Of course, another very famous case discussed at length in the literature is that of embryo selection in IVF and the permissibility of *selecting for* disability. Intentionally implanting embryos that one knows will develop into individuals with disabilities is also a case in which one causes a disabled person to exist instead of causing a non-disabled person to exist (where there's a commitment to cause a person to exist, and where one could easily cause a non-disabled person to exist instead). I'm not going to discuss this case, simply because I think the ethics of embryo selection introduce a lot of noise, and might well include complications that cut across the issue of whether we can permissibly cause disability. At the very least, it's important to note that there is clearly no obvious entailment from a mere-difference view of disability to the permissibility of selecting for disability.

Child Now: A woman, Ellen, knows that if she becomes pregnant now the child she conceives will be born disabled. If she waits six months to become pregnant, however, the child she conceives will be born non-disabled. Ellen prefers not to wait, so she becomes pregnant right away. She gives birth to a daughter, Franny, who is disabled.

Parfit's case is meant to be a puzzle for person-affecting ethics. The starting assumption is that Ellen does something wrong by choosing to get pregnant now, but there is no one such that Ellen does something wrong to that person. (She doesn't do something wrong to Franny, because Franny is better off existing than not existing, and had Ellen waited six months to conceive she would—presumably—have had a different child.)

The worry is that the mere-difference view cannot get the puzzle off the ground in the first place. It's supposed to be wrong for Ellen to choose to have a disabled child—that is, to cause a disabled person to exist rather than a non-disabled person to exist, when she could easily have done the reverse. But if being disabled is no worse than being non-disabled—if it is mere-difference rather than bad-difference—then why should we think Ellen's action is wrong?

We shouldn't. If disability is a mere-difference and not a bad-difference, then we should reject the background assumption meant to guide our intuitions in cases like Child Now. It isn't wrong to knowingly cause a disabled child to exist rather than a non-disabled child to exist.[19]

Does this commitment pose a problem for the mere-difference view? No—at least not any sort of additional problem not already present in the view itself. The idea that it is wrong to cause a disabled person to exist

---

Most people think there's no moral difference between being female and being male. And yet many people are uncomfortable with the idea of sex-based embryo selection. The permissibility of sex-based embryo selection isn't settled simply by the fact that it's no better or worse to be male than to be female, and vice versa. Likewise, it would be a mistake to think that the permissibility of selecting for disability simply falls out uncontroversially from a commitment to it being no worse to be disabled than to be non-disabled. The ethical issues surrounding embryo selection are complicated, and something I won't delve into any further here.

[19] A similar line on the non-identity problem is taken in Wasserman (2009).Wasserman bases his case on the role-morality of prospective parents and the 'ideal of unconditional welcome'. I'm sympathetic to much of what Wasserman says, but I make no positive claims here about the role-morality of prospective parents. My claim is much simpler: The defender of a mere-difference view of disability should reject the background assumptions of cases like Child Now.

rather than a non-disabled person to exist is predicated on the idea that it's worse to be disabled than non-disabled. This is something that the mere-difference view explicitly rejects. So it is certainly no argument against the mere-difference view that it cannot vindicate the intuition that Child Now is a case of wrongdoing, given that this intuition relies on the falsity of the mere-difference view.

But perhaps the intuitive reaction to Child Now can be strengthened. Here is a relevantly similar case from McMahan (2005):

The Aphrodisiac: Suppose there is a drug that has a complex set of effects. It is an aphrodisiac that enhances a woman's pleasure during sexual intercourse. But it also increases fertility by inducing ovulation. If ovulation has recently occurred naturally, this drug causes the destruction of the egg that is present in one of the fallopian tubes but also causes a new and different egg to be released from the ovaries. In addition, however, it has a very high probability of damaging the new egg in a way that will cause any child conceived through the fertilization of that egg to be disabled. The disability caused by the drug is not so bad as to make life not worth living, but it is a disability that many potential parents seek to avoid through screening. Suppose that a woman takes this drug primarily to increase her pleasure—if it were not for this, she would not take it—but also with the thought that it may increase the probability of conception; for she wants to have a child. She is aware that the drug is likely to cause her to have a disabled child, but she is eager for pleasure and reflects that, while there would be disadvantages to having a disabled child, these might be compensated for by the special bonds that might be forged by the child's greater dependency. She has in fact just ovulated naturally, so the drug destroys and replaces the egg that was already present but also damages the new egg, thereby causing the child she conceives to be disabled.

And you can imagine other cases along similar lines: The woman drinks alcohol, takes recreational drugs, etc., knowing that in so doing she will cause herself to have a disabled rather than non-disabled child. Intuitions that there is wrongdoing in cases like Aphrodisiac are arguably stronger than those in the basic Parfit-style cases. As McMahan says, 'most of us think that this woman's action is morally wrong. It is wrong to cause the existence of a disabled child rather than a normal child in order to enhance one's own sexual pleasure.'

Do cases like Aphrodisiac pose a problem for the mere-difference view? Before proceeding further, it's worth noting that when we're considering the merits of the mere-difference view, our intuitions about a case like Aphrodisiac may not be the best place to start. Aphrodisiac involves, as its central elements, both the actions of a potential mother and a woman's sexual pleasure. It's not too much of a stretch to think that our reactions to such a case might not be guided by the light of pure moral reason alone.

That being said, there may well be cases like Aphrodisiac that involve wrongdoing. But that doesn't mean that they involve wrongdoing simply because they involve causing a disabled rather than a non-disabled person to exist. Perhaps it is wrong 'to cause the existence of a disabled child rather than a normal child *in order to enhance one's own sexual pleasure*' (my italics). More plausibly, it may well be wrong to cause the existence of a disabled child in order to smoke, drink alcohol, etc. It can, familiarly, be wrong to do x for reason Φ, even if it is not wrong to do x simpliciter.

If the defender of the mere-difference view wants to agree that the woman in Aphrodisiac does something wrong, she can. And she can do so without committing herself to the claim that it's wrong to cause a disabled person to exist when one could easily have caused a non-disabled person to exist instead. Perhaps Aphrodisiac shows an unacceptable casualness about reproductive decisions or implies that the mother undervalues the extent to which being disabled will make her child's life *harder*, even if it does not automatically make it *worse*. And so on.

So while the defender of a mere-difference view certainly doesn't need to vindicate the claim that the woman in Aphrodisiac does something wrong, she can if she wants to. Just because it isn't wrong simpliciter to cause a disabled person rather than a non-disabled person to exist, it may still be wrong to cause a disabled person rather than a non-disabled person to exist *for specific reasons.*[20] There's no entailment from the general permissibility of causing a disabled person to exist to the permissibility of any and all instances of causing a disabled person to exist.

In Child Now, the advocate of a mere-difference view of disability should simply resist the idea that there is any wrongdoing. It's not wrong to cause a disabled rather than a non-disabled person to exist. The intuitive reaction that there is wrongdoing in Child Now can be strengthened, but the ways in which it can be strengthened introduce a lot of

---

[20] Similarly, for example, it wouldn't be wrong to knowingly conceive a child who will grow up to be gay, but it might well be wrong to intentionally do so because you are a big fan of *Glee*.

noise. In these amped-up versions of the basic case—like Aphrodisiac—we can say that there is wrongdoing without claiming that there is wrongdoing in virtue of causing a disabled person rather than a non-disabled person to exist.

5.5 Causing and 'Curing'

Here is a line of thought that may look tempting at this point. Let's abstract away from actions aimed at individuals, and simply consider the case of finding a way to remove or prevent a given disability (a 'cure', to use the value-laden term). It is a good thing, most people would say, to 'cure' disability. This makes disability importantly different from features like sexuality. It would *not* be a good thing to 'cure' minority sexualities. This undermines both the tenability of the mere-difference view and the type of argument that proponents of the mere-difference view tend to use in its defense.

If a scientist is working hard to develop a 'cure' for a disability, we say she is doing something good and praiseworthy. We give her grant money and government support. We hope she succeeds. But if a scientist is working hard on a 'cure' for gayness, we think she is doing something dystopian and horrible. We shun her from the academic community and take away her support infrastructure. We hope she fails miserably.

This discrepancy arises because we think it's a good thing to cause someone to be non-disabled. We think that we should work toward the ability to cause non-disability. In contrast, it's not a good thing to cause someone to alter their sexuality. We shouldn't work toward the ability to cause changes in sexuality. But if this is the case, then there is a fundamental difference between causing changes to a person's disability status and causing changes to a person's sexuality. And any such fundamental difference undermines the plausibility of the mere-difference view.

But *why* do we think it's a bad thing to develop 'cures' for being gay? I suspect that most, if not all, of our aversion comes from the bad effects we assume would go along—quite contingently—with the development of any such 'cure'. The very language of 'cure' is, of course, pejorative—it implies a change *for the better*. But let's assume that what's being researched is simply a drug that can alter sexuality. That is, imagine that scientists are developing a drug that can make people who experience exclusively same-sex attraction instead experience other-sex attraction.

Most of us would, I'll wager, think that this is a bad idea. And that's simply because we can easily imagine what would happen if such a drug were available. Young gay people would be pressured, even coerced, into taking the drug by prejudiced parents. Gay people from prejudiced backgrounds could simply take the drug, rather than learn to accept their sexuality. There would be immense social pressure, at least in many communities, for anyone who self-identified as gay to 'cure themselves'. In a situation where either the majority can change to accommodate the minority, or the minority can change to be like the majority, the minority isn't likely to fare very well.

But these consequences are only contingently associated with a drug that alters sexual attraction. It's not that there's anything intrinsically wrong with such a drug—it's that given the way our world actually is, with all its prejudices and social pressure toward conformity, such a drug would in fact have bad consequences. The same drug wouldn't have such consequences in a world that was fully accepting of gay people. In fact, insofar as choice and self-determination are to be valued, it could easily be said to have good consequences. It might be nice for people to be able to determine their own sexuality as they saw fit (and even change back and forth, as desired). The drug only has bad effects when it can be used as a way of undermining gay rights and depopulating the gay community.

Likewise, insofar as choice and self-determination are good things, it's good for people to be able to determine their own physicality. And so there's nothing intrinsically wrong with 'cures' for disability—at least if they are understood non-pejoratively simply as a mechanism for causing non-disability. The mere-difference view doesn't maintain that everyone who is disabled likes being disabled. And it's perfectly compatible with the mere-difference view that, even in an ableism-free society, some disabled people would still want to be non-disabled, just as it's perfectly compatible with the mere-difference view that disability will still be bad for some people (chapter 3). There's nothing wrong with—and much that's good about—a mechanism that allows such disabled people to become non-disabled if they wish (and allows, vice versa, non-disabled people to become disabled if they wish).[21]

---

[21] As, for example, the transabled desire.

But we *should* worry about what effects a concerted effort to develop such 'cures' for disability has in the actual, ableist world. There's nothing wrong with disabled people wanting to be non-disabled. And there's nothing wrong with those disabled people who want to be non-disabled seeking the means to make themselves non-disabled. But there *is* something wrong with the expectation that becoming non-disabled is the ultimate hope in the lives of disabled people and their families. Such an expectation makes it harder for disabled people—who in other circumstances might be perfectly happy with their disability—to accept what their bodies are like, and it makes it less likely that society's ableism will change. It's hard to accept and be happy with a disabled body if the expectation is that you should wish, hope, and strive for some mechanism to turn that disabled body into a non-disabled body. And it's unlikely that society will change its norms to accommodate disability if society can instead change disabled people in a way that conforms them to its extant norms.

As an example, the film *The Kids Are Alright*—about people with muscular dystrophy who were featured as 'Jerry's Kids' in the famous annual Jerry Lewis telethon, but later became protesters against the telethon—highlights exactly these problems. Many of the people with muscular dystrophy profiled in the film strongly object to the relentless focus on 'the cure' that was a feature of the yearly telethon, and are frustrated at how much of the money brought in by the Muscular Dystrophy Association is spent researching these magical 'cures'. It's not that they object to the existence of—or the search for—treatments that remove or prevent disability. It's rather that they think that focus on such treatments is distracting and unhelpful. What they want are things like: research on how to extend the lifespan of persons with Duchenne muscular dystrophy, better wheelchair technology, focus on helping people with muscular dystrophy find accessible jobs, more public awareness about accessibility, etc. These issues—far more than treatments that could make them non-disabled, they argue—are what matter to the day-to-day lives of people like themselves. Research 'for a cure' doesn't help them, and pronounced focus on such research further stigmatizes them (by communicating the assumption that 'a cure' is something they want or need).

Laura Hershey, a former 'Jerry's Kid', addresses the same issues in her now-famous article 'From Poster Child to Protestor'. Hershey objects to the massive amount of funding and research devoted to 'finding the cure' for her disability (rather than to developing assistive technology or helping disabled people find employment, for example). The 'search for the cure', she argues, is both practically and ideologically problematic. She writes:

I've encountered people who, never having tried it, think that living life with a disability is an endless hardship. For many of us, it's actually quite interesting, though not without its problems. And the majority of those problems result from the barriers, both physical and attitudinal, which surround us, or from the lack of decent support services. These are things that can be changed, but only if we as a society recognize them for what they are. We'll never recognize them if we stay so focused on curing individuals of disability, rather than making changes to accommodate disability into our culture.

She continues:

Sure, some people with muscular dystrophy do hope and dream of that day when the cure is finally found. As people with disabilities, we're conditioned just like everyone else to believe that disability is our problem . . . When so many of us feel so negative about our disabilities and our needs, it's difficult to develop a political agenda to get our basic needs met. The cure is a simple, magical, non-political solution to all the problems in a disabled person's life. That's why it's so appealing, and so disempowering. The other solutions we have to work for, even fight for; we only have to dream about the cure . . .

To draw a parallel, when I was a child and first learned about racial discrimination, I thought it would be great if people could all be one color so we wouldn't have problems like prejudice. What color did I envision for this one-color world? White, of course, because I'm white. I didn't bear black people any malice. I just thought they'd be happier, would suffer less, if they were more like me.

There may in fact be a discrepancy between how we view attempts to remove or eliminate disability and attempts to remove or eliminate gayness. But it's not obvious that there *should* be any stark discrepancy between the cases. Does this mean that the defender of a mere-difference view is committed to thinking that large swaths of medical research are morally corrupt? No. Much disability-related medical research aims to make life easier for disabled people—not to turn disabled people into non-disabled people. And, again, there's nothing wrong per se with research that aims to allow disabled people to become non-disabled. The point is simply that it's complicated. Given the way the world actually is, such research isn't the obvious and unequivocal good that many take it to be. Nor should it be looked to as the ultimate dream and wish of disabled people and their families, or the ultimate solution to the problems faced by disabled people.

5.6 Summing Up

I have argued that mere-difference views of disability do not license the permissibility of causing disability (and conversely, the impermissibility of removing disability) in any way that undermines the tenability of the mere-difference position. In some cases of causing disability, the mere-difference view can agree that causing disability is impermissible. In other cases, the mere-difference view can say that causing disability is permissible—but unproblematically so. And likewise, mutatis mutandis, for causing non-disability. There is no direct route from adoption of a mere-difference view of disability to objectionable (im)permissibilities.

Notably, though, the explanation for *why* at least some cases of causing disability are impermissible is interestingly different for mere-difference views than it is for bad-difference views. A defender of a mere-difference view can easily say that many cases of causing disability are impermissible. But it's never the case that causing a non-disabled person to be disabled is wrong simpliciter. That is, many cases of causing disability are wrong, but they aren't wrong *in virtue of* the causing of disability. They are, rather, wrong for reasons separable from disability in particular: They involve unjustified interference or unjustified risk-taking, for example. And I suspect it's this point that may be causing a lot of the confusion about what, exactly, mere-difference views are committed to. They can't say that a case of causing disability is wrong in virtue of the fact that the action causes disability—whereas bad-difference views can. But that by itself doesn't generate permission to go around causing disability. Lots of standard cases of causing disability can be wrong, according to mere-difference views, without being wrong *in virtue of* causing disability.

This point is an important one. There are many bad things that cause disability—poverty, lack of access to healthcare, malnutrition, pollution, etc. The advocate of the mere-difference view can, of course, agree that these things are bad. Moreover, she can agree that part of what makes them bad is the way in which they cause disability. But what makes these things bad isn't *merely* causing disability. It's causing disability where there is severe lack of accessibility and there are no economic resources to accommodate disability, it's causing disability where there is severe social stigma against the disabled, it's causing disability that will incur transition costs, etc. The badness isn't ever constituted merely by causing disability.[22]

The causation-based arguments I have been discussing are intended to undermine the mere-difference view, and to provide evidence in favor of the bad-difference view. They cannot do this. The various cases of causing disability—and the diverging viewpoints given by mere-difference and bad-difference views on these cases—give us no independent traction on the question of whether disability is a mere-difference or a bad-difference. You will only think that the cases in which a mere-difference view says it is permissible to cause disability are problematic if you think that disability is something that's bad or that makes you worse off. That is, you will only think that commitments of the mere-difference view with respect to causing disability are problematic if you are *already* committed to a version of the bad-difference view. Without further elaboration, at least, arguments both from causing disability and from causing non-disability are thus no threat—or at least no *independent* threat—to the tenability of mere-difference views of disability. They give us no independent traction on the question of whether mere-difference views are plausible.

---

[22] And this points to a problem with the rhetoric we often use in explaining the badness of these things. We often say something to the effect of 'Oh no! Look! Disability!' when we want to point to the bad effects of poverty, pollution, etc. But, for the reasons discussed in section 6.3, that rhetoric encodes a lot of bias.

6

Disability Pride

> Disability Pride is an integral part of movement building, and a direct challenge to systemic ableism and stigmatizing definitions of disability. It is a militant act of self-definition, a purposive valuing of that which is socially devalued, and an attempt to untangle ourselves from the complex matrix of negative beliefs, attitudes, and feelings that grow from the dominant group's assumption that there is something inherently wrong with our disabilities and identity.
>
> Sarah Triano (2006)

The dominant conception of disability in contemporary society is an explicitly normative one. Disability is tragedy. Disability is loss. Disability is misfortune.

Within this normative conception of disability, there is little room for understanding the experience of the thriving disabled person. And so we develop narratives for disability to accommodate the fact that many disabled people seem to thrive. We tell the story of the tragic overcomer—the plucky little cripple who beat the odds despite the personal tragedy of disability. We tell the story of the inspirational disabled person—the courageous cripple who persevered through so many hardships, and whose bravery we admire because of it. We tell the story of the saintly disabled person—the smiling cripple who endured so much with such beatific patience. This is how we understand the thriving disabled person. They are thriving *in spite of* disability. They are never simply thriving. And they are certainly never thriving—heaven forbid—partly *because of* disability.

We often think about our bodies as the outcome of a natural lottery. Some people played the natural lottery and got lucky. They have lithe, athletic, beautiful bodies. Some people fared less well. They're a little too short, their faces aren't symmetrical enough, they're too clumsy, their hair is weird. Disabled people, we assume, are a kind of lower bound to this sort of bad luck. They played the natural lottery and *they lost*. Some disabled people try to make the most of what they've got, and that's admirable. It shows good character to do your best with what you have. But that doesn't change the fact that disability is unlucky—that disabled people are only ever going to be doing their best with a bad deal.

I've previously argued that we should want both a metaphysics of disability (chapter 1) and a theory of disability's connection to well-being (chapters 2 and 3) that leave room for the coherence of *disability pride*. And I've been appealing to the importance of disability pride in understanding disability-positive testimony (chapters 3 and 4). I've also argued that the idea of *valuing* disability makes sense (chapter 3) and shouldn't be explained away. In this final chapter, I'm going to cash in on these promissory notes and argue for the importance of disability pride. Pride, I argue, is a crucial part of undermining the idea that disability is somehow essentially or inherently tragic. And in this respect, the benefits of pride are as much epistemic as they are emotive.

6.1 Hermeneutical Injustice

In *Epistemic Injustice*, Miranda Fricker identifies two main types of distinctively epistemic injustice. The first—already discussed in chapter 4—is testimonial injustice. In cases of testimonial injustice, we devalue the testimony of members of a particular group *in virtue of their membership of that group*, and we thus display prejudice against members of that group *as knowers*. But Fricker identifies a separate form of epistemic injustice she calls *hermeneutical injustice*. In cases of hermeneutical injustice, we harm people by obscuring aspects of their own experience. Our dominant schemas—our assumptions, what we take as common ground—about a particular group can make it difficult for members of that group to understand or articulate their own experiences qua members of that group.

Fricker begins her discussion of hermeneutical injustice with the case of a young mother who happened upon a feminist 'consciousness-raising' seminar in the early 1970s. The woman's account of her experience there is striking:

'People started talking about postpartum depression. In that one 45-minute period I realized that what I'd been blaming myself for, and what my husband had blamed me for, wasn't my personal deficiency. It was a combination of physiological things and a real societal thing, isolation. That realization was one of those moments that make you a feminist forever.' (2007, p. 149)

Prior to hearing a discussion of postpartum depression, this woman had only been able to frame her experience in terms of personal struggle; she had understood it as her own failing, both as a wife and as a mother. But the simple knowledge that her experience was shared by others, that it might have causes other than her own shortcomings, even just that it had a name—that level of social understanding was life-changing. And, as Fricker emphasizes, this sort of collective understanding was hard won. It was easy, in the late 1960s and early 1970s, to blame depression in young mothers on women's 'hysteria' or on a lack of proper maternal focus. It was less easy to see depression as a complex biopsychosocial phenomenon, and to appreciate the extreme physical and social pressures that motherhood incurred. In a context of sexist assumptions both about women's natural role and about women's mental fragility, 'these women groped for a proper understanding of what we may now so easily name as [postpartum] depression' (p. 149).

The case of the young mother is not merely a case of someone who happens to be ignorant of a term, or happens to have an undiagnosed condition (though it is certainly that as well). It's a case in which structural social features are 'wrongfully preventing her from understanding a significant area of her social experience, thus depriving her of an important patch of social understanding' (p. 149). Because of prevailing beliefs about women and mothers at the time, it's difficult for her to understand her own experience. And that lack of understanding *harms* her.

Fricker then considers the plight of employed women before the first sexual harassment court case had been brought to trial (and, indeed, before the term 'sexual harassment' had been coined). Again, these women struggled to make sense of and articulate their own experiences. They could say that their bosses' 'flirting' made them 'uncomfortable' and was 'inappropriate'. But what was difficult to express—even to themselves— was that what they were experiencing wasn't just unwelcome (but ultimately harmless) flirting. And perhaps even more importantly, the narrative of harmless interpersonal flirtation obscured how their experiences were a *systematic* problem faced by women in the workplace.

Fricker contrasts these sorts of cases to someone with a disease that is currently poorly understood by medical science. This person cannot fully understand an aspect of their experience, because the science that could explain their disease doesn't yet exist. Yet this person isn't the victim of epistemic injustice. They are, rather, simply epistemically unlucky. Dominant assumptions and stereotypes about people with this particular disease aren't preventing them from fully comprehending their experience. They aren't being epistemically disadvantaged qua person with that disease. They're just unfortunate enough to have a disease that's a mystery to contemporary medicine.

Hermeneutical injustice, Fricker argues, doesn't arise in any and all cases in which a person cannot understand part of their own experience. Rather, hermeneutical injustice involves cases in which people cannot understand part of their own experience specifically because they have been *hermeneutically marginalized*. That is, they are a member of a group about which prejudicial assumptions or stigmas are prevalent, and those stigmas and assumptions play a key role in interpreting the experiences of that group. And the net result is important gaps in knowledge.

According to Fricker:

What is bad about this sort of hermeneutical marginalization is that . . . it will tend to issue interpretations of [the marginalized group's] social experiences that are biased because insufficiently influenced by the subject group, and thus unduly influenced by more . . . powerful groups (thus, for instance, sexual harassment as flirting, rape in marriage as non-rape, post-natal depression as hysteria, reluctance to work family-unfriendly hours as unprofessionalism, and so on). (p. 155)

That is, when a minority is hermeneutically marginalized, we tend to interpret that group's experiences based on the opinions and stereotypes of the majority. The net result is that the marginalized group is unable to adequately influence the way in which their own experiences are understood.

6.2 The Weight of Normative Assumptions

'Oh, I'm so sorry to hear that!'
'Wow, that must be rough.'
'Is there hope for a cure?'
'Well, you seem to be doing really well, in spite of it all.'
'You must be so brave!'

These phrases—and many more like them—are well known to disabled people. They're the type of reaction you get when you explain or disclose a disability. They're how people react to your own personal tragedy. Oh, you're disabled? *I'm so sorry.*

And it's within this dominant schema of normative assumptions about disability that disabled people must try to understand their own experiences. Many disabled people are thus faced with the struggle of reconciling their own experiences with the ways in which the non-disabled frame those experiences. They are happy, but non-disabled people feel sorry for them. They live perfectly ordinary lives, but non-disabled people call them brave and inspiring. They have positive experiences of their bodies, but non-disabled people assume that their bodies must be a terrible burden. And so on.

This mismatch between expectation and lived experience isn't just a surprise or a curiosity. It's a deep-set epistemic burden. As Fricker remarks:

When you find yourself in a situation in which you seem to be the only one to feel tension between received understanding and your own intimated sense of a given experience, it tends to knock your faith in your own ability to make sense of the world. (p. 163)

Once again, in place of being disabled consider being gay. For gay people who grew up in a context where repressive or prejudicial conceptions of gayness were the norm, making sense of their own experiences of sexuality could be extremely difficult. Fricker, for example, discusses Edmund White's memoir *A Boy's Own Story*. White's book examines the prevailing stereotypes of 'the homosexual' that dominated his childhood—the outcast, the deviant, the psychiatric patient, the sinner. These stereotypes—which simultaneously terrified and fascinated him—were the only ways he knew to make sense of his own attraction to other men. And yet none of them fit, and none of them were what he wanted to be. Looking back, he reflects: 'I see now that what I wanted was to be loved by men, and to love them back, but not to be *a homosexual*' (p. 165, emphasis added). This statement—which sounds almost self-contradictory—is an expression of the deep-set tensions White encountered trying to understand his own experience of sexuality. To White, the idea of a positive, fulfilling self-identity as a gay man was so in tension with dominant stereotypes of 'the homosexual' that it simply didn't make sense. And it didn't make sense even in the face of his growing awareness that loving and being loved by men was a good thing. Similarly, for many disabled people the idea of a positive, fulfilling self-identity as a disabled person is so in tension with dominant stereotypes that it simply doesn't make sense. The only way to thrive as a disabled person is by 'overcoming' your disability.

6.3 Normatively Laden Distinctions

Here are two ways we can make prejudicial judgements. The first proceeds in two stages. We begin by making a purely descriptive distinction. Once that distinction is in place, we then go on to make normative (often prejudicial) judgements based on that distinction. So, for example, we make a descriptive distinction between people with red hair and people with non-red hair. Then we make the claim that people (especially women) with red hair are flighty, quirky, and overly emotional. Or we make a descriptive distinction between people who are from Spain and people who are not. Then we make the claim that people who are from Spain are particularly lazy. And so on.

In such cases, the distinction itself isn't normatively laden. Our understanding of the difference between, for example, redheads and non-redheads isn't *itself* couched in normative terms. Rather, we make a purely descriptive distinction, and then we make normative judgements that employ or are based on that distinction.

That sort of distinction can be contrasted to ways of drawing distinctions that aren't purely descriptive, but rather are (implicitly or explicitly) normativized. So, for example, if we draw a distinction between the sinners and the saints, we're not marking out a purely descriptive categorization and then going on to make a normative claim about that categorization. Rather, our very understanding of the distinction between the sinners and the saints is normative. We can, of course, make descriptive claims about either side of the distinction. The sinners do a, b, and c; the saints do x, y, and z. But such descriptive features aren't (or aren't by themselves) how we grasp or understand the distinction. Descriptive features like shade and tone of hair are how we understand the distinction between redheads and non-redheads. We may layer some normative baggage on top of that distinction, but the distinction itself is a descriptive one. Whereas descriptive features like actions and omissions aren't (or aren't by themselves) how we understand the distinction between saints and sinners. Normativity is built into the distinction itself.

I don't doubt that there's a spectrum of variation between the redhead/non-redhead distinction and the saints/sinners distinction. And there will no doubt be borderline cases—cases in which it's indeterminate or vague whether normativity is built into a given distinction. My claim is simply that there's a difference between the redhead/non-redhead distinction and the saints/sinners distinction, and that this difference is at least in part due to the role that normativity plays in characterizing the distinction.

Now consider the distinction between the *straight* and the *queer*. In mid-twentieth-century America, this distinction plausibly functioned more like saints/sinners than redheads/non-redheads. That is, it's not simply that we described a group of sexual practices and then made a normative generalization based on that distinction (for example, that those who engage in specific sex acts or experience specific forms of sexual attraction are in fact morally inferior to those who don't). Rather, normativity was built into the distinction itself.

There was normal, appropriate sexual attraction and sexual behavior. People who experienced this kind of sexual attraction and engaged in this kind of sexual behavior were *straight*. And then there were people who were *queer*. The very idea of being queer was constructed in contrast to normalcy. You weren't queer just in case you were part of a statistical minority when it came to sexual attraction, orientation, or behavior. So, for example, you weren't queer if you just had very little interest in sex, you weren't queer if you were into certain (socially sanctioned) kinks or fetishes, you weren't queer if you simply didn't experience much sexual attraction, etc. To be queer wasn't just to be unusual with respect to sexual attraction or behavior. To be queer was to be *deviant* with respect to sexual attraction or behavior.[1]

It might be argued that, while the distinction between queer and straight was normatively laden, the distinction between heterosexual

---

[1] I take no stand here on whether, in the case of normatively laden distinctions, the normativity is somehow built into the meaning of the terms used to pick out the distinction, or is instead something like an implicature. (Though see Väyrynen (2013) for discussion about related issues for thick normative terms.) It doesn't really matter for my purposes *how* the normativity is built in—it just matters *that* it is built in.

and homosexual was not. I'm skeptical about this, however. In mid-twentieth-century America, the distinction between heterosexual and homosexual may not have been as explicitly normative as the distinction between queer and straight, but it was at the very least *implicitly* normative. As White's dissection of the stereotypes surrounding 'the homosexual' makes clear, there was much more packed into the concept than simple descriptive content. That is, what it was to fall on the homosexual side of the homo/hetero divide was more than simply to experience same-gender attraction. Here, for example, is how gay rights activist Morty Manford recalled his experience of being gay in the 1960s:

> The whole society was telling us it was horrible. A homosexual was a flaky, vacuous, bizarre person...The newspapers referred to homosexuals and perverts as if they were one and the same. The official line from psychiatrists was that homosexuals were inherently sick.[2]

Homosexuality was classified as a psychiatric disorder: a type of sexual perversion. Labeling gay people as homosexuals was a way of pathologizing them and of classifying them as deviant. Indeed, due to its clinical history and its association with anti-gay propaganda, GLAAD currently advises that the word 'homosexual' is offensive, and asks that it be avoided.[3] The concept of 'a homosexual' in mid-twentieth-century America seems to have been deeply—if perhaps implicitly—normative, to the extent that it makes perfect sense for White to describe his own experience as desiring to be loved by men, and to love them back, but not to be *a homosexual*.

In much the same way, the distinction between the disabled and the non-disabled is, in contemporary society, a normativized one. Historically, many disabilities—particularly congenital disabilities—were considered morally laden.[4] To be born disabled was often considered a sign of some sort of sin, divine disfavor, or malfeasance. Such conceptions of disability are no longer prevalent in contemporary Western society, but they've been replaced by understandings of disability that are equally (though differently) normativized. Disability is understood as

---

[2] Quoted in Marcus (1992), p. 190.   [3] https://www.glaad.org/reference/offensive.
[4] Perhaps the most famous example comes from the New Testament: 'And then his disciples said "Rabbi, who sinned, this man or his parents, that he was born blind?"' (John 9:2).

misfortune, as bad luck, as a natural impediment. Homosexuality was *deviance*; disability is *tragedy*.

And so disabled writer and activist Eli Clare (2008) writes about his childhood experience of disability:

I've told my share of stories about shame. All too young, I understood my body as irrevocably different: shaky, off balance, speech hard to understand, a body that moved slow, wrists cocked at odd angles, muscles knotted with tremors. But really, irrevocably different is a half lie; actually what I came to know was bad, wrong, broken, in need of repair. All the taunting, gawking, isolation, all the rocks hurled at me, all the pitying words, I stored them in my bones; they became the marrow, my first experience of shame.

There are lots of ways you can be physically 'different' or unusual—you can be tall or thin or freckled or red-haired. But, as the term itself suggests, our standard understanding of disability encompasses more than just being physically unusual in some specific way. There is ability, and then there is *dis*-ability: lack of ability, impaired ability, broken ability. As discussed in chapter 1, this characterization of disability is inadequate; disability can't be explained simply via lack of ability. And yet it's a major part of how many people understand disability (just as, for so many years, disorder or deviance was a major part of how many people understood gayness).

It shouldn't be surprising, then, when successful, thriving disabled people want to distance themselves from disability. Why wouldn't you want to distance yourself from lack and misfortune, especially if you see yourself as flourishing? As disability activist Mary Johnson acutely observes in *Make Them Go Away*:

Haven't you heard someone say, 'Oh, I don't consider myself disabled'? How many times have you said it yourself about someone? It's meant as a compliment. What does that mean? It means that saying someone is disabled is in a way an insult . . .

'Don't call me disabled,' Nick Ackerman told reporters. The Iowa college senior, who had used prosthetic legs since an accident in early childhood, who won the NCAA Division 3 wrestling championship, told a reporter that 'I don't have a disability, I have ability and I'm going to use it' and that 'I always thought I was normal.'

An admiring New York Times obituary reported that Celeste Tate Harrington, 'a quadriplegic street musician whose buoyant personality and unremitting chutzpah brought astounded smiles to everyone who watched her play the keyboard with her lips and tongue on Atlantic City's Boardwalk,' 'didn't consider herself disabled.' Nana Graham was born with 'undeveloped legs and feet that curved inward and upside down.' Her legs were amputated when she was 13. But her daughter told a reporter Graham was 'not handicapped.' Hearing-impaired actress Vanessa Vaughan insisted she was not disabled and refused to be interviewed by the Toronto Star for an article about disabled performers. Wheelchair tennis star Dan Bennett, 'born with spina bifida, leaving him without use of his legs,' did not consider himself disabled. 'The more we play, the more words like "handicapped" and "disabled" can begin to disappear,' wheelchair tennis player Joe Babakanian told a reporter . . .

The obituary for Bob L. Thomas, chief justice of the 10th Circuit Court of Appeals in Waco, Tex., noted that he had achieved 'success in law and politics despite total paralysis in all but his left hand,' having 'contracted polio at the age of 15.' He used a wheelchair until his death, yet a colleague remarked that he didn't consider himself disabled. 'He had an absolute determination to overcome his disabilities,' said another.

When Louisvillian Dan Massie died, a story noting his role as a 1970s disability activist reported that although his wife pushed him everywhere in his chair, he 'didn't act as if he was disabled.' 'He didn't take a penny of Social Security disability money,' a friend told a reporter. 'He sold jewelry on street corners and at festivals, and earned all his money.' . . .

People do not want to identify as disabled and will do almost anything to avoid it. If we act normal and don't get involved in that disability rights stuff, then we're not really disabled, we think. If we keep on trying to recover, then, we think, we're not truly disabled. President Roooovelt, even though he could not walk unaided, nevertheless called himself a 'cured cripple.' It was his way of doing the same thing. (2003, pp. 63–5)

It's important to note here that the issue isn't merely terminological or classificatory. When a person says 'I don't really think of myself as disabled,' they aren't, in general, saying that they don't think the word 'disabled' applies to them or that they don't think they have a disability. They recognize that they have a physical condition that is generally picked out by our word 'disability', and which marks them out as physically unusual. They will use bathroom stalls, parking spaces, and seats on public transportation marked as reserved for the disabled. They will enter disability-centric sports events. And so on. Nor is it, at least in most cases, that they object to the term 'disabled' in favor of some other term such as 'differently-abled' or 'crip'.

When a person says 'I don't really think of myself as disabled' or we say of a person 'I've never really considered him disabled,' it's not really a claim about how we use the word 'disabled'. Nor is it a claim that—perhaps despite appearances—the person in question does not have a physical trait that would or should be classed as a disability. Rather, we're making a value judgement. To say that you've never thought of yourself as disabled is to say that you refuse to cast yourself in a negative light. To say to someone that you've never considered them disabled is to pay them a compliment.

That we don't think twice about such rejections of disability—that we expect them, and even reward them—shows just how deeply our under-standing of disability is normativized. Imagine if Madeleine Albright, upon being asked what it was like to be the first woman to be Secretary of State, had answered 'Well, I don't think of myself as a woman—I've always been determined to overcome my gender.'[5] Or, when asked a similar question about race instead of gender, imagine that Colin Powell had responded 'Well, I've never really considered myself Black—I've always been determined to overcome my race.' We'd be surprised at such statements, to say the least. But it's exactly what we *expect* from successful, barrier-breaking disabled people.

6.4 Normatively Laden Distinctions and Hermeneutical Injustice

As Edmund White grew up, he experienced an increasing tension between dominant stereotypes of same-gender attraction and his own experience of such attraction. He wasn't deviant, and he wasn't dis-ordered. He simply loved men, and wanted men to love him back. Yet the prevailing understanding of what it was to be *a homosexual* made this

---

[5] Interestingly, there are many historical examples of these sorts of disavowals of woman-hood (which are, I should emphasize, distinct from rejection of a specific gender identity). And, perhaps unsurprisingly, they are prevalent in socio-historical contexts where being a woman was pathologized—where women were considered inherently inferior to men (or even *deformed* men). Most famously perhaps, Queen Elizabeth I is said to have declared in her speech at Tilbury: 'I know I have the body of a weak, feeble woman; but I have the heart and stomach of a king.' Other examples include several of the popular saint narratives from the Middle Ages. A common theme for many female saints—including St. Margaret, St. Thecla, and St. Uncumber—was that they had somehow 'overcome' their womanhood in various ways (sometimes by disguising themselves as men, sometimes even by being blessed for their saintliness by characteristics marked as 'male', including—in the case of Uncumber—a large beard). These cases, of course, raise questions about whether these individuals really were women, or instead were persons who accepted a different gender identity. But one thing that's clear is that the *narratives* surrounding these saints characterized them as women who deserved special praise for having overcome their (inferior) gender.

aspect of his experience difficult (if not impossible) to articulate—both to others and to himself.

And it's not hard to see why this would be the case. In the context of dominant stereotypes of gayness as deviance or dysfunction, a positive experience of gayness is difficult to make sense of. You're dysfunctional, but that's not a bad thing. You're a deviant, but that's something you think is good for you. And so on. It all starts to sound a bit like the mantra of the Villains' Support Group from the film *Wreck-It Ralph*: 'I'm bad, and that's good. I'll never be good, and that's not bad.'

Gay people were, in this respect, subject to hermeneutical injustice. Aspects of their own experience—namely, what it was to be a flourishing, thriving gay person—were obscured by dominant social prejudices. Stereotypes employed by the powerful majority (straight people) made it difficult for the minority (gay people) to understand and articulate something important about themselves. And the net result was harm to gay people.

Similarly, disabled people are continually faced with dominant assumptions about disability—disability is loss, disability is lack, etc. And these dominant assumptions can be in deep-set tension with their own more positive experiences of disability—making those positive experiences of disability difficult to articulate and understand. If disability is tragedy, then the best you can do as a disabled person is *overcome* tragedy, or flourish *in spite of* tragedy.

That there might be good things about being disabled, and that many of the bad things are the result of social rather than physical impediments, are obscured by this narrative of personal tragedy. And the net result is harm to disabled people. This isn't a purely theoretical point. There's a growing amount of empirical evidence suggesting that how disabled people feel about their own identity as disabled people matters greatly to their well-being. For example, current research suggests that, for disabled people, non-acceptance of disability is correlated with depression (and predicts future depression),[6] that positive disability identity predicts self-esteem,[7] and that positive disability identity predicts satisfaction with life.[8] But precisely what our dominant narratives of disability demand is that disabled people don't accept disability (that

---

[6] Townend et al. (2010).   [7] Nario-Redmond et al. (2013).

[8] Bogart (2014) interprets her findings as follows: 'Results suggest that rather than attempting to "normalize" individuals with disabilities, health care professionals should

they be determined to 'overcome' it, or that they 'refuse to see themselves as disabled'). And those same narratives make positive disability identity invisible—or perhaps even oxymoronic—for many disabled people.

Hermeneutical injustice arises when dominant stereotypes and assumptions prevent a marginalized group from understanding an aspect of their own experience (and, as a result, from articulating that experience to others). The dominant understanding of disability is an inherently normativized one—disability is loss, lack, or unfortunate departure from normalcy. And the consequence of such normativized conceptions of disability is that the experience of thriving disabled people becomes obscured and difficult to understand. The consequence, that is, is hermeneutical injustice for disabled people.

6.5 Hermeneutical Justice and Pride

Here is a hypothesis: Prejudicial assumptions based on purely descriptive distinctions are easier to dislodge than those based on normatively laden distinctions. I base this hypothesis on the very simple observation that it is easier to provide counterexamples to the former than to the latter. You tell me that blonde women are unintelligent; in response I give you a long list of intelligent blonde women. You tell me that people from New York are rude; in response I give you a long list of polite New Yorkers (perhaps together with some remarks on contextual variation in norms of politeness). And so on.

But suppose that, in the 1950s, you told me that homosexuals were deviant. How would I respond to this? How could I even begin to present cases that would be interpreted as counterexamples? What I would be trying to show you are cases in which someone experienced same-gender attraction but is not in any way deviant because of that. Yet the dominant assumptions of the (heterosexual) majority made such cases practically invisible. To give you a counterexample, I need to show you a case of someone who experiences same-gender attraction and has same-gender sex, but isn't sexually deviant. But the distinction between 'heterosexual' and 'homosexual' was, at the time, so normatively laden that this was

foster their disability self-concept. Possible ways to improve disability self-concept are discussed, such as involvement in the disability community and disability pride.'

tantamount to showing you a case in which someone is sexually deviant, but not sexually deviant.

And so my hypothesis is that in this latter kind of case—the case of prejudicial judgement based on normatively laden distinctions—prejudices are harder to combat. If I'm right about this hypothesis, then it represents a further bad effect of hermeneutical injustice. Not only are people prevented from articulating aspects of their own experience, but the way in which they are prevented from doing so can sometimes further entrench and perpetuate the very stereotypes and prejudices that caused that gap in understanding to arise. If I can't fully understand what it is to be a moral gay person, a rational woman, a flourishing disabled person, then I'm not able to adequately respond to the social stigmas that label gay people as deviant, women as hysterical, disabled people as tragic.

To address a hermeneutical injustice based on a normatively laden distinction, we first need to find a way to reframe that distinction. I can't fully understand what it is to be a thriving, flourishing gay person if I understand gayness as a deviation or perversion from the heterosexual norm. I can't fully understand what it is to be a powerful, strong woman if I understand womanhood as a weaker, frailer version of manhood. And so on.

Again, though, reframing the distinction isn't merely a matter of presenting counterexamples. The gap in our understanding—the hermeneutical injustice—tends to render counterexamples invisible. If a normatively laden distinction is entrenched, it becomes very difficult to see that the distinction doesn't hold. And so we need to do more than simply present cases where the distinction's taxonomy fails. We need to turn the distinction on its head. We need to radically recast it in a way that shows that its normative assumptions are mistaken.

And this, I contend, is one of the central functions of *pride*. By 'pride' here I mean the politically motivated celebration of difference, rather than something like a feeling of innate superiority. Pride, in the context of social marginalization, isn't the demand that we recognize that the marginalized group is somehow inherently blessed or special. It is, instead, better thought of as something like *permission to celebrate*. We often celebrate things without thinking they're something that makes us better or superior; we can be proud (in some sense) of having red hair, of being weirdly good at Settlers of Catan, of having an enormous comic book collection, of having a good 10k time, etc. These are things we can celebrate about ourselves without thinking they make us better than people who lack such features. Pride, in the context of social marginalization, can then be thought of as the claim that it's permissible to celebrate a marginalized feature in this way. Some feature—race, sexuality, disability, etc.—that dominant norms tell you that you should be ashamed of or apologetic about is, in fact, something it *makes sense* to celebrate.

In the mid-twentieth century, the dominant conception of 'homosexuality' was strongly medicalized. Same-gender sexual attraction was a psychological disorder. Maybe it was nobody's fault, and maybe nobody should be blamed for it, and maybe some people were even born that way, but it was still a type of disorder. But in backlash to this, another conception of being gay emerged. Maybe being gay wasn't a 'disorder'. In fact, maybe being gay could be a good thing. Within the gay community, the subversive idea that we can celebrate being gay—that being gay is something to be *proud of*—took shape.

Gay pride was an open, public refutation of the conception of gayness as disordered or deviant sexuality. If gayness was deviance from the straight norm, then it could at most be tolerated or grudgingly accepted. But gay pride wasn't asking for tolerance or grudging acceptance. Gay pride was asking for—demanding, even—*celebration*. Same-gender attraction was something that was meant to be shameful and secret and something that you talked about only with your psychiatrist and your doctor. But gay pride was having parties about it in the street.

Pride parades and rainbow flags and openly 'out' culture did more than suggest that there are some gay people who are not deviant or disordered. It helped us to understand how our way of thinking about the gay/straight distinction was confused—confused in a way that obscured the positive, enriching aspects of being gay. Gay pride didn't merely present us with examples of gay people who didn't think of themselves as deviant. Rather, it gave us examples of gay people—and a gay culture— who rejected the dominant understanding of gayness as deviation from the heterosexual norm.[9]

---

[9] Once again, I take no stand on whether and to what extent the gay pride movement was trying to redefine our terms or change their meaning. Certainly in some cases, such as the reclaiming project for 'queer', meaning change does seem to be a specific target. But it

The primary goals—and the primary benefits—of pride movements are often characterized as emotional ones. Pride movements help marginalized groups work through their feelings of shame. Pride movements help marginalized groups vocalize their feelings of anger at their unjust treatment. Pride movements help marginalized groups feel a sense of collective solidarity. And so on.

I don't dispute that these are important aspects of pride movements. But if I'm right, one of the most important contributions of pride movements is an epistemic one. That is, the benefits of pride movements are not merely emotional or affective—what or how we *feel*. Pride movements also affect what we can *know*.

And if this is right, it also provides a reply to the worry that pride requires an objectionable kind of identity politics.[10] Emphasis on pride needn't involve any sort of commitment to the idea that there is a deeply felt, universal experience had by members of marginalized groups. There needn't be any sense of 'identity' that is somehow essential to membership in a marginalized group—or which is characterized by shared feeling or shared affinity—in order to motivate pride.[11] Rather, all that is needed is that some people are viewed as defective or inferior by broader social norms because of features that mark them out as members of a particular social group. By advocating pride, members of such social groups can reject these norms. They can say that the very same features that dominant norms say should make them feel ashamed—feel *less than*—are ones that it makes sense to celebrate. In doing this, they aren't just promoting positive feelings; they're demanding epistemic justice. That is, they're demanding that norms and stereotypes about them be better informed by their own

---

would be a gross mischaracterization to say that the gay pride movement was merely concerned with redefining some words. And that's because, insofar as they were focused on meaning shift, the meaning shift was normative—they were focused on what our words *ought* to mean, and on the *injustice* in their current meanings.

[10] For discussion of this worry as it specifically relates to disability, see Davis (2013).

[11] Tommie Shelby (2005) eloquently discusses these issues as they relate to race. 'Given that there is [racial prejudice],' he argues, 'proving to others, and perhaps more importantly to oneself, that one is not ashamed of being classed with other blacks may only appear to be ... a kind of racialist chauvinism ... Yet it is possible to sustain black pride without believing that achievement is determined, to any significant extent, by race membership' (pp. 96–7).

experiences. ('Nothing about us without us,' as the disability rights movement would say.)

6.6 Disability Pride

Disability activist Tammy S. Thompson (1997) describes how she first became involved with the disability rights movement:

I've spent many years on a mission to cancel out my disability by frantically stacking up achievements, hoping that someday I would find that final, magic accomplishment which would absolve me of the sin of being disabled.

Loneliness and longing for fulfillment have been the constant threads in my life, motivating countless escape attempts. I guess I thought that if I were successful enough, I'd escape from the 'less than' feeling that quivers in my guts. I've felt that my disability is a debt to others that I could never be powerful enough to repay—that no matter how good I am, I will always need others to do things for me that I cannot do for myself. No matter what I did, I collided with that hard fact. I couldn't seem to accept it and carry on without shame. Then one day, riding the bus, I met a fellow with a disability who was proud. He was comfortable with himself and his disability. Disability pride—wasn't that an oxymoron? I had to find out, so I got involved in the independent living movement he told me about.

Participating in the Center for Disability Leadership program brought me up to speed and launched me into the disability rights movement. My life and my thinking were liberated. I got connected with powerful, wonderful people who were also disabled. These disability warriors taught me a new way to live that frees me from my past.

Similarly, filmmaker and activist Bonnie Sherr Klein (2001) recalls her first experience at a disability pride event, a few years after becoming disabled after a major stroke:

A gutsy, nervous young woman with the thick drawl of cerebral palsy is emcee. Not only is her speech different, but a new language is being spoken here. I feel like a privileged eavesdropper at first, but she is speaking for me and about me. Or is she? She cues us for a chant. 'Disabled and . . .' The crowd responds: PROUD! My throat jams on the word mid-chant. Is this honest? Who am I trying to fool? It's one thing to accept, but another thing to be proud. I'm proud of surviving and adapting maybe, but am I proud of being disabled? But it feels good to be shouting with hundreds of other bodies who look happy despite—because of?—their 'deformities'. Or is the word 'differences'? Or is it 'our'? (p. 75)

Sherr Klein found the idea of disability pride perplexing at first, but eventually embraced it—going on to become an active member of the disability pride movement and the creator of the film *Shameless: The Art of Disability*. She reflects:

In retrospect, the 'clicks' in my consciousness about disability parallel my coming to feminist consciousness two decades earlier. For a long time I denied I was disabled and kept my distance from other 'cripples' in the hospital gym because I was an exception to the rule. Later, I was sure I could 'overcome' it; I would be supercrip (superwoman); I would support the rights of other people with disabilities but *I* was not oppressed. As time passed, I experienced with great pain the ways in which other people's attitudes and societal barriers disempowered me. At first, I internalized the oppression and lost all self-esteem. Then, as I . . . discovered my commonality with other women (and men) with disabilities, I began to see more clearly. With solidarity came strength. (p. 77)

Disability pride doesn't merely offer examples of disabled people who are flourishing. Disability pride offers the radical suggestion that our entire way of thinking about disability is confused. And so, for example, the Chicago Disability Pride parade (currently the largest event of its kind in the world) offers the following explanation, opening with a quotation from the parade's founder, Sarah Triano:

Disability is a natural and beautiful part of human diversity in which people living with disabilities can take pride. That's a personal and radical concept. Persons with disabilities must live and breathe it in order to communicate it to one another and society.

The sad sack, the brave overcomer, and the incapable are worn-out stereotypes the parade refutes by giving us a time and space to celebrate ourselves as we are. First, we want to show the world the incredible joy that exists in our lives. We are part of the richness and diversity of this country and the world. The Parade is an international celebration of our continued and continuing survival. We also, by marching in this parade, are giving the world a chance to express pride in us, too! We will not hide behind doors. We are in the street![12]

If disability is tragedy, then there are very limited ways in which we can understand the experiences of flourishing disabled people. We have to think of them as having 'persevered through' tragedy, as having 'overcome' tragedy, as being very brave in the face of tragedy. Disability pride

---

[12] http://www.disabilityprideparade.com/whypride.php.

rejects these tropes of brave acceptance and perseverance. Disability pride calls for *celebration*.

The point is not—as discussed in chapter 3—that there are no bad effects of disability. We are, all of us, limited by our bodies. Whatever way your body is, there will be bad effects of having a body that's like that. But the disabled body is a pathologized body. It's a body that departs from 'normal' in ways we assume are bad or suboptimal. Disability pride rejects this pathologization. As disabled people, we are forever being told that there is something about our bodies that is lacking, that is *less than*. Disability pride says it doesn't have to be that way. Disability pride says that we may have *minority* bodies, but we don't have—we refuse to have—tragic bodies.

Bibliography

Adams, Rachael and Reiss, Benjamin (forthcoming) *Keywords in Disability Studies*. New York: NYU Press.

Alanen, Lilli and Witt, Charlotte (2004) *Feminist Reflections on the History of Philosophy*. Dordrecht: Kluwer Academic Publishers.

Albrecht, Gary (2006) *The Encyclopedia of Disability*. London: Sage Publications.

Amundson, Ron (1992) 'Disability, handicap, and the environment'. *Journal of Social Philosophy* 23, pp. 105–18.

Amundson, Ron (2000) 'Against normal function'. *Studies in History and Philosophy of Biological and Biomedical Sciences* 31C, pp. 33–53.

Ananth, Mahesh (2008) *In Defense of an Evolutionary Concept of Health*. Aldershot: Ashgate.

Appiah, Anthony (1996) 'Race, culture, and identity: misunderstood connections', in Appiah, K. A. and Gutmann, A., eds. *Color Consciousness: The Political Morality of Race*. Princeton, NJ: Princeton University Press, pp. 30–105.

Arneson, Richard (1999) 'Human flourishing versus desire satisfaction'. *Social Philosophy and Policy* 16 (1), pp. 113–42.

Atkinson, Rebecca (2007) 'Do I want my sight back?' *The Guardian*, July 17.

Atkinson, Rebecca (2008) 'Is deafness a disability?' BBC Online, April 2, http://www.bbc.co.uk/ouch/features/is_deafness_a_disability.shtml.

Bagenstos, S. and Schlanger, M. (2007) 'Hedonic damages, hedonic adaptation, and disability'. *Vanderbilt Law Review* 60 (3), pp. 745–97.

Barford, A., Dorling, D., and Shaw, M. (2006) 'Life expectancy: women now on top everywhere'. *British Medical Journal* 332 (7545), p. 808.

Barnes, Colin and Mercer, Geoff (1996) *Exploring the Divide*. Leeds: The Disability Press.

Barnes, Elizabeth (2014) 'Fundamental indeterminacy'. *Analytic Philosophy* 55 (4), pp. 339–62.

Barnes, Elizabeth (forthcoming) 'Realism and social structure'. *Philosophical Studies*.

Bates, M., Edwards, T., and Anderson, K. (1993) 'Ethnocultural influences on variation in chronic pain perception'. *Pain* 52 (1), pp. 101–12.

Baumann, C., Novikov, V., Regard, M., and Siegel, A. (2005) 'Did Fyodor Mikhailovich Dostoevsky suffer from mesial temporal lobe epilepsy?' *Seizure* 14, pp. 324–30.

Baynton, Douglas (2013) 'Disability and the justification of inequality in American history', in Davis, Lennard J., ed. *The Disability Studies Reader*. London: Routledge, pp. 17–33.

Becker, Lawrence (2000) 'The good of agency', in Frances, L. and Silvers, A., eds. *Americans with Disabilities: Implications of the Law for Individuals and Institutions*. New York: Routledge, pp. 54–63.

Benito-Leon, J., Morales, J. M., Rivera-Navarro, J., and Mitchell, A. J. (2003) 'A review about the impact of multiple sclerosis on health-related quality of life'. *Disability and Rehabilitation* 25 (23), pp. 1291–1303.

Bettcher, Talia Mae (2009) 'Trans identities and first person authority', in Shrage, Laurie, ed. *You've Changed: Sex Reassignment and Personal Identity*. Oxford: Oxford University Press, pp. 98–120.

Blorn, Rianne, et al. (2012) 'Body identity integrity disorder'. *PLoS One*, April 13.

Bogart, Kathleen (2014) 'The role of disability self-concept in adaptation to congenital or acquired disability'. *Rehabilitation Psychology* 59 (1), pp. 107–15.

Boonen, A., van den Heuvel, R., van Tubergen, A., Goossens, M., Severens, J. L., van der Heijdel, D., and van der Linden, S. (2005) 'Large differences in cost of illness and wellbeing between patients with fibromyalgia, chronic low back pain, or ankylosing spondylitis'. *Annals of the Rheumatic Diseases* 64, pp. 396–402.

Boorse, Christopher (1976) 'Health as a theoretical concept'. *Philosophy of Science* 44 (4), pp. 542–73.

Boorse, Christopher (1997) 'A rebuttal on health', in Humber, J. M. and Almeder, R. F., eds. *What is Disease?* Totowa, NJ: Humana Press, pp. 1–134.

Boorse, Christopher (2014) 'A second rebuttal on health'. *Journal of Medicine and Philosophy* 39 (6), pp. 683–724.

Bosveld, Sarah (2015) 'Becoming disabled by choice, not chance'. *The Toronto Sun*, June 8, http://www.torontosun.com/2015/06/08/becoming-disabled-by-choice-not-chance-transabled-people-feel-like-impostors-in-their-fully-working-bodies.

Bovens, Luc (1992) 'Sour grapes and character planning'. *The Journal of Philosophy* 89, pp. 57–78.

Bradley, Ben (2007) 'A paradox for some theories of welfare'. *Philosophical Studies* 133 (1), pp. 45–53.

Bradley, Ben (2013) 'Objectivist theories of wellbeing', in Eggleston, B. and Miller, D., eds. *The Cambridge Companion to Utilitarianism*. Cambridge: Cambridge University Press, pp. 220–39.

Brown, Steven (2002) 'What is disability culture?' *Disability Studies Quarterly* 22 (2), pp. 34–50.

Brownlee, Kimberley and Cureton, Adam, eds. (2009) *Disability and Disadvantage*. Oxford: Oxford University Press.

Bruckner, Donald (2009) 'In defense of adaptive preferences'. *Philosophical Studies* 142, pp. 307–24.

Bruno, M. A., Bernheim, J. L., Ledoux, D., Pellas, F., Demertzi, A., and Laureys, S. (2011) 'A survey on self-assessed well-being in a cohort of chronic locked-in syndrome patients: happy majority, miserable minority'. *BMJ Open* 1 (1), pp. 1–9.

Buchanan, A., Brock, D., Daniels, N., and Winkler, D. (2000) *From Chance to Choice: Genetics and Justice*. Oxford: Oxford University Press.

Burkhardt, C. S., Clark, S. R., and Bennett, R. M. (1993) 'Fibromyalgia and quality of life: a comparative analysis'. *The Journal of Rheumatology* 20 (3), pp. 475–9.

Campbell, Stephen (2016) 'The concept of wellbeing', in Fletcher, Guy, ed. *The Routledge Handbook to the Philosophy of Well-Being*. London: Routledge, pp. 402–14.

Campbell, Stephen and Wahlert, Lance (2015) 'Is disability conservationism rooted in status quo bias?'. *American Journal of Bioethics* 15 (6), pp. 20–2.

Chang, Ruth (2002) 'The possibility of parity'. *Ethics* 112, pp. 659–88.

Chang, Ruth (2004) 'All things considered'. *Philosophical Perspectives* 18, pp. 1–22.

Clare, Eli (2001) 'Stolen bodies, reclaimed bodies: disability and queerness'. *Public Culture* 13 (3), pp. 359–65.

Clare, Eli (2008) 'Resisting shame, making our bodies whole'. Keynote address, Trans Health Conference, http://eliclare.com/what-eli-offers/lectures/resisting-shame.

Collins, Patricia Hill (1990) *Black Feminist Thought in the Matrix of Domination*. Boston, MA: Unwin Hyman.

Corbett, Jenny (1994) 'A proud label: exploring the relationship between disability politics and gay pride'. *Disability and Society* 9 (3), pp. 343–57.

Crisp, Roger (2006) 'Hedonism reconsidered'. *Philosophy and Phenomenological Research* 73 (3), pp. 619–45.

Daniels, Norman (1985) *Just Health Care*. Cambridge: Cambridge University Press.

Davis, Lennard J. (1995) *Enforcing Normalcy: Disability, Deafness, and the Body*. London: Verso Press.

Davis, Lennard J. (2013) 'The end of identity politics and the beginning of dismodernism', in Davis, Lennard J., ed. *The Disability Studies Reader*, 4th edition. London: Routledge, pp. 263–78.

Decosterd, I., Allchorne, A., and Woolf, C. (2002) 'Progressive tactile hypersensitivity after peripheral nerve crush'. *Pain* 100 (1–2), pp. 155–62.

Devlieger, Patrick (1995) 'Why disabled? The cultural understanding of physical disability in an African society', in Ingstad, Benedicte and White, Susan Reynolds, eds. *Disability and Culture*. Berkeley: University of California Press, pp. 94–107.

Devlieger, Patrick and Albrecht, Gary (2000) 'Your experience is not my experience: the concept and experience of disability on Chicago's Near West Side'. *Journal of Disability Policy Studies* 11 (1), pp. 51–60.

Dorsey, Dale (2010) 'Preferences, welfare, and status quo bias'. *Australasian Journal of Philosophy* 88 (3), pp. 535–54.

Dotson, Kristie (2011) 'Tracking epistemic violence, tracking practices of silence'. *Hypatia* 26 (2), pp. 236–57.

Edwards, S. D. (2004) 'Disability, identity, and the "expressivist" objection'. *The Journal of Medical Ethics* 30 (4), pp. 418–20.

Eggleston, B. and Miller, D., eds. (2013) *The Cambridge Companion to Utilitarianism*. Cambridge: Cambridge University Press.

Eiesland, Nancy (1994) *The Disabled God: Toward a Liberation Theology of Disability*. Nashville, TN: Abingdon Press.

Elster, Jon (1983) *Sour Grapes: Studies in the Subversion of Rationality*. Cambridge: Cambridge University Press.

Eyre, Sarah (2012) 'A few awesome things about being disabled'. *xoJane*, May 17, http://www.xojane.com/healthy/disabilitys-unexpected-silver-linings.

Fadiman, Anne (1997) *The Spirit Catches You and You Fall Down*. New York: Farrar, Straus and Giroux.

First, M. and Fisher, C. (2012) 'Body identity integrity disorder: the persistent desire to acquire a physical disability'. *Psychopathology* 45 (1), pp. 3–14.

Fleischer, Doris Zames and Zames, Frieda (2011) *The Disability Rights Movement*. Philadelphia, PA: Temple University Press.

Fletcher, Guy, ed. (2016) *The Routledge Handbook to Philosophy of Well-Being*. London: Routledge.

Frederick, Shane and Loewenstein, George (1999) 'Hedonic adaptation', in Kahneman, D., Diener, E., and Schwarz, N., eds. *Wellbeing: The Foundations of Hedonic Psychology*. New York: Russell Sage Foundation, pp. 302–29.

Fricker, Miranda (2007) *Epistemic Injustice*. Oxford: Oxford University Press.

Glucklich, A. (2001) *Sacred Pain*. Oxford: Oxford University Press.

Hahn, Harlan and Belt, Todd (2004) 'Disability identity and attitudes toward cure in a sample of disabled activists'. *Journal of Health and Social Behavior* 45 (4), pp. 453–64.

Harman, Elizabeth (2007) 'Harming as causing harm', in Roberts, M. and Wasserman, D., eds. *Harming Future Persons. International Library of Ethics, Law, and New Medicine* 35, pp. 137–54.

Harman, Elizabeth (2009) '"I'll be glad I did it" reasoning and the significance of future desires'. *Philosophical Perspectives* 23 (Ethics), pp. 177–99.

Harris, John (2001) 'One principle and three fallacies of disability studies'. *The Journal of Medical Ethics* 27 (6), pp. 383–7.

Hart, L., Hart, B., and Bergin, B. (1987) 'Socializing effects of service dogs for people with disabilities'. *Anthrozoos* 1 (1), pp. 41–4.

Hartman, Chandra (2013) 'Are lesbian, gay, bisexual, and transgender patients at higher risk for mental health disorders?'. *Evidence-Based Practice* 16 (3), p. 7.

Haslanger, Sally (2000) 'Gender and race: (what) are they? (What) do we want them to be?'. *Nous* 34 (1), pp. 31–55.

Haslanger, Sally (2014) *Resisting Reality*. Oxford: Oxford University Press.

Heathwood, Chris (2007) 'The reduction of sensory pleasure to desire'. *Philosophical Studies* 133 (1), pp. 23–44.

Heathwood, Chris (2013) 'Subjective theories of wellbeing', in Eggleston, B. and Miller, D., eds. *The Cambridge Companion to Utilitarianism*. Cambridge: Cambridge University Press, pp. 199–219.

Heathwood, Chris (2016) 'Desire fulfillment theory', in Fletcher, Guy, ed. *The Routledge Companion to the Philosophy of Well-Being*. London: Routledge, pp. 148–60.

Hershey, Laura (1993) 'From poster child to protester'. *Spectacle*, www.independentliving.org/docs4/hershey93.html.

Holmes, Martha (2004) *Fictions of Affliction: Physical Disability in Victorian Culture*. Ann Arbor: University of Michigan Press.

Howard, Dana (2015) 'Transforming others: on the limits of "you'll be glad I did it" reasoning'. *Res Philosophica* 92 (2), pp. 341–71.

Howe, David P. (2011) 'Cyborg and supercrip: the Paralympics technology and the (dis)empowerment of disabled athletes'. *Sociology* 45 (5), pp. 868–82.

Hughes, Bill and Patterson, Kevin (1997) 'The social model of disability and the disappearing body: toward a sociology of impairment'. *Disability and Society* 12 (3), pp. 325–40.

Ingstad, Benedicte and White, Susan Reynolds (1995) *Disability and Culture*. Berkeley: University of California Press.

Jeffers, Chike (2013) 'The cultural theory of race: yet another look at Du Bois's "The Conservation of Races"'. *Ethics* 123 (3), pp. 403–26.

Jenkins, Katharine (forthcoming) 'Amelioration and inclusion'. *Ethics*.

Johnson, Harriet McBryde (2003) 'Unspeakable conversations'. *New York Times Magazine*, February 16.

Johnson, Harriet McBryde (2005) *Too Late to Die Young: Nearly True Tales from a Life*. New York: Picador Press.

Johnson, Mary (1998) 'Pride and identity'. *The Ragged Edge*, March/April.

Johnson, Mary (2003) *Make Them Go Away: Clint Eastwood, Christopher Reeve, and the Case against Disability Rights*. Louisville, KY: The Avocado Press.

Kahane, Guy (2009) 'Non-identity, self-defeat, and attitudes to future children'. *Philosophical Studies* 145 (2), pp. 193–214.

Kahane, Guy and Savulescu, Julian (2009) 'The welfarist account of disability', in Brownlee, Kimberley and Cureton, Adam, eds. *Disability and Disadvantage*. Oxford: Oxford University Press, pp. 14–53.

Kahane, Guy and Savulescu, Julian (2011) 'Disability: a welfarist approach'. *Journal of Clinical Ethics* 6 (1), pp. 45–51.

Kahneman, D., Diener, E., and Schwarz, N. (1999) *Wellbeing: The Foundations of Hedonic Psychology*. New York: Russell Sage Foundation.

Kim, Jaegwon (1992) 'Multiple realizibility and the metaphysics of reduction'. *Philosophy and Phenomenological Research* 52 (1), pp. 1–26.

Kingma, Elselijn (2010) 'Paracetamol, poison, and polio: why Boorse's account of function fails to distinguish health and disease'. *British Journal for the Philosophy of Science* 61 (2), pp. 241–64.

Kittay, Eva (forthcoming) 'Dependency', in Adams, Rachael and Reiss, Benjamin, eds. *Keywords in Disability Studies*. New York: NYU Press.

Krag, Erik (2013) 'Health as normal function: a weak link in Daniels's theory of just health distribution'. *Bioethics*. Published online December 21, 2012.

Krahn, L., Hongzhe, L., and O'Connor, K. (2003) 'Patients who strive to be ill: factitious disorder with physical symptoms'. *American Journal of Psychiatry* 160 (6), pp. 1163–8.

Kristiansen, K., Vehmas, S., and Shakespeare, T. (2009) *Arguing about Disability: Philosophical Perspectives*. London: Routledge.

Ladau, Emily (2013) 'The complexities of "curing" disabilities', *Words I Wheel By*, August 15, http://wordsiwheelby.com/2013/08/complexities-of-cures/.

Lamé, I. E., Peters, M. L., Vlaeyen, J. W. S., Kleef, M. V., and Patijn, J. (2005) 'Quality of life in chronic pain is more associated with beliefs about pain, than with pain intensity'. *European Journal of Pain* 9 (1), pp. 15–24.

Lawrence, Anne (2006) 'Clinical and theoretical parallels between desire for limb amputation and gender identity disorder'. *Archives of Sexual Behavior* 35 (3), pp. 263–78.

Lewis, David (1999) 'Many but almost one', in *Papers in Metaphysics and Epistemology*. Cambridge: Cambridge University Press, pp. 164–82.

Linton, Simi (1998) *Claiming Disability: Knowledge and Identity*. New York: NYU Press.

Linton, Simi (2006) *My Body Politic*. Ann Arbor: University of Michigan Press.

Lobentanz, I. S., Asenbaum, S., Vass, K., Sauter, C., Klösch, G., Kollegger, H., Kristoferitsch, W., and Zeitlhofer, J. (2004) 'Factors influencing quality of life in multiple sclerosis patients: disability, depressive mood, fatigue and sleep quality'. *Acta Neurologica Scandinavica* 110 (1), pp. 6–13.

Loewenstein, G. and Schkade, D. (1999) 'Wouldn't It be nice? Predicting future feelings', in Kahneman, Daniel, Diener, Ed, and Schwarz, Norbert, eds.

Wellbeing: The Foundations of Hedonic Psychology. New York: Russell Sage Foundation, pp. 85–105.

McCracken, Lance (1998) 'Learning to live with the pain: acceptance of pain predicts adjustment in persons with chronic pain'. *Pain* 74 (1), pp. 21–7.

McDaniel, Kris (2010) 'A return to the analogy of being'. *Philosophy and Phenomenological Research* 81 (3), pp. 688–717.

MacLehose, William (2006) 'Aristotelian concepts of gender', in Schaus, Margaret, ed. *Women and Gender in Medieval Europe.* New York: Routledge, pp. 35–6.

McMahan, Jeff (2005) 'Causing disabled people to exist and causing people to be disabled'. *Ethics* 116 (1), pp. 77–99.

McRuer, Robert and Wilkerson, Abby (2003) *Desiring Disability: Queer Theory Meets Disability Studies.* Special issue of *GLQ: A Journal of Lesbian and Gay Studies* 9 (1–2).

Mader, Bonnie and Hart, Lynnette (1989) 'Social acknowledgement for children with disabilities: the effect of service dogs'. *Child Development* 60 (6), pp. 1529–34.

Mallon, Ron (2004) 'Passing, travelling, and social reality'. *Nous* 38 (4), pp. 644–73.

Marcus, Eric (1992) *Making History: The Struggle for Gay and Lesbian Equal Rights, 1945–1990, An Oral History.* New York: HarperCollins.

Marcus, Neil (1992) *Storm Reading.* By Neil Marcus, Roger Marcus, and Rod Lathim. Access Theatre, Santa Barbara, CA. Performance.

Mattlin, Ben (2012) *Miracle Boy Grows Up: How the Disability Rights Movement Saved My Sanity.* New York: Skyhorse Publishing.

Mauer, Marc (2010) 'The advantage of uncertainty'. Presidential address, Annual Convention of the National Federation of the Blind, July 8, https://nfb.org/images/nfb/publications/bm/bm10/bm1008/bm100806.htm.

Metzler, Irina (2005) *Disability in Medieval Europe.* London: Routledge.

Meyer-Bahlburg, H. F. L., Migeon, C. J., Berkovitz, G. D., Gearhart, J. P., Dolezal, C., and Wisniewski, A. B. (2004) 'Attitudes of adult 46,XY intersex persons to clinical management policies'. *The Journal of Urology* 171 (4), pp. 1615–19.

Miller, Sarah Alison (2010) *Medieval Monstrosity and the Female Body.* London: Routledge.

Mills, Charles (1998) *Blackness Visible.* Ithaca, NY: Cornell University Press.

Milner, Ilene and Feldman, Marc (1998) 'Factitious deafblindness: an imperceptible variant of factitious disorder'. *General Hospital Psychiatry* 20 (1), pp. 48–51.

Mitra, Sophia (2006) 'The capabilities approach and disability'. *The Journal of Disability Policy Studies* 16 (4), pp. 236–47.

Moran, Mark (2011) 'Data sounds alarm on gay teens' heightened suicide risk'. *Psychiatric News* 46 (9), pp. 9–28.

Morse, J. and Morse, R. (1988) 'Cultural variation in the inference of pain'. *Journal of Cross-Cultural Psychology* 19 (2), pp. 232–42.

Murakami, Haruki (2009) *What I Talk About When I Talk About Running: A Memoir*. New York: Vintage.

Mustanski, B., Garofalo, R., and Emerson, E. (2010) 'Mental health disorders, psychological distress, and suicidality in a diverse sample of lesbian, gay, bisexual, and transgender youths'. *American Journal of Public Health* 100 (12), pp. 2426–32.

Nario-Redmond, M., Noel, J., and Fern, E. (2013) 'Redefining disability, reimagining the self: disability identification predicts self-esteem and strategic responses to stigma'. *Self and Identity* 12 (5), pp. 468–88.

Nebel, Jacob M. (2015) 'Status quo bias, rationality, and conservatism about value'. *Ethics* 125 (2), pp. 449–76.

Nussbaum, Martha (1993) 'Non-relative virtues: an Aristotelian approach', in Nussbaum, M. and Sen, A., eds. *The Quality of Life*. Oxford: Oxford University Press, pp. 242–69.

Nussbaum, Martha (2001a) 'Symposium on Amartya Sen's philosophy 5: adaptive preferences and women's options'. *Economics and Philosophy* 17 (1), pp. 67–88.

Nussbaum, Martha (2001b) *Women and Human Development: The Capabilities Approach*. Cambridge: Cambridge University Press.

Oliver, Mike (1996) *Understanding Disability: From Theory to Practice*. London and Basingstoke: Palgrave Macmillan.

Oliver, Mike and Barnes, Colin (2012) *The New Politics of Disablement*. London and Basingstoke: Palgrave Macmillan.

Palter, Robert (1995) 'Hume and prejudice'. *Hume Studies* 21 (1), pp. 3–24.

Parfit, Derek (1984) *Reasons and Persons*. Oxford: Oxford University Press.

Paul, L. A. (2014) *Transformative Experience*. Oxford: Oxford University Press.

Phelps, Michael and Cazeneuve, Brian (2008) *Beneath the Surface*. Champagne, IL: Sports Publishing, LLC.

Ptito, M. and Kupers, R. (2005) 'Cross-modal plasticity in early blindness'. *The Journal of Integrative Neuroscience* 4 (4), p. 479.

Pyeritz, Reed (2012) 'Evaluation of the adolescent or adult with some features of Marfan Syndrome'. *Genetic Medicine* 14 (1), pp. 171–7.

Rawls, J. (1955) 'Two concepts of rules'. *Philosophical Review* 64 (1), pp. 3–32.

Roy, A. W. N. and MacKay, G. F. (2002) 'Self-perception and locus of control in visually impaired college students with different types of vision loss'. *Journal of Visual Impairment & Blindness* 96 (4), pp. 254–66.

Samuels, Ellen (2013) 'My body, my closet: invisible disability and the limits of coming-out discourse', in Davis, Lennard J., ed. *The Disability Studies Reader*, 4th edition. London: Routledge, pp. 316–32.

Sandhal, Carrie and Auslander, Philip (2005) *Bodies in Commotion: Disability and Performance*. Ann Arbor: University of Michigan Press.

Sathian, K. (2000) 'Practice makes perfect: sharper tactile perception in the blind'. *Neurology* 54 (12), pp. 2203–4.

Satz, Ani B. (2006) 'A jurisprudence of dysfunction: on the role of "normal species functioning" in disability analysis'. *Yale Journal of Health Policy, Law, and Ethics* 6 (2), pp. 221–67.

Saunders, P. U., Pyne, D. B., Telford, R. D., and Hawley, J. A. (2004) 'Factors affecting running economy in trained distance runners'. *Sports Medicine* 34 (7), pp. 465–85.

Savulescu, Julian (2015) 'Bioethics: why philosophy is essential for progress'. *The Journal of Medical Ethics* 41 (1), pp. 28–33.

Schaus, Margaret (2006) *Women and Gender in Medieval Europe*. New York: Routledge.

Schott, Robin May (2004) 'Feminist rationality debates: rereading Kant', in Alanen, L. and Witt, C., eds. *Feminist Reflections on the History of Philosophy*. Dordrecht: Kluwer Academic Publishers, pp. 101–16.

Scotch, Richard (1988) 'Disability as the basis for a social movement: advocacy and the politics of definition'. *Journal of Social Issues* 44 (1), pp. 159–72.

Searle, John (1969) *Speech Acts: An Essay in the Philosophy of Language*. Cambridge: Cambridge University Press.

Sen, Amartya (1985) *Commodities and Capabilities*. Oxford: Oxford University Press.

Sen, Amartya (1990) 'Justice: means vs. freedoms'. *Philosophy and Public Affairs* 19 (2), pp. 111–21.

Sen, Amartya (1993) 'Capability and well-being', in Nussbaum, M. and Sen, A., eds. *The Quality of Life*. Oxford: Oxford University Press, pp. 30–53.

Shakespeare, Tom (1996) 'Disability, identity, and difference', in Barnes, Colin and Mercer, Geoff, eds. *Exploring the Divide*. Leeds: The Disability Press, pp. 94–113.

Shakespeare, Tom (2006) *Disability Rights and Wrongs*. Oxford: Oxford University Press.

Shakespeare, Tom (2013) 'The social model of disability', in Davis, Lennard J., ed. *The Disability Studies Reader*, 4th edition. London: Routledge, pp. 214–21.

Shakespeare, Tom (2014) *Disability Rights and Wrongs Revisited*. London: Routledge.

Shelby, Tommie (2005) *We Who Are Dark: The Philosophical Foundations of Black Solidarity*. Cambridge, MA: Harvard University Press.

Sherr Klein, Bonnie (2001) 'We are who you are: feminism and disability', in Ryan, Barbara, ed. *Identity Politics in the Women's Movement*. New York: NYU Press, pp. 71–7.

Shrage, Laurie (2009) *You've Changed: Sex Reassignment and Personal Identity.* Oxford: Oxford University Press.

Siebert, Valeri (2014) 'Michael Phelps: the man who was built to be a swimmer', *Telegraph*, April 24, http://www.telegraph.co.uk/sport/olympics/swimming/10768083/Michael-Phelps-The-man-who-was-built-to-be-a-swimmer.html.

Silvers, Anita (1998) 'Formal justice', in Silvers, Anita, Wasserman, David, and Mahowald, Mary, eds. *Disability, Difference, and Discrimination: Perspectives on Justice in Bioethics and Public Policy.* Oxford: Rowman and Littlefield, pp. 13–145.

Silvers, Anita (2001) 'A neutral ethical framework for understanding the role of dis-ability in the life cycle'. *The American Journal of Bioethics* 1 (3), pp. 57–8.

Silvers, Anita (2003) 'On the possibility and desirability of constructing a neutral conception of disability'. *Theoretical Medicine and Bioethics* 24 (6), pp. 471–87.

Singer, Peter (2004) 'Ethics and disability: a response to Koch'. *Journal of Disability Policy Studies* 16 (2), pp. 130–3.

Stensman, R. (1985) 'Severely mobility-disabled people assess the quality of their lives'. *Scandinavian Journal of Medical Rehabilitation* 17 (2), pp. 87–99.

Stone, Share Dale (2005) 'Reactions to invisible disability: the experiences of young women survivors of hemorrhagic stroke'. *Disability and Rehabilitation* 27 (6), pp. 293–304.

Stramondo, Joseph (2011) 'Doing ethics from experience: pragmatic suggestions for a feminist disability advocate's response to prenatal diagnosis'. *International Journal of Feminist Approaches to Bioethics* 4 (2), pp. 48–78.

Swain, John and French, Sally (2000) 'Toward an affirmation model of disability'. *Disability and Society* 15 (4), pp. 569–82.

Tammet, Daniel (2007) *Born on a Blue Day: Inside the Extraordinary Mind of an Autistic Savant.* New York: Simon and Schuster.

Thompson, Tammy S. (1997) 'Escape from shame'. *Mouth Magazine* 43, July.

Thomson, Rosemarie Garland (1997a) *Extraordinary Bodies: Figuring Physical Disability in American Culture and Literature.* New York: Columbia University Press.

Thomson, Rosemarie Garland (1997b) 'Disability, identity, and representation: an introduction', in *Extraordinary Bodies: Figuring Physical Disability in American Culture and Literature.* New York: Columbia University Press, pp. 5–18.

Thomson, Rosemarie Garland (2012) 'The case for conserving disability'. *The Journal of Bioethical Inquiry* 9 (3), pp. 339–55.

Townend, E., Tinson, D., Kwan, J., and Sharpe, M. (2010) 'Feeling sad and useless: an investigation into personal acceptance of disability and its association with depression following stroke'. *Clinical Rehabilitation* 24 (6), pp. 555–64.

Tremain, Shelley (2002) 'On the subject of impairment', in Shakespeare, T. et al., eds. *Disability/Postmodernity: Embodying Disability Theory.* London: Continuum, pp. 32–47.

Triano, Sarah (2006) 'Disability pride', in Albrecht, Gary, ed. *The Encyclopedia of Disability*. London: Sage Publications, pp. 476–7.

Turnbull, Clare and Hodgson, Shirley (2005) 'Genetic predisposition to cancer'. *Clinical Medicine* 5 (5), pp. 491–8.

Väyrynen, Pekka (2013) *The Lewd, the Rude, and the Nasty: A Study of Thick Concepts in Ethics*. Oxford: Oxford University Press.

Vehmas, Simo and Mäkelä, Pekka (2009) 'The ontology of disability and impairment', in Kristiansen, Kristjana, Vehmas, Simo, and Shakespeare, Tom, eds. *Arguing About Disability: Philosophical Perspectives*. London: Routledge, pp. 43–56.

Viane, Ilse et al. (2003) 'Acceptance of pain is an independent predictor of mental well-being in patients with chronic pain: empirical evidence and reappraisal'. *Pain* 106 (1–2), pp. 65–72.

Wasserman, David (2009) 'Ethical constraints on allowing or causing the existence of people with disabilities', in Brownlee, Kimberley and Cureton, Adam, eds. *Disability and Disadvantage*. Oxford: Oxford University Press, pp. 319–51.

Wendell, Susan (1989) 'Toward a feminist theory of disability'. *Hypatia* 4 (2), pp. 104–24.

Wendell, Susan (1997) *The Rejected Body: Feminist Philosophical Reflections on Disability*. London: Routledge.

Wendell, Susan (2001) 'Unhealthy disabled: treating chronic illnesses as disabilities'. *Hypatia* 16 (4), pp. 17–33.

Woodward, Christopher (2016) 'Hybrid theories', in Fletcher, Guy, ed. *The Routledge Handbook of Philosophy of Well-Being*. London: Routledge, pp. 161–74.

Zack, Naomi (1997) 'Race and philosophic meaning', in *RACE/SEX: Their Sameness, Difference, and Interplay*. London: Routledge, pp. 29–43.

Index